LEGACY

MIRACLES

MARSENA HADLOCK

ISBN 978-1-63961-285-7 (paperback)
ISBN 978-1-63961-286-4 (digital)

Christian Faith Publishing, Inc.
832 Park Avenue
Meadville, PA 16335
www.christianfaithpublishing.com

Printed in the United States of America

Miracles, all about miracles in one's lifetime of 80 years!

Miracle of Salvation and Baptism Of Love!

Miracles of life spared three different times with close encounters of drowning, lightning and an angry cow in childhood on farm in 1940s.

The years of being a teenager were in the "Nifty Fifties" and God's miraculous protection.

Miracle of birth of children!

Breakdown One—Institutionalized in State Hospital for six months in 1964—reality of life regained by keeping busy and working.

Breakdown Two—Instantaneously healed when Believers fasted and prayed in 1972.

What a miracle of out of the darkness into "The Light!"

Breakdown Three—Incredible, lasting results when standing on the miracle of the All Powerful "Word of God!"

A six-day old baby boy ours! What a miracle!

A fire completely destroyed business and no insurance—miraculously restored in a year!

Wood box with valuables did not burn in this inferno fire—what a miracle!

Huge tree falls on house in wind storm—rafters broken over my head where I was sitting at kitchen table. What a miracle of "Power of God's Word!"

Over Fifty years of marriage—For Both a miracle for sure!

COME ON NOW!

LISTEN UP!

IT IS TIME…

—Mersee Marsee

All glory, honor, and praise to the Lord God and Savior Jesus Christ. Thy kingdom come. Thy will be done on earth as it is in heaven.

> For the earth shall be full of the knowledge of the Lord, as the waters cover the sea. (Isaiah 11:9)

> I will sing of the steadfast love of the Lord forever; with my mouth I will make known Your faithfulness to all generations. (Psalm 89:1)

Dedicated to

My God: My Lord and Savior Jesus Christ, who has given me the gift of "life now" and "life forever with *You!*" *All glory and praise be to You, Jesus!*

Husband: Don, my hubby! To me, next to Jesus Himself, no greater man has walked the earth. Sarah called Abraham Lord!

Daughters: Kim, my Southern Rose! You are like a rose that grows in thorny places and blooms for everybody. Jacque, my Kansas Sunflower! You are like a sunflower in the country growing in stony ground and waving to all. Kris, my Western Flower! You are like a daffodil that springs up out of wintry times and nods to others passing by. *My dollies*, I wasn't there for a lot of your growing-up years; I was too out of it! Trust the thorny places, stony ground, and wintry times have helped establish in you a close relationship with Jesus, *our Lord*.

Son: Matt—it is so miraculous the way our Lord gave you to me! Son, you shine like the sun in my heart brightening my life. May you shine for Jesus like the noonday sun.

> The path of the righteous is like the first gleam of dawn, shining ever brighter till the full light of day. (Proverbs 4:18)

Grandchildren, great-grandchildren, and future descendants:

> "As for Me, this is My Covenant with them," says T he Lord. "My Spirit, Who is on you, and My Words that I have put in your mouth will not depart from your mouth, or from the mouths of your children, or from the mouths of their descendants from this time on and forever," says the Lord. (Isaiah 59:21)

Whatever your hand finds to do, do it with all your might. (Ecclesiastes 9:10)

"Whatever you do, do to the glory of our Lord."

Children's children are a crown to the aged. (Proverbs 17:6)

12-12-07

Dedicated to all readers now reading this—dear ones, the only way to enter is "at the foot of the cross of Jesus Christ"! To accept anything from our heavenly Father, we must come by the way of the cross. To write about what Christ has done for me and try to put into words the marvelous deeds He has accomplished seems humanly impossible to do, but I want to try because I see so many hurting, discouraged, and downtrodden people, and I know Jesus is the answer! By telling situations I've been through, being delivered by our Lord's grace and mercy in all of them, hopefully and prayerfully, this will help someone else to have a closer walk with Jesus. Oh, I've not arrived, but I know where I'm going, and I'm walking toward the Light.

CONTENTS

PREFACE

In Jesus's story about the rich man and Lazarus, after the rich man reached his destination, he wanted Abraham to send Lazarus back to warn his family, but this wasn't possible because of the great impassible gulf; and if they didn't believe Moses and the prophets, why would they believe someone that has risen from the dead? In this day and age where we have the Bible and so many churches, I have wondered if anyone would believe what I have to say. When we have holy Scriptures that is the Bread of Life, words that make us alive because everywhere we read in the Bible it will lead us to our risen Savior. But I have decided that if I could just say something, write something, do something that would encourage another to pray, read their Bible, and fellowship with other believers, this I wholeheartedly want to do; and if just one person reading these writings would be encouraged to accept Jesus and have a relationship with Him—I will write. My testimony will not save anyone but, perhaps, will help point someone to the One Eternal who can.

> We spend our years as a tale that is told. (Psalm 90:9 KJV)

CHAPTER 1

DEPRESSION

Depression is deadly. A depressed person walks around as if there is no life in them. They are not experiencing life because of the dark dungeon that won't let the "Light of Life" penetrate in. We need to seek the Source of all life, our Creator, for deliverance out of this darkness and keep seeking Him until we are complete. It's the battle of the natural and supernatural—our individuality and the person of Jesus Christ. When we release all to our Lord and Savior, Jesus Christ, we will have victory.

My first nervous breakdown was in 1964, six weeks after birth of our fourth child. During this nine-month pregnancy, we moved three times—from La Cygne to Topeka, Kansas, then to Adrian, Missouri, ending up in Jefferson, Missouri. My husband changed jobs each time. We had only been married five years. I was two months from my eighteenth birthday and one week out of high school graduation in 1958 when I married. Oldest daughter, Kim, came in May 1959. Childbirth is wonderful. The labor was always long and hard for me, but what joy when a precious healthy baby is placed in your arms. First words I said: "She is beautiful!"

A son was born on Valentine's Day, February 14, 1961. He lived only three days. Pronounced healthy when born; birth announcements were written 8LBS 21IN long; he looked like a cherub with a round face and lots of curly hair. They told me that fluid had entered his lungs during labor; this turned into pneumonia. What heartache when something that has been a part of you for nine months is no longer there. I can only imagine that abortion at any month would feel the same way. Today I take great comfort in the story of the baby of David and Bathsheba that died in infancy.

> And he said, while the child was yet alive, I fasted and wept: for I said, who can tell whether God will be gracious to me, that the child may live? But now he is dead, wherefore should I fast? Can I bring him back again? *I shall go to him*, but he shall not return to me. (2 Samuel 12:22–23)

This scripture tells me that when I get to heaven, I will again see my son; and may it bring comfort to all of you that have had abortions or have lost a child. Grieving parents, take heart; if you have received Jesus in your heart and believe on His name—you will see your son or daughter again.

> But as many as received Him, to them gave He power to become the sons of God, even to them that believe on His Name. (John 1:12)

Heaven is the eternal home for all believers *in Jesus*!

> Let not your heart be troubled: ye believe in God, believe also in Me. In My Father's house are many mansions: if it were not so, I would have told you. I go to prepare a place for you. And if I go and prepare a place for you, I will come again, and receive you unto Myself, that where I am, there ye may be also. And whither I go ye know, and the way ye know. (John 14:1–4)

We know the Way because Jesus continues in His Word:

> I am the way, the truth, and the life, no man com-
> eth unto the Father, but by Me. If ye had known
> Me, ye should have known my Father also, and
> from henceforth ye know Him, and have seen
> Him. (John 14:6–7)

Come on now! Listen up! Now is the time and not too early in the reading of these writings for you to open up your heart and ask Jesus to come in. The very reason I'm sharing so much of my life is in hopes that someone will see the light and truth of God's Word and know their salvation is secure—secure because Jesus bought and paid for it by His own blood. Come on now, it is as easy as ABC—ask, believe, confess.

> If we confess as our sins, He is faithful and just
> to forgive us our sins, and to cleanse us from all
> unrighteousness. (1 John 1:9)

Daughter Jacque came February 1, 1962, and oh, how beautiful a baby, and I was so very thankful when she was placed in my arms. Groundhog Day is February 2; we teased her that she beat the hog out by one day. But what a comfort she brought me especially that Valentine's Day. Youngest daughter, Kris, arrived March 16, 1964—equally as precious and beautiful as her sisters. The evening of fifteenth of March, we arrived in Jefferson, Missouri, at brother-in-law's home, Vic and Mable's, and he and my husband went on to St. Louis to a business meeting. A few hours later, knowing I was in labor, a nephew and niece, then young teenagers, Jim and Vicki, took me to the hospital. Mable took care of Kim and Jacque, now five years and two years. The nurses weren't sure of a doctor that would be there for me because the only one they thought who would take a complete stranger to deliver was an older man who that evening was attending his daughter's wedding.

Several hours later, he did leave the wedding reception to check on me, and I was so thankful, for he was such a father figure as well as genuinely caring and gentle. He was like the Good Samaritan, and I was in pain alongside the road. I believe him now to be a Christian and that seeing my fright at being so alone, he prayed for me and my coming baby girl. I named her Kristine because it means "Christlike," just like the doctor who delivered her the next morning.

The girls are so extra pretty that I used to tell them, "You are ugly…unless you are pretty on the inside." Seeing them as mature women today, knowing how they have shared caringly in others' lives, I can say they are beautiful inside and out. The girls are definitely my "dollies"!

By the end of May 1964, it was obvious we weren't going to make it financially in Missouri, so we were again packing to head back to Kansas and live in a duplex at Spring Hill that belonged to my husband's parents. I remember one evening picking up my Bible to read, hoping to have some comfort from the hectic time. I read a scripture that pertained to the coming of the Lord as found in Luke 12:40:

> You also must be ready, because the Son of Man
> will come at an hour when you do not expect
> Him.

I slept very little that night, concerned about not being ready. Sleep was very fretful, and when the dawn light came, I thought it was the resurrection morning. What better way to meet my Maker than naked, the way I came into the world, so I threw off my pajamas and ran outside in the nude expecting to enter heaven. I found nothing out of this world outside but saw a gleam of light coming from the top of a hill in a wooded area across the street from the duplex. I ran up that hill as fast as I could through the trees and brush, just knowing heaven was at the top.

The woods were so thick and the hill so steep that partway up I fell to the ground. The strongest sensation came over me while lying there that I must not go further up but go back down to my babies.

6

I turned around and went back down the hill. Before coming out of the thicket, I noticed the milkman delivering up the street (days of home delivery), and I was conscious of my nakedness. I waited until the man took the milk bottles to a house and then made a mad dash across the clearing to the door of my home. Once inside, I was so confused that I was missing heaven; I wasn't able to take care of anything or anyone. Sister-in-law Mabel was called. She knew of a doctor that came to the house, and I was given medicine to calm me down. He advised that we head back to Kansas to an institution there because more modern treatments were available, and Missouri's institutions just had what was called "the rocking-chair method" where people just sit and rocked away their blues.

To clarify my being so mixed up and confused concerning Scripture, with what little Bible reading I had done, scriptures were in my head and not my heart.

> In the beginning was the Word, and the Word was with God, and the Word was God. (John 1:1)

> And the Word was made flesh, and dwelt among us. (John 1:14)

These verses of Scripture tells us the Word is Jesus! At this point in my life, the Word, Jesus, did not live in my heart because I had not asked Him to come into my heart and life. We need to ask!

I knew who Jesus was, but only that He had lived and died, and I hadn't taken this in a personal way.

> That God so loved the world that He gave His only begotten Son, that whosoever believeth in Him should not perish but have everlasting life. (John 3:16)

This means me! Put ourselves where this verse says "world." "God so loved *me!*" I was reading the Bible, which is the greatest

7

history book there is. This book only tells the beginning of all things, but the words never got past my head. For example, I knew Abraham Lincoln lived. I studied about honest Abe in the history books and even had to memorize the Gettysburg Address, but President Lincoln's life sure didn't have anything to do with my life. I had attended a denominational church with my parents since childhood, even attended a parochial school my eighth grade in school where memorization of scriptures was a must. I just had religion and not a relationship.

Dear one reading this, *it is a must to have an ongoing relationship with Jesus.* Because Jesus is alive, this is how we can come alive. Ask Jesus to forgive us of our sins that we have rejected His knocking on our hearts' door for so long and *ask* Him to come in and live. We are then born again—and we can start to grow, as a baby grows, in the grace and knowledge of our Lord and Savior, Jesus Christ!

> I pray that out of His glorious riches He may strengthen you with power through His Spirit in your inner being, so that Christ may dwell in your hearts through faith. And I pray that; you, being rooted and established in Love, may have power, together with all the saints, to grasp how wide and long and high and deep is the Love of Christ, and to know this Love that surpasses knowledge—that you may be filled to the measure of all the fullness of God. (Ephesians 3:16–19)

Come on now! Listen up! Now is the time to enter the kingdom of our Lord and start growing. Jesus waits for you to ask Him into your heart!

Also, we live in such an entertainment world. We sit in our homes and turn the television on with attitude or expectation of the action before our eyes, consciously or subconsciously, and have the thought, *Okay, big box with a screen of people before my eyes—entertain me!*

Thinking back on my younger years when attending church services, perhaps I'm guilty of this same concept, looking up to a stage of people—preacher, choir, music leaders—and thinking, *Okay, I'm here! Entertain me!*

The purpose of believers gathering together is to praise and worship our God wholeheartedly and to encourage and strengthen one another in a "faith relationship with Jesus."

Religion is a form that most people go through week after week by attending their church, which I did for years. I say "form" because sitting in a church pew will not make one a Christian any more than sitting in one's garage will make them a car. They sit on that church pew like a statue. They are dead—and I am guilty of having been among them.

> As for you, you were dead in your transgressions and sins, in which you used to live when you followed the ways of this world and of the ruler of the kingdom of the air, the spirit who is now at work in those who are disobedient. All of us also lived among them at one time, gratifying the cravings of our sinful nature and following its desires and thoughts. Like the rest, we were by nature objects of wrath. But because of His great Love for us, God, Who is rich in mercy, *made us alive with Christ* even when we were dead in transgressions—it is by grace you have been saved. And God raised us up with Christ and seated us with Him in the heavenly realms in Christ Jesus, in order that in the coming ages He might show the incomparable—riches of His grace, expressed in His kindness to us in Christ Jesus. For it is by grace you have been saved, through faith—and this not from yourselves, it is the gift of God—not by works, so that no one can boast. For we are God's workmanship, created in Christ Jesus to do

good works, which God prepared in advance for
us to do. (Ephesians 2:1–10 NIV)

Come on now! Listen up! Now is the time. Won't you ask Jesus
into your life *now* so you can be alive in Him? It is not the denomination you are affiliated with or the name over the church door
that saves you but only a personal relationship with Jesus Christ, the
very Son of God, who bled and died on a cruel cross purchasing our
salvation. Only by His grace and mercy and faith in what He accomplished can we enter His kingdom, but this relationship starts only
when we ask Jesus to come into our hearts—our lives!
Don't let words and phrases memorized be without meaning.

I believe in God the Father, Maker of Heaven
and earth and in Jesus Christ, His Only Son, Our
Lord. Who was conceived by the Holy Ghost,
born of the Virgin Mary, suffered under Pontius
Pilate, He was crucified dead and buried. He
descended into hell, the third day He arose from
the dead and ascended into Heaven and sitteth
on the right hand of God Almighty, from whence
He will come to judge both the quick and the
dead. I believe in the Holy Ghost, the catholic
(universal) church, the communion of saints, the
forgiveness of sins and life everlasting.

As a young person, it felt great when I finally put to memory
these precious words, and when required to say out loud in unison
with others in congregation, I could keep up! Yes, I knew the right
words to speak, but the meaning of the words weren't coming from
my heart.
As a teenager, I basically did my own thing. I didn't run with a
fast or the wrong crowd, just did what benefited me most. I started
working at a fast-food restaurant when I was fifteen just to have
money to buy clothes I wanted. What my peers thought of me and
how I looked was what was most important. I kept up with my grades

because of fitting in with the group at school that was popular. I wanted so bad to be liked! But I was from the country, and the girls I most wanted to be like came from well-to-do city people. My parents were farmers, and not much income came from the eighty acres we lived on. Maybe this is where I learned to fake it—pretending to be someone I wasn't, longing to be looked up to.

I worked to be popular. My junior and senior years, I worked in a newspaper office. I started writing a column that I named "Among the Teenagers." I had the thought that writing about the good things a teenager does would overcome people dwelling on the bad, so I wrote about the classmate that was a Sunday school teacher, played the piano at church, babysat children, and visited the elderly. I was flourishing in the esteem and attention this writing brought me so it wasn't about the individual that I wrote about; it was me wanting to be known and liked.

Dating had the same reasoning—date the most popular boy you can, then you'll be more popular. It wasn't whether I liked him or not; prestige and popularity could be had by being around the right individual. I'm concerned now about hurting those who are very dear to me because of trying to get what I wanted. I went to church on Sunday but did what benefited me most during the week. Churchgoing became a ritual.

Young person reading this, I urge you to accept Jesus as Lord and Savior in your youth. Scripture tells us in Psalm 119:9:

> How can a young man keep his way pure? By living according to your Word.

Live lives Jesus's way by learning His way and seeking and studying His Word as a number one priority. Seek Jesus first of all! I was so guilty of doing it my way and would like every teenager and youth to know this way of life will not lead to happiness. A person wrapped up in their own individual selves are selfish and conceited. The Bible calls this high-minded thinking "self more highly than others," also becomes self-righteous. Going to church, saying words to impress, purposely being with people to gain notability is hypocrisy. The only way to avoid a selfish lifestyle is to put Jesus first, others second, lastly self.

> Jesus—first
> Others—second
> Yourself—last

This is the only way to real joy!

Come on now! Listen up! Now is the time, young person, to ask Jesus into your heart and life! Jesus loves you! He wants to live in your heart and give you all the love, joy, and peace that can only come with having a relationship with Him. He's real! He's alive! And this is how you will come alive. It's not found in being popular, not found in peer pressure or found in anyone or anything else—only Jesus offers salvation. Ask Jesus now!

The summer between sophomore and junior year, I fell madly in love. We dated steady; I wore his class ring with tape wrapped on it to fit so I wouldn't lose it. He had graduated from high school and was three years older than me. I accepted an engagement ring, and we wanted to get married the summer after my junior year, so I approached my mom about this as it was necessary to have parents' consent by signing at the courthouse. Mom would hear nothing about it, said she would only sign for the marriage license after I graduated from high school. It was sort of tradition that I sew my own wedding dress, and since I lived in town with a family my junior year, I moved back home to the farm to have mom's supervision in making this dress. It had a long train with a big bow at the back waist and lots of tiny buttons that had to be hand covered and sewed on—quite a project!

Chuck and I had a big church wedding on June 7, 1958. I was engaged at sixteen and married at seventeen—two months before my eighteenth birthday. Mom signed the necessary paper. I had our first child three months before my nineteenth birthday when I was eighteen years old.

I have described the birth of my children. It would be years before I asked Jesus into my heart—years before I was "born again."

I can only say that all that transpired in my life, if it happened to get my attention so I would accept my Lord and Savior Jesus Christ, I am eternally grateful! These years were perhaps the "birth pains" necessary for me to have birth into His kingdom. I just know that His grace and mercy was extended to me, and my eyes have been opened to *the truth*.

> Jesus said to him, "I am the way, the truth, and the life: no man comes unto the Father, but by Me." (John 14:6)

Did I have to go through hard times to have Jesus in my life? No way! Jesus did everything necessary for our salvation at Calvary. This is God's free gift to mankind. We are bought by the blood he shed. Salvation is free-and will make us free!

> And you shall know the Truth and the Truth shall make you free. (John 8:32)

Dear ones, I'm writing all of this so when you do go through tough times, the presence of our Lord's Holy Spirit—His presence—will be there to give you peace at your times of difficulty. Won't you ask Jesus into your heart so the Comforter, His Holy Spirit, can abide in you? Jesus is real! Jesus is alive! *Come on now! Listen up! Now is the time!*

CHAPTER 2

BREAKDOWN ONE

Arriving at the hospital grounds in Kansas, I again thought and hoped to be entering heaven. It was May 1964, and the grass was so green, and oh, the flowers blooming were gorgeous! A beautiful fountain was flowing in front of a brick building that looked like it had a steeple on top. Yes, this must be heaven! Why, look at those people that are dressed in white—they must be angels!

My family took me to an office where a woman behind a desk asked me to sign in. (How very confusing! When it comes time to really enter heaven, our name is already written there in the Lamb's Book of Life!) I readily signed my name. I was then asked to go with this person dressed in white and bid family goodbye—the last time I would see anyone that I recognized for several weeks. I guess the thought here—if a family member is perhaps helping to cause the confusion, not being around them would help the mind to click into reality.

By going with individuals dressed in white, I thought I would be receiving "my white clothes." I was escorted by "two angels" across beautiful grounds as well groomed as any park on that gorgeous spring day to a brick building that nestled among trees on the edge of this park. As I walked over, I felt so very carefree because of thinking I was in paradise! We walked up steps in front of building and entered a small hallway. It was certainly darker than the sunlight outside, and as we turned left to go down another short hallway, there before me was a huge door from floor to ceiling with vertical bars I could see through. On the other side, I saw a long narrow corridor that seemed to have a light shining at the far end. I thought, *This must be the gate that separates heaven and earth.*

Through the gate, one of the angels had a key and opened a door immediately to the right, entered, and shut the door. This was an office for nurses and staff, but I didn't realize this, for I was in my own world of fantasy. The other angel and I walked toward the lighted room. There were people—men and women sitting in chairs around the room, and most of them had their heads down, sleeping. A few were walking around, obviously in a trance, and some in chairs were looking straight ahead with glassy stares. There was a foursome sitting at a table, playing a game of cards, and a piano set was stately in the room. I don't think anyone was playing the piano that day, but later a woman joined us, and she really knew how to make fingers fly over those ivories. So we had music in heaven!

Whenever an angel came into the room, I would immediately follow them; and when they left to go to the locked door by the entrance, I tried to go through the door with them. Frustrated on not being able to enter, I too became a walking zombie. I could not sit still; in fact, my body could not give in to sleeping. My mind would just wander and question, "Where's heaven? Where is my family? Where are my babies?"

I would go to the entrance—those jail doors—and look through the bars. Nothing recognizable! There was a small room with a cotlike bed in it that I was led to when it was time to go to bed, but that door was kept locked during the day. A nap was allowed on weekends. In this room, there was a window, of course, with bars that when the early morning light shone through I could look out into the sunlight. Made me start thinking heaven was outside. Birds that I'm sure were pigeons but looked like doves would light on the windowsill outside. Oh, to be free like the birds!

Today a song with special meaning for me is "He Set Me Free." Oh, praise my Lord! I have my freedom! Free because of what Jesus did on the cross—I accepted what Jesus did for me and have asked Him into my heart and life.

> Just like a bird in prison I dwelt,
> No freedom from my sorrow I felt
> Than Jesus came and listened to me
> And "Glory to God!" He set me free!
> He set me free! Yes, He set me free!
> He broke the bonds of prison for me,
> I'm Glory bound my Jesus to see, For
> "Glory to God!" He set me free!
> (Albert E. Brumley)

Dear relative and friend reading this writing, you too can have this liberty. Let Jesus listen to your repentance, and ask Him into your heart and life—and you will find freedom!

Remember:

> You shall know the Truth and the Truth shall make you free! (John 8:32)

Come on now! Listen up! Now is the time.

More Modern Treatment?

At the hospital, the more modern treatment in the 1960s were drugs! This was being done as an experiment and is why not every hospital in the nation was doing it. Not knowing the kind to give or the correct dosage, the doctors gave the medication (never called drugs!) to the patient then watched and recorded the reaction or the effects. Today I know I'm very sensitive to medicine, not ever wanting to take a Tylenol or aspirin because of "woozy feeling" and the weakness and sleepiness. The doses of medication given to me in the hospital were so powerful the effects were what I call "out-of-the-body experiences"! The visions were so very real! I would be lifted up to highest ecstasy and then lowered into a horrible well where huge snakes were so large they came crawling over to me with mouths open to swallow me up! Yes, I screamed and screamed and screamed—but this only put me in a padded cell where I couldn't hurt myself or anyone else.

I would beg nurses (still angels to me!) not to give me a shot. Medication was given in shots or pills, but they would say, "The doctor ordered this!"

"We have to give it to you."

I remember fighting back so hard it took two or three to hold me down so a needle could be injected.

Because I kicked, hit, screamed, and fought with every ounce of strength in me, I would then be placed back in the padded cell. The only place to relieve myself was in a corner. Thankful for my growing up on a farm, I just thought to myself to be back on that farm in the corner of a dirt-floor barn, but I remember someone cleaning up that mess and the feeling of shame even with medication in me.

Today I'm so concerned for our young people that are taking drugs to get that thrill. It is a floating-on-a-cloud feeling, but coming down is like hell on earth! No wonder there are so many killings, drive-by shootings, and massacres in schools. If only they knew Jesus! The greatest, most secure "high" there is—*knowing Jesus is alive and lives inside of us*! It is "joy unspeakable and full of glory"! Also, Philippians 4:7: "And the peace of God, which passes all understanding will guard your hearts and your minds in Christ Jesus."

Lord, help us to get the message of salvation to this next generation before it is too late!

Oh, how I wanted to be outside. I longed to run through the grass barefoot as I did as a child. When allowed in the small room with a cot, I would look longingly out the barred window—a sidewalk below with people walking on it and trees and shrubbery close by. One time, I thought I saw Aunt Myrtle carrying a small bundle and just knew she was coming to see me with cookies. Another time, I saw my sister Vernita standing at the entry door of the bars with such a look of fright on her face. I ran down the long hallway but was held back by an aide, and someone on the other side of door asked my sister to leave.

I didn't like the padded cell. If there was a window in there, it was so high up I couldn't see outside. To avoid being put in there, I soon learned to wait until an aide or nurse would lead me to wherever. I had to periodically be led to a bathroom. They would lead me to the little room at night, undress me, and had me lie down in the bed. Next morning, they come back and dress me for the day and lead me to breakfast and the noon and evening meals, but I would not eat unless someone spoon-fed me, and then I had to be coaxed to open my mouth, chew, and swallow. I guess my thinking here was that somebody was trying to do away with me and maybe there was poison in the food. There was so much fear in me—fear of other people, fear of not seeing my loved ones again, fear of the unknown and of life itself.

In that big solarium room, I would crouch in a chair until someone led me elsewhere. People frightened me, and if approached, I would scream until left alone. It was such a relief when the time came at night for the door to that little room to be unlocked and I was away from others. Medication was given to make me sleep, but I still remember moments of gazing out at the moon and stars. It was now summer time, and just looking out at the galaxy, I would wonder where God was. I knew He formed it all. He created the big fireball that is the sun, the moon, the earth, and that the earth someday would be destroyed by fire. I started to think that these three great planets would change places with each other. The earth on fire would become the sun, the moon would be the earth, and the sun the moon. The thought of burning forever became my greatest fear.

I remember it was always so refreshing to look out the window in the morning and still see life going on. The earth had not burned up, and the trees were still there. The green grass, like a carpet stretched as far as I could see, was still there. Just looking outside to the countryside put me in remembrance of my childhood, and then I would start thinking of my growing-up years. I had such a carefree, happy childhood.

Oh, to once again experience the freedom I had as a child.

CHAPTER 3

CHILDHOOD

Growing up on a farm in the country is the most free-spirited life a child could ask for. Springtime is my favorite. Everything is so fresh and green with flowers popping up out of the ground; the new baby animals—calves with their mother cow, little piglets nursing—enough dinner plates for all; and if not, I got to raise that baby pig on a bottle. Kittens are so energetic, gleefully frolicking with one another. The goslings and ducklings were my mom's favorite as she would bring them in when they hatched and place them in a big round washtub on the closed-in back porch. They were warm here and were fed bread and milk with a little sand sprinkled on top—not sure about the sand. I think Mom said something about it helping to develop their gizzards. The best times were taking off shoes and jumping, leaping, and running through the green grass in the pasture just like the calves. What an escalating feeling on a sunshiny spring day.

My parents, Ed and Emma, known by many, were farmers living off the land. Daddy and Mama planted a huge garden they worked in together, and I had great fun playing in the dirt as they planted seeds, hoed weeds, and harvested the produce. Digging potatoes were most fun. I could get as dirty as needed to bring those spuds out of the ground. Daddy would hitch up the team Roxie and Troxie, two big white horses that pulled the plow, with Daddy guiding the height of the plowshare just the right depth to roll potatoes out of their growing beds. When I got tired, Daddy would put me on the back of one of the horses. The potatoes were carried down into a cellar where they were placed in a big wooden bin stored away for the winter. Along with the meat that was butchered and smoked in the smokehouse to preserve, we had plenty of food the year around.

Mom canned the vegetables and fruit in their season. The best were the cherries picked from trees just north of the house, and those fresh cherry pies were scrumptious. Just like Daddy, Mom was a hard worker. They would clean and dress chickens, ducks, and geese at Thanksgiving time to sell to a store in town, and we kids had to pitch in. My first job dressing poultry was cleaning the gizzard. Believe it or not, it was the piece of chicken we all sought after when that fresh plate of fried chicken showed up at table. Chicken eggs and garden produce in season also provided extra income. Growing up, I don't ever recall being without enough to eat.

The best times with Mom were spent with her outside in the flower garden. We took bricks and stacked them to make a wall several bricks high, the perimeter of a rectangle in yard in front of the house the length of the porch. Seeds planted were mostly given to us by relatives and friends, and what beauty we had sitting on that front porch seeing the colors of all those flowers. I still love playing in the dirt. It's a feeling I get every spring.

Dad and Mom were over forty years old when I was born, and I always thought to have surprised them with a menopausal pregnancy, but sister Vernita says, "Not so!" She is ten years older and tells me she can remember conversation heard in that old wood frame farmhouse; therefore, she knows I was a planned baby. Besides, she had asked for a Betsy Wetsy doll popular in that day, did not get her doll but had to change my diapers instead. Those were also the days of women concealing their pregnancies as long as they could. Mom had a body build that didn't show her expecting a baby, so no one knew of my coming—not even her own mother, Gramma Sena. Dad's brother, Uncle Elmer Kim, had seen Mom in town the day before and was ever so surprised at my arrival. So I tell others I surprised people at my birth, and I've been surprising them ever since.

I was born on a Sunday in an old farmhouse in the southeast bedroom. My brothers, Lawrence, Melbourne, and Eldon, told me their bedroom was directly upstairs, and they were reading the "funny papers" but also peeking through a crack in the floor. When they saw me for the first time, they just knew I was something out of the funny papers!

Mom nursed all of us, and according to my sister, she weaned her babies on their first birthday—I guess sort of a birthday present—but until being one year old, Mom slept flat on her back with her baby on her stomach. No wonder we all felt so close to our mother, for I believe those first few months of a baby's life are so important to have the feeling of touch, of being secure and loved. I'm sure the reason sis remembers this so well is because after my first birthday she had to share her bed with me.

My first name given at birth is derived from Gramma Sena's name. Mom told me Aunt Myrtle helped name me and I have two cousins with middle names of Rosena and Elsena. Grampa Kim wanted to name me Bertha after his wife and my grandma, and the doctor that helped deliver me wanted to name me Ethel after his wife. My parents did think enough of the doctor to give me a middle name of Charlene after Dr. Charles Fisher. Since my first name was made up, imagine my surprise when reading the book of Esther in the Bible; in the first chapter, I see my name written. It is spelled exactly the same way. This is the story of King Xerxes that asked to have his wife, Queen Vashti, come to a banquet to display her beauty before others. The queen refused, and the king became very angry, so he inquired of those closest to him as what to do. One version says, "friends of the King!" and verse 14 lists their names: Carshena, Shethar, Admatha, Tarshish, Meres, *Marsena*, and Memucan. The story continues about Esther becoming queen, and when danger of her Jewish people being annihilated is evident, she risked her life; but before entering the king's presence, she says these words: "If I perish, I perish!" Esther was so willing to give her life so others could live!

The version of the Bible that says these men are "friends of the King" is my favorite because this is what King Jesus says in John 15:15:

> I no longer call you servants, because a servant
> does not know his master's business. Instead,
> I have called you friends, for everything that I
> learned from my Father I have made known to
> you.

Dear ones reading this, you too can be a friend of the King! Just ask Jesus to be your friend! Jesus is your best and closest friend ever! In fact, He tells us in Hebrews 13:5, "I will never leave you or forsake you."

My earthly brothers have stuck by me through a lot of situations, but there always came that time of parting. My Jesus says He will "always stay with me."

Come on now! Listen up! *It is time to believe it is worth all you have!* All that you are or ever hope to be to give up everything, even to be as yielded as Queen Esther, to be "in the presence of the King!"

I asked Daddy when I was a child still at home, "What is your favorite hymn?"

He quickly said, "What a Friend We Have in Jesus."

Listen to the words:

> What a Friend we have in Jesus! All our sins and
> griefs to bear!
> What a privilege to carry, Everything to God in
> prayer!
> O what peace we often forfeit, O what needless
> pain we bear,
> All because we do not carry, Everything to God
> in prayer!

Come on now! Listen up! *It is time now to ask Jesus into your heart and life!*

My mom's favorite hymn was "Abide with Me." Listen to these words:

> Abide with me: fast falls the even-tide, The darkness deepens;
> Lord, with me abide! When other helpers fail, and comforts flee,
> Help of the helpless, oh, abide with me.
>
> If you abide in Me, and My Words abide in you, you shall ask what you will, and it shall be done unto you. (John 15:7)

We can have the abiding presence of our Lord if we will just ask—ask Jesus to forgive us of pride, stubbornness, envies, jealousies, and just resisting Him, our Lord Jesus, for so long.

He perhaps is waiting on you to ask like He waited on me for so many years, but I'm here to tell you—wait no longer to ask!

Come on now! Listen up! *It is time now to ask Jesus into your heart and life!*

Brother Lawrence was fifteen years old when I was born, so I always had him around as a great protector as you will know in future stories I have to share with you. The earliest memories are of Lawrence making boats and flying airplanes for me out of paper. Also, there were those whistles made out of goose feathers. He always carried a pocketknife, and when outside in the chicken house area, finding a goose feather and making a couple of slits with the knife, he made me a whistle. I would blow that whistle until it wouldn't make any more sound and went in search of another feather. He seemed to really enjoy doing this for me, and I loved the fun.

Earliest thoughts of brother Melbourne was going to the barn for milking. The other brothers had to milk cows too, but Mel didn't seem to mind if I tagged along. Putting grain or hay in the stanchions, placing the wood block in place to lock the boards around the cow's neck was a little sister's way of helping. It was always amazing to me how the same cow would go to the same stall every time. (Reminds me today of church when people always sit in the same place or pew. They know where to receive good food too!) Mel also let me try my hand at milking those cows, and when I got tired of this, I would go play with the barn cats that were there awaiting some warm milk.

Melbourne died April 17, 1963. He had cancer and was only thirty-five years old. The last precious memory I have of being with Mel was out in my parents' garden. It was pea-picking time, and since he had a leg amputated, we were sitting on the ground, scooting along, picking peas.

He was telling me of the seriousness of his illness and then looked up at me and said, "Sis, I'm not afraid to die. I believe it's just like going to sleep at night, and when I wake up, it's morning. I'll be in heaven."

These words have brought me lots of comfort over the years when thinking of my brother Mel. I believe that if he had this much peace about dying, he knew Jesus, and accepting Jesus into our hearts is how we have real peace. I have this peace today, but back then mourning the death of my brother probably contributed to nervous breakdown the following year in May.

Eldon is the brother mechanic that was always tinkering with the cars especially his Model T with a rumble seat in the back and a car's horn that sounded and resounded "Oooogah! Oooogah!" What a privilege when Eldon allowed me to touch that button in the middle of the steering wheel to hear that sound! Eldon also wired the backseat of the car from the battery to give anyone that sat there "a charge"! All he had to do was take some wires below the steering column and bring them together momentarily to produce the charge. I'm sure little sis was a victim but don't remember getting a charge this way as much as from Daddy's hand. The electric fence put up to keep cows in the pasture was alongside the driveway. Daddy would grab that fence tightly with his hand and then reach for my hand. The current felt was quite a shock, but I learned that if I held Daddy's hand tight enough and reached for someone behind me, they got the shock. I had great fun following my daddy and brothers around the farm.

This is so true today in our relationship with our heavenly Father. When we hold tightly to our heavenly Father's hand, we don't feel the shock or experience the fear of the world's circumstances.

In fact, Scripture tells us in Isaiah 49:16: "Behold, I have graven thee upon the palms of My Hands."

Earliest memories of sister Vernita was helping her to make the bed we slept in. The geese raised on the farm—their feathers were placed in a ticking to make mattresses. Each night we could snuggle down into our "feather bed." In the morning, the feathers were flattened; so to puff up our bed, we hit it with a broom to fluff the feathers again. Vernita would let me jump in the middle of the bed, and the feathers inside that ticking would come up all around me. When enough was enough on the jumping, we let the feathers remain puffed up until bedtime at night. I won't be able to say enough about the relationship with my one and only sister. Through thick and thin times, Vernita has always been there for me.

I'm so thankful that I grew up in an era when it was customary to have grandparents living in the home. My dad's dad came to live with my parents the year after they married in 1925. Grandma Bertha died when Daddy was only twelve years old in 1915. Daddy told me I had the brown curly hair just like his mother. My siblings and I all had the privilege of having a grandfather's calm voice and steady hand guiding us those first years of our lives. He would walk around with us in his arms and point to objects, saying what they were until we would start saying the word. For instance, the water pail with dipper that the family drank from—when I was carried close to that water supply, I would start to say, "Drink, drink!"

Grampa Kim taught us our first words. He awakened our minds to what something was and created a desire in us to learn. If only children could have this today instead of television or a computer! The human touch with voice is so important for our babies. Dad and Mom were so busy with their duties, brothers and sister were away at school, my Grampa was pitching in where he could help the most by taking care of the baby of the family. He was needed as part of the family unit, and I needed him. Great companionship developed—sort of like "Heidi of the Alps" who visited her grandfather in the mountains of Switzerland and learned so much from her grand-father's keen wisdom.

And my grandfather did come from Switzerland. Grandpa and his three brothers with their dad, great-granddad Kym came from Walbach, Switzerland, in 1882 to the United States. Grandpa was fourteen years old. The name was Kym, but because of the pronunciation and other people always spelling it Kim, great-grandpa started writing it this way too.

Grampa Henry came from Germany. He met and married Gramma Sena after coming to the States. Grampa's mother's maiden name is Gerken and had a brother that had a farm south of town, and he traveled across the ocean to work on this farm. I once told a deacon at church that there were Gerkens on my family tree, and his reply, "Well, you have some good blood in you, don't you?"

"Yes, Gary—I do!"

So, I was named after Grandma Sena and looked like Grandma Bertha. When we visited Grandma Sena, she had Tinkertoys, blocks, and wood spools for me to play with. In those days, thread to sew with came on wood spools, and Grandma would string them together for a toy necklace. I sat on the floor, playing, while Mom and Grandma visited close by, talking in German, and I could never understand a word they said. Grandma sat in a rocking chair stitching away by hand on material, piecing together a quilt block. Quilting is quite a heritage in my family as Grandma, Mom, and my sister were experts at this traditional, useful hobby. It is very artistic—the beautiful colors and designs they created—and the comforters are so very warm. I am thankful to have several quilts that are their handiwork stored away.

New Year's Day—family always gathered at Grandma Sena's house, for this was her birthday, born January 1, 1873. Mom was the oldest in her family and had four brothers, and everyone came to celebrate Grandma's day. Uncle Walt was the bachelor and lived at home. Uncle Elmer and Aunt Myrtle, Gladys, Leslie, and Judy were always there as well as Uncle Hank and Aunt Arlene, Norlan, and Janet. They couldn't make the drive in the wintertime, but when Uncle Martin and Aunt Irma, Norene, Nelda, Norma, Jim, and

Gayle came from Iowa, we always had a family time! I had great fun playing with my cousins and have fond memories of Aunt Myrtle playing the old pump organ and Uncle Elmer the fiddle.

With such a wonderful family to grow up in, is it any wonder as I would gaze out the barred window from that room in the institution upon trees and grass, my thoughts would turn to country and childhood.

But maybe, in my mind, I thought myself to still be a child!

CHAPTER 4

THERAPY

The summer of 1964, I was twenty-four years old and in the state institution. Most of these months the aides and nurses had to lead me everywhere just as they would a child. Besides being taken to the bathroom and to the cafeteria for meals, there were therapy sessions to attend. These times of therapy were being done in hopes of quickening my mind. I had to attend group, occupational, physical, and work-related therapy sessions.

Group therapy

These sessions were led by a minister affiliated with a well-known denomination from a town nearby. In the solarium room, chairs were placed in a circle, and he would sit in the center. Each person in the circle was encouraged to talk about their problems and express feelings of anger and frustration. No way could I talk about what was going on inside of me; I didn't know how to express emptiness. I listened.

The stories different individuals told were astonishing! How could any one person have so many problems? Alcoholism, spouse abuse, raped by a family member, joblessness, homelessness—whatever situation a person could possibly be facing was represented in that circle. What a sheltered life I had been living! I think when such hardcore stories were shared in this group, a person listening would think they had no problem at all because of the severity of situations others were in. At least, this is the way I felt.

The man in the center of the circle would watch expressions of people's faces when a problem was talked about. If an individual gasped, rolled their eyes, or changed chair positions and acted disgusted in anyway on what they were hearing, he would turn to that individual and say, "What do you think they should do about this situation?"

I gasped on a story of adultery, and when I couldn't reply, just shook my head back and forth sideways, trying to say no, this minister said, looking straight at me, "It's okay to have extramarital affairs. It will add spice to one's own marriage!"

Another time, the story was about verbal spouse abuse—an argument taking place between husband and wife, and the wife had to leave in order to avoid physical abuse. Of course, she was in that circle. I was really taken back when the leader-minister looked at me again and said, "Marsena, what you need to do is tell a person to go to 'hell' now and then, not that you really mean it. It's just a way of saying, 'Get off my back!'"

I don't think I ever shared in this group. I was just so miserable, wanting to see my family, my children, and escape from this place, longing to have whatever needed to be made right in my life to happen so I could go home!

Maybe therapy was working.

Dear ones! Come on now! Listen up! It is time to realize how very specific the Word of God is on adultery and a lot of other lifestyles. To tell someone it's okay to do something contrary to Scripture is a very dangerous thing to do. If a person heeds the advice of another human being instead of God's Word, they could be doomed. For the Bible reads,

> Now the works of the flesh are manifest, which are these; Adultery, fornication, uncleanness, lasciviousness, idolatry, witchcraft, hatred, variance, emulations, wrath, strife, seditions, heresies, envying, murders, drunkenness, reveling,

and such like; of the which I tell you before, as I have also told you in time past, that they which do such things shall not inherit the kingdom of God. (Galatians 5:19–21 KJV)

Now the doings (practices) of the flesh are clear (obvious); they are immorality, impurity, indecency, idolatry, sorcery, enmity, strife, jealousy, anger (ill temper), selfishness, divisions (dissensions), party spirit (factions, sects with peculiar opinions, heresies), envy, drunkenness, carousing, and the like. I warn you beforehand, just as I did previously, that those who do such things shall not inherit the Kingdom of God. (Galatians 5:19–21 AMP)

The group therapist saying, "It's okay to tell someone to go to 'hell'" is just as dangerous. To say those words of direction to someone else is standing in judgment of another, and proclaiming this sentence in anger or hatred makes one guilty of the above scripture in Galatians 5:19–21. Our lifestyle should, to the best of our ability, represent our Lord Jesus. Speech from our mouth should flow freely with the love of Jesus to win another into His kingdom. Scripture tells us in Matthew 7:1: "Judge not, that you be not judged."

Study note from Life in the Spirit KJV by Donald C. Stamps

Matthew 7:1—Judge not. Jesus condemns the habit of criticizing others while ignoring one's own faults. Believers must first submit themselves to God's righteous standard before attempting to examine and influence the conduct of other Christians (Matthew 7:3–5). Judging in an unjust manner also includes condemning a wrongdoer without desiring to see the offender return to God and His ways (Luke 6:36–37).

1.   Christ is not denying the necessity of exercising a certain degree of discernment or of making value judgments with respect to sin in others. Elsewhere we are commanded to identify false ministers within the church (v.15) and to evaluate the character of individuals (Mat 7:6; cf. John 7:24; 1Cor 5:12; see Gal 1:9 note; 1Tim 4:1, note; 1John 4:1).

2.   This verse must not be used as an excuse for laxity in exercising church discipline (see Mat 18:15, note).

(As you will read later in these writings, I did tell someone or something to go to hell and felt justified and freedom in my spirit after doing so—my freedom deliverance!)

Occupational therapy

The instructor wanted us to work with our hands and think with our minds. We were encouraged to work puzzles, play cards or games, count items, stack blocks, mold clay, etc. I was given a piece of clay to work with in my hands to get the feel of it then was asked to throw this piece of clay down on a board on the table we were standing over and to think of someone we were mad at. I couldn't think of anyone to be mad at. I finally thought of myself. I didn't like me! I didn't like what I had become. I hated myself. So I threw that piece of clay down as hard as I could—again, again, and again—and I ended up as a heap on the floor. I guess my action was the reaction they were looking for.

Physical therapy

This in time was my favorite because it involved action of walking outside and swimming in a pool. Both are still two of my favorite things to do. We also played volleyball in the gym, but the greatest was those long walks on the grounds among the trees and on the sidewalks that surrounded the buildings. The supervisor of the group was always talking to us, whether we communicated back or not, and I loved her chatter. One day, walking back to our building from one of those walks, she started singing songs. Several in the group joined in. A song in particular—the words were

> So let the sun shine in, face it with a grin, smilers
> never lose and frowners never win, so let the sun
> shine in face it with a grin, open up your heart
> and let the sun shine in.

Up to this point, I could not express myself in any way. I couldn't smile! I sure couldn't laugh or even cry! But something about the singing made me think of songs from my childhood, and I started crying like a dam was bursting. It felt so good! I had such a release, and what a relief! This was such a breakthrough of gaining progress on the road to my health being restored. Today, in singing this song, I like to think of "opening up your heart and letting the *Son*_shine in—Jesus Christ, the Son of God"!

Work therapy

The institution was self-supporting. On the acreage was farm ground where crops were raised, a dairy farm with milking cows, a huge greenhouse where food could be raised year around. There was the kitchen where all food was prepared and the cafeteria, a canteen to purchase snacks, and the clothing, sewing, and mending-of-clothes shop. They had a fire station and carpenter's shop. I know the place was subsidized by government funds, but the place appeared to be quite a self-sufficient community. The clothing shop became my work area, and I think tons of clothes were donated for the patients to wear. There were all sizes of everything and even baby clothes for a patient to give to their children. Every article of clothing had to be sorted and placed in its particular category. At the start of going there, my mind would not function to comprehend where to place items. I would get frustrated, give up, and go sit it out usually on the floor. I am thankful that those in charge didn't give up on me. Before leaving the hospital, I saw a woman's coat that looked like "lamb's wool." I took the coat home, cut it up, and made a coat and hat for my youngest baby girl. I remember the color was a beautiful light blue-gray.

Weekend visits

I believe the best therapy was when I could once again see my loved ones. Saturdays and Sundays were the days designated for family visits. Chuck came with talk about working once again with his dad, Claude, and brother, Claudie. They are a four-generation family of doing plaster and stucco work. Margie, brother Mel's widow, was keeping the girls, and Chuck helped bring them for visits also. I couldn't say enough about Margie's efforts during this time. Melbourne II was six years old, my daughter Kim five years, Jacque two years, and Kris, only a few months old, and Margie was an extremely busy mom to all of them. My mom and Chuck's mom, Faye, also helped to see the girls were well taken care of.

I remember one beautiful summer day having a picnic on the hospital grounds. Brother Eldon and wife, Peggy, children, Debbie and Bill, were there from their overseas home. Peggy was pregnant with Tena. Eldon worked for an airline as a mechanic instructor, and their homes abroad were in Addis Ababa, Ethiopia; Beirut, Lebanon; and Jeddah, Saudi Arabia. My mom and dad along with sister Vernita and husband, Reed, also came. I didn't contribute much to the conversation, only talked when asked a direct question that could be answered with one word like yes, no, or okay—but it sure was great to see family! After going home from the hospital, I learned friends had tried to visit but could not because only immediate family was allowed.

Breakthrough

By the end of the summer, I had earned the rights, with permission, to go on walks by myself. I say "earned" because you had to prove to the staff the capability of being trusted. This was accomplished by taking care of all body needs, keeping my room clean, going to meals and therapy sessions without being told to do so, basically being a person—a human being. Whenever possible, I would walk on the green grass among the trees. This one particular day, I knelt to pray. I had thought of God as way up above the blue sky but not sure He knew who I was, kneeling on that Kansas turf. I don't remember what I prayed, but to mark the occasion, I picked up two small twigs from a tree, hewed out part of the middle section of one and toward the top of the other with a fingernail, and placed them together to form a cross. I was so happy with my crude cross, knowing this had meaning and hope for me that I took it back to my room, cleared everything off the dresser, and placed the cross there. My excitement was short-lived! An aide came into the room, saw what I had on the dresser, and said to another with her, "Well, she must be about twelve years old now!" But I didn't want to be a child!

Upon hearing what the aide said, I took the cross off the dresser—it was just twigs anyway—and threw it in the trash can. I then placed perfume, powder, pictures that had been given me, and a calendar upon the dresser.

I wanted to be a woman, not a child. I wanted to be a wife and mother. I'll show that aide!

Nervous breakdown

What is a nervous breakdown? Someone explained to me it was like a heart attack—only it is a mind attack. The mind converts back to being a baby, perhaps even back in the womb. When is a baby the happiest? Mine were so happy when they were naked—hence, I took my clothes off. They were so happy in the bathtub—hence, content surrounded by water as a baby in the womb. I had to be spoon-fed like a baby and led around by someone's hand like a toddler child. I couldn't verbally ask for something I needed; an overseer had to assume the need just like we do children. When an aide saw me acting like a twelve-year-old, she expressed what she saw—a childlike action of playing with twigs or sticks. We can only assume what to know about another individual by what they say or by their actions. Maybe this is why the expression "action speaks louder than words."

What was inside of me is still hard for me to say. I only had the feeling of a lost child all by themselves, shut up in a deep, dark cave. I toured a cave once, and the tour guide turned off all the lights just to show how dark it is down in a cave. You cannot see your hand in front of your face! This is how I felt. I was down to the depths of who knows where with no hope of climbing out. It seemed as if there was no door, no light, nothing in front of me to show the way; but down in that darkness, if someone bumped into me, I would scream—hopeless and fearful at the same time!

This is why I sat most of the time and crouched on the floor in a corner if I could. I didn't want to come into contact with anyone or anything. Lots of scary things are in deep, dark places! There was such a depth to my darkness that I was constantly scared and frightful of my surroundings, and sound—all sounds were magnified. If a train whistle could be heard in the distance, I would think a train was coming through the building and I had better get up and run. Of course, someone would catch me, and the bodily contact would make me scream. The screaming and fighting with the person that stopped me would place me back into a padded cell. What was going on inside of me was pure torture!

If I did allow a person to touch me, they had to approach me with slow movements like a loving touch and a calm voice. The "sweet talk" would make me feel content, especially coming from a large, stately woman, and I actually would let them put their arms around me like a mother does her child. As long as this person had time to hold me, I was comforted.

I don't know how long I was in this frame of mind, but at some point in this period of time, the doctors told my family the doubts of me ever fully recovering. My breakdown was so severe. I know of cases where somewhere in the broken mind of a breakdown the mind locked and no entry can be made. The person is locked into the inside of their own mind, and the real world of reality cannot enter. They see visions inside and even talk with imaginary people, make-believe characters, and animals. Some even imagine themselves to be that animal. In the Bible, we have the story of Nebuchadnezzar in Daniel 5:21:

> And he was driven from the sons of men; and his heart was made like the beasts, and his dwelling was with the wild asses—(wild donkey): they fed him with grass like oxen, and his body was wet with the dew of heaven.

This verse of Scripture goes on to tell us this man lived like this until he recognized lordship of the Most High God:

> Till he knew that the Most High God ruled in the kingdom of men, and that he appointed over it whomsoever he will.

I am so thankful for the childhood that I had, for one of the breakthroughs that I remember was prompted by a song from my youth: "So let the sun (Son) shine in, face it with a grin." Hearing these words helped to bring my mind closer to reality, but was the Son, Jesus, also knocking at my heart's door to enter? Was Jesus on this particular day, wanting to enter my life and take away all my fears? And the day when I put the twigs together to form a cross! How could I know the cross to have special meaning unless my parents and family members taught me and took me to church where explanation of the meaning of the cross was told? How else could I have identified with a little cross made of twigs if this information was not embedded in the "back of my mind"?

Dear family member and friends reading this, come on now! Listen up! *It is time to realize that everything we have spiritually, physically, mentally, emotionally, and financially is because of the cross Jesus died on for you and me!*

> But my God shall supply all your need according to His riches in glory by Christ Jesus. (Philippians 4:19)

Jesus came to earth because of our Father's love, and because Jesus died and rose again, we can live and never die!

> For God so loved the world, that He gave His only begotten Son, that whosoever believeth in Him should not perish, but have everlasting life. (John 3:16)

Jesus wants to be Lord of our kingdom! Nebuchadnezzar wasn't restored to sanity until he knew that "the Most High God ruled in the kingdom of men."

Most of us growing up in church are taught to say the Lord's Prayer:

> Our Father which art in Heaven, Hallowed be Thy name, Thy Kingdom come, Thy will be done in earth, as it is in Heaven. Give us this day our daily bread. and forgive us our trespasses, as we forgive those who trespass against us. And lead us not into temptation, but deliver us from evil: For Thine is the Kingdom, and the power, and the glory, forever! Amen! (Matthew 6:9–13)

Oh, dear ones reading this! Pray this prayer with all the meaning your heart can possibly give to uttering these words. Don't be as a child when first learning this prayer so often said in unison to be saying words just because you were asked from a pulpit or to be quoting a recitation. Come on now! Listen up! *It is time to give special emphasis to whom prayer is addressed. This is our Father who loved us so much he gave us his son so that we can have life!*

How reverently and with great awe should these words be said! In our lives, in our kingdoms, no other name should be so lifted up and so hallowed; and when you say the words "Thy kingdom come," realize what you are asking! For, dear ones, you are asking the King, who created the whole universe to come and establish His kingdom in your heart! There is no end to His blessings that can be so graciously bestowed by His hand on you.

You may go through tough times, but with Jesus inside you, His love and peace will sustain and keep you.

> For He shall give His angels charge over you, to
> keep you in all your ways. (Psalm 91:11)

CHAPTER 5

BACK IN THE WORLD

I was told that I would soon be considered to go home on weekend visits. If everything went well, they would lengthen my stay at home to a week and then increase weekly and monthly. We lived in a small duplex in Springhill, Kansas, and the weekend visits went very well and then back to the hospital during the week for daily therapy sessions. When leaving for the home visits, the hospital staff would caution me to be sure and take my medication as prescribed. It was the fall of 1964 when time came for the month-long stay at home. I did okay at first, then I couldn't make myself go outside where people were. We lived on a busy street, so I avoided even the yard outside of the duplex. Going to the grocery store where lots of people were was not even considered. It just seemed to me that wherever people were, especially strangers, they were looking at me like they knew I was insane. I thought they were staring at me and maybe pointing at me and thinking, *Look at that nut from the insane asylum!*

I stayed in bed, covered up my head with a pillow to try to shut out all sights and sounds. If I could be like an ostrich that sticks my head in the sand, maybe my mind would quit thinking and I would be well. Again, my mind would play tricks on me with sounds and with voices of people that came to visit. I didn't leave the bedroom when visitors came, so I imagined their talk was negative and critical about me. One day when alone at home, I decided I had had enough of myself and would just do away with me! I tied a small rope to the top of the doorjamb and then around my neck and kicked the chair out from under me. The rope came loose, and I fell to the floor. I went back to bed, thinking of myself as more of a failure. I couldn't succeed at even doing away with myself. The next day, I was taken back to the hospital institution, this time with "suicidal tendencies."

Back in the routine of therapy sessions, I also had psychological meetings with psychiatrist. I still wonder how an ink blot on a piece of paper, folding the paper in half, and then describing what image or shape the ink blot had become is a test of someone's mind. I would rather be outside looking up at the clouds in the sky and imagining a big chariot or ship to float upon. I read my first psychology book when in high school back in the 1950s, and Sigmund Freud had to be psycho himself to develop the investigation of analyzing human's thought process. With psychology a person is able to blame his situation on his upbringing, culture, surroundings, and other people and still not get to the deep-rooted problem of sin! We will have in-depth feelings of insecurities, blaming others, and faultfinding until we recognize our sins and give them all to Jesus, who is the only one that can wash us clean.

Come on now! Listen up! It is time to realize the darkness of the enemy of our souls. I had darkness so deep within me for so long that when I finally allowed the "light of the gospel" to shine in by asking Jesus Christ to come and live in me, only then did I receive deep, deep satisfaction and peace within.

The Word of God, our Bible, is the only true source and fact to base our past, present, and future lives on. Within the pages of Scriptures, we will find all that is needed to live life on this earth that sustains health for our mentality as well as all emotional and psychological behavior. If we let our minds dwell on the contents of the Word of God, we will come into "perfect peace"!

> Thou wilt keep him in perfect peace, whose mind
> is stayed on Thee; because he trusted in Thee.
> (Isaiah 26:3)

The Word is Jesus!

> In the beginning was the Word, and the Word
> was with God, and the Word was God. (John 1:1)

And then read on down in the same chapter to verse 14:

> And the Word was made flesh, and dwelt among
> us, (and we beheld His Glory, the Glory as of the
> only begotten of the Father), full of grace and
> truth.

Come on now! Listen up! It is time to make common sense with
our minds that the Creator of all things who even created you in your
mother's womb wants life for you!

> For you created my inmost being, you knit me
> together in my mother's womb. (Psalm 139:13
> NIV)

By asking our Creator, Jesus, to come into your heart and life,
He knows how life was intended to be lived! Believe Him! Believe
His Word!

> All scripture is given by inspiration of God, and
> is profitable for doctrine, for reproof, for correc-
> tion, for instruction in righteousness. (2 Timothy
> 3:16)

> For all have sinned and fall short of the Glory of
> God. (Romans 3:23)

> For the wages of sin is death, but the gift of God
> is eternal life in Christ Jesus Our Lord. (Romans
> 6:23)

If we confess our sins, He is faithful and just and will forgive us our sins and purify us from all unrighteousness. (1 John 1:9)

Behold, I stand at the door, and knock: if any man hear my voice, and open the door, I will come in to him, and will sup with him, and he with Me. (Revelation 3:20)

Yet to all who received Him, to those who believed in His Name, He gave the right to become children of God. (John 1:12)

Come on Now! Listen up! Now is the time to believe the Word of God!

I stayed at the institution for about a month more that year but was home in time for Thanksgiving. It was during this time I starting smoking cigarettes. A doctor told me it might help my nerves, and he himself smoked. Another individual said I looked sophisticated with a cigarette in my hand. I so desperately wanted to be like what I thought to be a woman of success and a normal human being, and if smoking showed others the air of sophistication and not an insecure, timid person—I would smoke. After all, when at the movies, just "look at all those beautiful movie stars who smoked"!

Sometime during this month, I decided that I could make it at home by keeping busy. Mom had often quoted a saying: "You need to keep busy. This keeps the devil away!"

My intentions were to get a sewing machine out and sew clothes for everybody in the family and just keep busy so as not to think! This I did.

To leave the hospital institution, I didn't wait for approval to leave but signed myself out. When I entered, I had signed myself into the facility and legally could sign out.

I want to say there is a compassionate group of individuals who work with mental patients. I have several people in mind when I think of the care they gave, and today they are known in their communities as very active participants. They are "givers"—people who give of themselves in helping others to have life. Thank you, Donna! Thank you, Wes!

What concerns me about our hospitals, institutions, and nursing homes is the medication (drugs!) that are given to sedate. I realize that in a lot of cases, the sedation is necessary to keep a person from harming themselves or bring harm to others, but it is so heart-wrenching to me to walk in these places and see lifeless human beings. Several years after my institutional stay, I went back as a volunteer. I so wanted to help those who were there in somewhat the same state of mind I had been in, but as a volunteer, I could not give a hug or touch the patient. A warm hug brought much comfort to me—and I could not mention the name of Jesus at all. I heard a statement and quoting, "Mental institutions have a lot of people that are confused about Jesus Christ!" This is a lie straight from the enemy's camp. Confusion is caused by the devil! If Jesus could be mentioned and talked about by a born-again believer, a lot of these people could be "set free"!

> And ye shall know the truth, and the truth shall
> make you free. (John 8:32)

Before my mother passed away in September 1984, I tried keeping her in my home to avoid the nursing home. A lot of other circumstances at the time—the girls were teenagers and young women establishing their own homes, a young son approximately four years old and a husband who is self-employed and I am the bookkeeper. Mom was full-time care. She would call out in the night for me, and I would go to her bedside and try to comfort her. About the third day, she fell by the bed and couldn't get up on her own. It was all that my youngest daughter, Kris, and I could do to lift her back up off the floor into the bed.

Exhausted and discouraged about the situation, I visited with the doctor that was caring for Mom.

He said, "Most people that work in a nursing home do only an eight-hour shift, not twenty-four hours a day!"

I reluctantly put Mom in the nursing home close to our home where I could stop by frequently. She withdrew and didn't know or would recognize any of us. Mom developed pneumonia and was taken to the hospital where antibiotics and nutrients were given intravenously. She got better and started to recognize her surroundings and each of us. My sister Vernita, always alert to medical situations, realized that Mom, since in the hospital, had not been given any sedation medication. We asked the doctor when Mom went back to the nursing home if the staff, by "doctor's orders," could refrain from giving her drugs.

The doctor's answer: "I don't think there is a nursing home in all these United States that would accept a patient unless they could be sedated!"

CHAPTER 6

WORLDLY SUCCESS

The hum of the sewing machine was kept quite busy for several months, and I made my mind dwell on the task at hand, taking care of the girls and keeping house. Chuck accepted the manager position of a service station in town, and we moved there. A dear friend, Rena, along with Carol and Norma, had visited me in Springhill, and they had taken me out in the country that fall to pick up pecans. When making our home in town, Rena encouraged me to join a sorority that she was active in. These women—Rena, Carol, Mary, Bettie, Norma, and Betty O—helped me to regain confidence of being with other people, and I began to think of ways to keep my mind focused by doing a job that I could make money to help our financial situation.

I sold cosmetics from door to door; it was a country route and I only did one campaign and I started applying for office work. Typing was something I really enjoyed when in high school, so I had an interview at the office of a factory there in town. I was so nervous when taking the typing test I got on the wrong row of keys and, of course, flunked the test; but due to the person directing the interview who was so kind and understanding and close friends, I didn't get discouraged. I applied for a cashier's position at a small loan company in a neighboring town, but here I had to take an "aptitude test." This alarmed me! On the work application, I had to list health history and stated about my stay in a mental institution—but what if something showed up in this testing that would say, "She isn't fit for employment"? I was scared! Imagine my surprise when the manager of this loan office called me and said he had heard from home office and that the aptitude test that I had taken was the second highest ever recorded in the whole company. I had the job! Wow! I was on the way!

I enjoyed getting up every morning and going to work. Small cash loans were given, and it became my job to search out a person's background for qualification of a loan. I still remember the occupation at most risk to make loans to were ministers and policemen. The office was upstairs over a bank, and I soon made friends with the women there. A company that bottled milk was a half block down the street, and I soon made a friend in Caroline who worked in the office there. She was a single mom and had four children—David, Randy, Vicky, and Becky. I've had the pleasure of watching them grow up and attended all their weddings. I still remember Caroline telling me that to make ends meet, she bought a pound of hamburger and divided it into fourths. With each fourth she made hamburger gravy to feed her family.

On the main street of this town was a little drugstore where workers would gather midmorning for a coffee break. Women from a larger loan company that dealt mainly in real estate loans were usually there, and I became acquainted with them as well. I shared with them how very much I liked my job but missed being in my hometown because of the distance away from my little girls. They were preschool and grade-school age, and I would like a job closer to them so I could more easily attend school functions.

One morning, one of the women from this larger loan company told me their manager wanted to see me. I thought it had to do with a loan Chuck and I had with them because we recently had purchased a house and received a loan from this company. Again, imagine my surprise when Mr. Chet offered me a position at their branch office in my hometown. Brought to mind a saying of my parents: "Always do what is right because you never know who is watching!"

The woman in charge of this branch office was quitting because of a husband's transfer to another state, and the job was mine if I wanted it. The business offered savings accounts and the real estate loans and I would make appointments and an official loan officer would come and meet with the customer. Frank would come over once a day for these appointments, and I did the savings department. I basically was alone most of the day but worked closely with the women in home office (Mary and Betty were tops!) by telephone for daily a cashier's drawer had to balance and also those end-of-the month reports and, yes, periodically facing those official bank examiners. Every evening on my way home from work, I would put the day's income in night depositor with local bank—a lot of responsibility but sure made me feel important! In fact, the women at the local bank said I was making more money than they were, and some of them had worked at the bank for years. Success! Oh, I really thought I had arrived!

I worked in the same town where my girls attended school. We were making payments on a large two-story Victorian house that I loved and had great plans to redecorate. We were also making payments on a red-and-white 67' Chevrolet Impala. Chuck was now working for the county sheriff's department as a deputy—a job he really seemed to enjoy—and we were members of a church where he was active in the choir. Life appeared to be good. We were in debt like everyone else. I thought we had finally arrived at success as far as the status quo was concerned. Chuck was even elected president of a local organization. Yep! I finally made it! I was just as good as anybody.

The clubhouse for this organization was at the lake, and I remember going there to a masquerade party. Phyllis Diller was a famous television comedienne in the 1960s, and I went to a party impersonating her. I had bleached blond hair which I ratted to stick out, lots of heavy makeup on my face, wore a gold-glittering sheath dress and carried a long cigarette holder with, of course, a lighted cigarette. Alcohol, or booze, was what was called "refreshments." And most everybody had plenty of this refreshment and was really feeling the effects. We were acquainted with everyone there; after all, we were a small town. One woman in particular and I had shared those "womanly talks" before, and we started to visit. We went outside where it was more quiet, and north of the building was a ditch that we sat down in. Our backs were leaning on one bank of the very small ravine with our legs lying against the other bank, feet sticking out in the air. We were comfortable for our little visit.

It was a beautiful star-filled night, and the moon made the lake glisten. We talked about our children—the most talked about subject of most women. We talked about our husbands, things going on in the community, and happenings and circumstances of other people's lives. We must have visited for hours. Then the thought came to me, *Had I really arrived at success? I was sitting in a ditch!* I then got sick to my stomach.

But then maybe it was the effects of the "refreshment."

Come on now! Listen up! It is time to realize the world will not bring peace and happiness.

The world with all its advertisements is telling us to buy something new to be happy and to gain satisfaction. We are led to think a new or larger house is needed. We need a new car, new furniture, new clothes with more style because fashion is of most importance. But then, dear ones, how long does it take before we think something else is needed and we keep ourselves in a cycle of wanting and getting? There is always the temptation to get more, more, and more!

Precious family and friends, listen up! It not only works this way with material things but cravings for something to satisfy a deep inner want with alcohol, nicotine, the thrill of gambling. Just look at all the casinos that beckon for participants. People are even hooked on caffeine. I need another cup of coffee or cola drink, and if we don't get a kick or an extra charge from coffee or cola, we can always get caffeine by eating chocolate. Oh, how I like a good piece of smooth brown chocolate! Cravings for food runs rampant in this nation! Come on now! Listen up! What if every time a desired craving entered our thinking, instead of all the mentioned above, we *craved Jesus*—craved being closer to Jesus than ever before! Crave a closer relationship with Jesus!

The "side effects" are above what we can imagine or think—all the love, joy, peace we can ever imagine or think living and working inside of us!

> Now unto Him that is able to do exceedingly abundantly above all that we ask or think, according to the power that worketh in us. (Ephesians 3:20)

What power? The power of Jesus living within! Come on now! Listen up!

> We mutter and sputter; we fume and we spurt.
> We mumble and grumble; our feelings get hurt.
> We don't understand things; our vision grows dim.
> When all that we need is a "moment with Him"!

Come on now! Listen up! *Jesus is the only one who really satisfies!*

> Peace I leave with you, my peace I give unto you: not as the world gives, give I unto you. Let not your heart be troubled, neither let it be afraid. (John 14:27)

Oh, dear ones reading this. Jesus is the answer! Jesus saves, Jesus keeps, and Jesus satisfies! When you ask Jesus into your heart and life, you are asking someone who is alive—because He is alive! This is how we can have life and become dead to the things of the world and to that which tempts us. Jesus only gives peace inside.

> Turn your eyes upon Jesus! Look full into His wonderful face.
> And the things of earth will grow strangely dim
> In the light of His glory and grace.

These things I have spoken unto you, that in Me you might have peace. In the world you shall have tribulation: but be of good cheer; I have overcome the world. (John 14:33)

CHAPTER 7

OFFENCES

Rejection: Not being wanted is a very deep hurt.

Just before our tenth anniversary in 1968, Chuck came home one day and said he loved another. The secretary at work was his ideal woman. The hurt went so deep I was stunned, immobilized, dead in my tracks for action, but I knew keeping busy was what I had to do. After all, I had to think of the girls. I knew of a woman whose husband had placed her in the state institution, declared her insane, and received custody of their children. This was not happening to me! I loved my children and would fight to stay above these circumstances so as to have them.

I had my weak moments because my stomach was in such knots I couldn't eat. I had to keep my strength up because I needed the livelihood and had to keep working. I'm so thankful for the people at home office, for they were so understanding; and with Grandma's café across the street, she sent her grandson over almost every day with a tray of food. Thank you, Troy!

I didn't like going out the noon hour. I didn't want to face people that would try to console me, and I would end up in one of those crying spells. I went to work every day and headed straight home in the evenings to my girls. I only missed one day of work during the whole proceedings, and that was the day I had to go to the courthouse and stand in front of the judge for the divorce. Work, again, was a solace for me.

I did seek counseling from our pastor. He said I had the grounds for divorce that the church could approve and that he was so close to Chuck and I that he wanted me to go to Kansas City to a Christian counseling service. This I did. The appointment time came, and meeting the counselor for first time, I found out he was a psychiatrist and the method of treatment was hypnosis. Immediately, alarm came to me. What on earth did hypnosis have to do with my situation? I had enough of all these psychiatry methods a few years back.

I did sit down in a chair, and he proceeded to wave a watch in front of me back and forth, but I was so determined that this man was not entering my subconscious mind. In fact, he wasn't entering my mind because I kept my mind busy thinking of other things. I had had enough of horrible and evil thoughts that had affected my mind in the state hospital and didn't want anyone messing up my mind again so that I would have to go back to that institution.

After a while, he gave up and said, "Well, this isn't getting us anywhere!"

I think I left to be more bewildered and hurt than ever. But from this, I have learned that everything that says to be Christian may not be! We need to be aware of "wolves in sheep's clothing"!

> Watch out for false prophets. They come to you
> in sheep's clothing, but inwardly they are fero-
> cious wolves. (Matthew 7:15 NIV)

My big concern was the girls—how were they coping with their daddy no longer living with us? I had been awarded the house, furniture, and car from the court proceedings but had to sell the house because I couldn't keep up with the payments. We moved to a little duplex on the east end of town. Sorority sisters and their husbands help make the move. A local trucking company furnished a truck, and Dr. O repaired a dresser and hooked up a washer and dryer. The duplex was next door to a little neighborhood grocery store and across the street from a girls' school academy where the girls and I could ride bicycles through the beautiful grounds. Friends Dan and

Rena lived around the corner. Yes, this was a neighborhood where the girls could be safe.

The owner of the little grocery store became known to our family as Granny Alta. A widow, she lived upstairs over the store and was a tremendous blessing to us. If I had to work late, I could count on her to watch Kim, who walked home from school. Kim stayed alone until I left work and picked up Jacque and Kris at their babysitters. I spent many a consoling and encouraging time with Granny Alta by having those "comfort talks." A very optimistic person, defeat was not in her vocabulary. In fact, when she was in her eighties, she tells me, "I'm not going to get old!" And she never did, proving to me that aging is somewhat of an attitude. I once asked her if she had a secret to her longevity, if she ate a certain food or took special vitamins.

She said, "Well, I eat onions in some form every day!"

She loved children but didn't have any of her own. Teenagers could easily talk with her along with her many friends. After I accepted Jesus into my heart and life, the Lord gave me the privilege of leading Granny Alta into His kingdom. Praise the Lord! She not only "didn't get old," Granny Alta didn't die! She was over ninety years of age when she passed from this life in March 1986, just keeled over with heart failure into the waiting arms of her Savior, Jesus Christ.

> Jesus said to her, "I am the resurrection and the life. He who believes in Me will live, even though he dies; and whoever lives and believes in Me will never die." (John 11:25–26)

It was Christmas of 1968. I attended the service at my church and went home to an empty home because the girls were with their dad and his family. Christmas is supposed to be family time with the children laughing and playing around a tree with their newly opened gifts. The emptiness I felt was devastating. I felt so alone. I knelt beside my bed and prayed, "O, Lord! Send me a Christian husband and daddy for my girls!"

At this time, I still thought our Father was up in heaven and Jesus was at His right hand waiting to come back to earth to judge the quick and the dead. In other words, He was up there, and I was down here and wasn't sure He interacted with people. He was God! He didn't have to pay any mind to my circumstances. But I did feel better after I prayed.

I now know that great mercy was given me for as I write this, this godly person has been my husband for over fifty years. Thank you, Lord!

CHAPTER 8

GOOD-LOOKING DUDE

In February 1969, I was standing behind the cashier's counter and gazing out the front windows that overlooked the park square. I watched as a good-looking dude got out of a station wagon parked across the street and was walking toward the front entrance of the loan company. When he walked in, grinning as he came up to the counter, he said, "My name is Don H, and I would like to see the manager, Mr. Frank."

Being a good secretary, I told him the boss wasn't in and if he would like to make an appointment, please tell me his address, phone number, and desired business transaction. He gave the information and started asking me questions—my name, if I lived in town, and how long had I worked there. I told him and also how much I enjoyed my town and my work.

He then asked the sweetest question ever asked me by a man: "Are you available for dating?"

I somehow stammered out, "Well, yes!" And then he asked what some of my interest were, what did I like to do for hobbies. I first told him about my daughters and how important in what I did would first be their well-being and then I liked to read, sew, crochet, and play around on the piano, but I really liked being outside. Walks and bicycle riding in the spring and fall, swimming in the summer, and this being winter, I told him about a recent outing I had with friends at Mt. Blu, a snow-skiing place west of Lawrence, Kansas, that created artificial snow to operate. A person would grab a rope on a pulley at the bottom of the hill, and with skis on and tightly gripping the rope, you could be pulled to the top of the hill where you skied back down and my problem being I didn't know how to stop my skis when reaching the bottom. In fact, one of the friends I had gone with to Mt. Blu, Lynn, was waiting in line at the bottom of the hill to grab the pulley rope to ascend back up the hill. I was on skis going fast down the hill when I saw I was headed directly to hit him. All I could do was holler at him, "Lynn, Lynn, I can't stop!" He moved up about a foot, and I sailed over the back of his skies.

I may have met Don before in passing like at the service station but didn't know until this day that I was talking to a most avid outdoor sportsman. Fishing, hunting, swimming, waterskiing, scuba diving and snow skiing were his forte. He did ask me out, and our first date was to a wrestling match at the municipal auditorium in Kansas City, Kansas. I now tell people, "We've been wrestling ever since!"

On this first date, he asked me if I had loved my ex-husband.

I responded directly, "If I didn't, I don't know what love is all about!"

Our second date included the girls, and since Don was a volunteer fireman, we attended a dinner with the firemen and their families in our town. Don carried Kris in his arms with Kim and Jacque following into the banquet room, and I was behind them.

Entering the room, Don announced with a loud voice, "I brought my family too!"

It seemed like every eye in the place turned to stare at us. This was "only our second date"! After eating, with two other couples— Bob and Donna, Jack and Moreen—Don and I and the girls went roller-skating at the rink.

Come on now! Listen up! When I told Don on our first date that "I didn't know what love was all about," this was so true because I didn't know Jesus in a personal way; I just had religion. I had thoughts in my head who God was and rituals put to memory who God was, but My Jesus didn't have permanent residence.

Oh, dear ones reading this! Be sure—be very sure—you are in tune with your Creator and you have a relationship with Jesus! The sweet fellowship with Jesus inside is worth more than anything! If you haven't done so, won't you ask Jesus into your heart and life now? He wants to enter your innermost being and give you love.

Come on now! Listen up! It is time.

> Beloved, let us love one another: for love is of God; and every one that loveth is born of God, and knoweth God. He that loveth not knoweth not God; for God is Love. In this was manifested the love of God toward us, because that God sent His only begotten Son into the world, that we might live through Him. Herein is Love, not that we loved God, but that He loved us, and sent His Son to be the propitiation for our sins. (1 John 4:7–10)

Come on now! Listen up! Jesus went to the cross so we could be reconciled to the Father. Jesus took all of our sins upon Himself to remove sin from us. What we need to do is to

- ask forgiveness of our sins,
- believe Jesus had taken our sin upon Himself,
- confess this has been accomplished.

> That if thou shalt confess with thy mouth the Lord Jesus, and shalt believe in thine heart that God hath raised Him from the dead, thou shalt be saved. For with the heart man believeth unto righteousness; and with the mouth confession is made unto salvation. (Romans 10:9–10 KJV)

A definition I like for the word *righteousness* is "right relation-ship." Through what Jesus did on the cross, we are restored to a right relationship with our Father. After accepting Jesus and what He did, we keep ourselves in a right relationship by prayer, talking and communicating with the Father in Jesus's name, and by study of His Word. We need to read and study His Word until the Word—Jesus—is digested into our being, into our hearts, and then we keep our hearts with all diligence. This will be *life* for us!.

> Jesus answered, "I am the way and the truth and the *life*. No one comes to the Father except through me." (John 14:6)

> My son, attend to My Words, incline thine ear unto My sayings. Let them not depart from thine eyes; keep them in the midst of thine heart *for* they are *life* unto those that find them, and health to all their flesh. Keep thy heart with all diligence; for out of it are the issues of *life*." (Proverbs 4:20–23 KJV)

Come on now! Listen up! Now is the time to get *life and ask Jesus into your heart*!

Granny Alta was a godsend. She stayed with the girls a lot so Don and I were free to go places. We enjoyed each other's company, and I was blessed when our times together did include the girls. This was important to me. The stairs going up to Granny Alta's apartment was just a few feet from the front door of our duplex. It would usu-ally be after closing time of the little grocery store she had when she would see Don drive up and get out of his vehicle.

She would holler some cheery greeting and say, "If you need me, you know where to find me!"

At times, I thought, *She is really taken with this man!* I know she was over seventy-five years old.

One day when Granny Alta and I were having one of those private discussions, she told me, "You know, Don has the clearest complexion. Why—the skin on his face is as smooth as a baby's behind!"

She then started calling him "Donnie Babe." Kris, only four years old, started calling him this as well. Don then started calling her "Kissie Krissie," and she usually obliged with a kiss.

Three couple friends were also fascinated with learning to snow ski. A trip was planned to go to Tan Tara Resort in the Ozarks. Before reservations were made, I told my friend Bev my hesitation in going because of the room situation. The couples going—Loren and Bev, Rex and Judy, Bob and Sheila—were married. Those gals told me no problem; it was just a weekend, and their husbands wouldn't mind for Don to room with one of them. Loren and Bev has daughters the ages of mine, and we left the children with a reliable babysitter at their house. We left town immediately following work on Friday evening, and after stopping for the evening meal arrived at the hotel at bedtime. Those gals had a sneak surprise for me! Each couple had keys for their rooms, and they handed the last key to Don and I, laughing gleefully, and left us in the hallway outside the vacated room. It was too late to drive back home and so tired after working all day and traveling there. We unlocked the door and went in. I was so thankful to see two beds in the room!

This resort also had artificial snow for skiing but a single chair lift for going back up the hill. Don had been to the big ski areas in Colorado and expressed the thought of us going there. He said the month of March there was still lots of snow in the mountains of Colorado. I knew getting off from work wouldn't be a problem, but I couldn't go unless there was a chaperone. I had young girls to rear and needed to be a good example. Chuck's sister Hazel and husband Jim lived in Littleton just outside of Denver and readily agreed for us to stay with them. I can't say enough about Chuck's family for still considering me in the family. The first part of March 1969, Don and I had five glorious days in Colorado. Granny Alta stayed with the girls.

The first morning at the ski area, Don put me in a class where I learned the snow-plow position to stop downhill skis. I was so amazed at the vastness of the slopes. Jim, Hazel, and their children, Claudia, Andy, and Charles, were wonderful hosts! They even went to the mountains with us where we all had a great day snowmobiling. I loved the mountains, and skiing and snowmobiling are such exuberating sports.

On the way back across Kansas, it was nighttime, and I remember looking over at Don driving and seeing his profile with the bright moonlight shining behind him. I thought what a wonderful man he was and how easily I could fall in love, but I was fearful of rejection and kept my distance. After a couple of dates, Don even called me "door hugger" because I didn't sit close to him in the car. I just didn't want to be hurt, and I felt down deep what I would tell my daughters when they started dating in those teenage years:

"Dating is like going hunting. The hunt's over when you get the game."

CHAPTER 9

OPEN HEART'S DOOR

During a lot of our dates or times together, we attended services at a local full-gospel church. This was all so new to me as I didn't remember having any knowledge of the books of Acts and Revelation that are in our Bibles. But what immediately spoke to my heart at the onset of going there was the music. These people didn't just sing songs about Someone, they sang as if singing directly to Someone! I was touched and amazed! And then, a way that really ministered to me was the children's church. My girls were so excited about the stories and songs they were learning and started singing them at home. I hadn't seen my girls so happy in months!

Pastor Vic and Marge have two girls, Laurie and Cherie, the same ages as Jacque and Kris, and these girls were having some good times getting acquainted. Kim started being interested with children's church, helping with the puppet stories. We got her a dummy puppet, and she started to learn how to be a ventriloquist. Don and I were fellowshipping with couples and having a great time, two couples—Les and Pat and Dave and Georgiea—the guys are brothers, sons of Harry and Helen. Don's Grandmother Yoell was the best of friends with Helen's family, the Earnst family. In fact, Grandmother Yoell named her daughter Helen (Don's mother) after this Helen. My grandfather Kim worked on the farm of the Earnst family southwest of town. After my parents' passing, my sister was cleaning out the old farm house and found a birth announcement telling of the birth of Les. Both Don's and my family had in previous generations close connections with this family.

The ultimate was the evening at a revival service in March 1969 when I went forward under conviction of the message just heard and knelt at the altar and *asked Jesus into my heart and life*. I felt so good! I cried! Realizing conviction was lifted, I cried more—sobbing! What a relief! No pressures, *just love*!

Now why a woman cries when she is happy, I don't know; but this time, it was like what Mom used to say: "Crying is like washing windows of a house. The windows are dirty, and after washing them, you can always see out a lot better!"

As I knelt there crying, I became conscious of two individuals on either side of me. I felt such a closeness of fellowship that felt like something inside of me was identifying with what these two women had. They commenced to pray, thanking the Lord for my newfound salvation and also that He would continue to bless my life. A sweet, sweet Spirit was there! The moment was so cleansing, peaceful, and calm—just like the calm after a terrible storm! I am so thankful that our Lord blessed us with two precious sisters that night who have always been there for me, and I now know, Marge and Georgiea, that we are in His kingdom together forever!

All I can say is I have never felt so *complete* and *clean*. The completeness was like everything in me was now connected. My inner being had come together! I was a whole human being! I can only describe this like Ezekiel's dry bones:

> The hand of the Lord was upon me, and carried me out in the spirit of the Lord, and set me down in the midst of the valley which was full of bones. And caused me to pass by them round about: and, behold, there were very many in the open valley; and, lo, they were very dry. And he said unto me, "Son of man, can these bones live?" And I answered, "O Lord God, thou knowest." Again, he said unto me, "Prophesy upon these bones, and say unto them, 'O ye dry bones, hear

the word of the Lord. Thus saith the Lord God unto these bones; "Behold, I will cause breath to enter into you, and ye shall live: And I will lay sinews upon you, and will bring up flesh upon you, and cover you with skin, and put breath in you, and ye shall live; and ye shall know I am the Lord."'" So I prophesied as I was commanded; and as I prophesied, there was a noise, and behold a shaking, and the bones came together, bone to his bone. And when I beheld, lo, the sinews and the flesh came up upon them, and the skin covered them above: but there was no breath in them. Then said he unto me, "Prophesy unto the wind, prophesy, son of man, and say to the wind, 'Thus saith the Lord God; "Come from the four winds, O breath, and breathe upon these slain, that they may live."'" So I prophesied as he commanded me, and the breath came into them, and they lived, and stood up upon their feet, an exceeding great army. Then he said unto me, "Son of man, these bones are the whole house of Israel: behold, they say, 'Our bones are dried, and our hope is lost: we are cut off for our parts.' Therefore, prophesy and say unto them, 'Thus saith the Lord God; "Behold, O my people, I will open your graves, and cause you to come up out of your graves, and bring you into the land of Israel. And ye shall know that I am the Lord, when I have opened your graves, O my people, and brought you up out of your graves, And shall put my spirit in you, and ye shall live, and I shall place you in your own land; then shall ye know that I the Lord have spoken it, and performed it," saith the Lord.'" (Ezekiel 37:1–14)

Come on now! Listen up! It is time to come alive! In verse 14, the Word of God tells us,

And shall put My Spirit in you, and you shall live!

When a person asked Jesus, who is God into their hearts, His Spirit is given birth!
That which was dead now has a start of life!
Come on now! Listen up! Listen to how Jesus tells this to Nicodemus:

> Jesus answered and said unto him, "Verily, verily, I say unto thee. Except a man be born again, he cannot see the kingdom of God." Nicodemus saith unto him, "How can a man be born when he is old? Can he enter the second time into his mother's womb, and be born?" Jesus answered, "Verily, verily, I say unto thee, Except a man be born of water and of the Spirit, he cannot enter into the Kingdom of God. That which is born of the flesh is flesh; and that which is born of the Spirit is Spirit. Marvel not that I said unto thee, Ye must be born again. The wind bloweth where it listeth, and thou hearest the sound thereof, but canst not tell whence it cometh, and whither it goeth: so is every one that is born of the Spirit." (John 3:3–8)

Oh, dear family and friends! It's like a spark that sets one's heart on fire and you burn with desire for more of Him. More of Jesus! More of His Precious Holy Spirit! More of His Word in our hearts and lives that we please our Lord in kingdom ways!

> Thy Word have I hid in mine heart, that I might not sin against Thee. (Psalm 119:11)

Not only did I feel more connected but clean! The cleansing is so remarkable!

Dear ones, being "born again" makes one clean as a newborn baby!

> Therefore if any man be in Christ, he is a new creature: old things are passed away; behold all things are become new. (2 Corinthians 5:17)

The cleansing that takes place is the washing away of all guilt, shame, hurts, and crud of the past! We won't have to think on those things out of our past anymore! We only have to look ahead and to our Lord's kingdom ways! When we do look back and let our mind dwell on the past, this is when we can have problems. My daddy, when plowing a furrow, would always look straight ahead at a certain object. If he would look back for very long, the furrow would become crooked. We can't look back and make a straight line ahead.

> Jesus replied, "No one who puts his hand to the plow and looks back is fit for service in the Kingdom of God." (Luke 9:62 NIV)

Dear ones, when we accept Jesus Christ into our hearts and lives, the cleansing makes us so clean that we do not have to think about the dirt of our past anymore!

Listen to the story of Jesus and the woman at the well in Samaria.

> There cometh a woman of Samaria to draw water: Jesus saith unto her, "Give me a drink." (For His disciples were gone away unto the city to buy meat.) Then saith the woman of Samaria unto Him, "How is it that thou, being a Jew, askest drink of me, which am a woman of Samaria? For the Jews have no dealings with the Samaritans." Jesus answered and said unto her, "If thou knewest the gift of God, and Who it is that saith to thee, Give Me a drink; thou wouldest have asked

of Him, and He would have given thee living water." The woman saith unto Him, "Sir, Thou hast nothing to draw with, and the well is deep: from whence then hast thou that living water: Art Thou greater than our father Jacob, which gave us the well, and drank thereof himself, and his children, and his cattle?" Jesus answered and said unto her, "Whosoever drinketh of this water shall thirst again: But whosoever drinks of the water that I shall give him shall never thirst; but the water that I shall give him shall be in him a well of water springing up into everlasting life." (John 4:7–14)

Look at the last part of verse 14 again: "*in him a well of water springing up into everlasting life.*"

Dear ones, do you know what an artesian well is? Listen to this definition:

> A well drilled through impermeable strata to reach water capable of rising to the surface by internal hydrostatic pressure. (*American Heritage Dictionary*, Second College Edition)

The Holy Spirit can penetrate through all the hardcore crust of sin, saturating the very depth of our beings with His cleansing love that rises up within us to immeasurable joy!

> Surely God is my salvation; I will trust and not be afraid. The Lord, the Lord, is my strength and my song; He has become my salvation. With joy you will draw water from the wells of salvation. (Isaiah 12:2–3)

Great love, joy, and peace has come to my life by my acceptance of Jesus! My Jesus is God of love! My Jesus is Prince of peace!

And when going through adverse circumstances, Jesus is my strength because just knowing Him gives joy!

> For the joy of the Lord is your strength. (Nehemiah 8:10)

Dear ones, we don't have to wait until we are in a church building at an altar. Why not make an altar where you are right now? If you can't get on your knees, kneel in your heart, for what He is looking for is a yielded heart! Be honest with Him! He knows everything that is going on anyway. Just say, "Forgive me of all my sins! I ask You, Jesus, to come into my heart and life and keep me in Your kingdom ways!"

And then, dear one, tell Jesus, "Thank you!" Start thanking Jesus that He went to the cross for your sins to purchase your salvation. For you see, dear one, when we confess to Jesus and then start praising and thanking Him, "*Belief is more established into our hearts. Thankfulness opens our hearts to His presence and our minds to His thoughts.*"

Come on now! Listen up! It is time to ask Jesus into your heart and life!

This is what I call, "Sip, sap, sup!" When we cook a pot of soup on the stove, as chef, we taste it before we serve it to see if we need to add any more ingredients. When we "*sip,*" we taste! Come on now! It is time to

"*Sip*"

> O taste and see that the Lord is good: blessed is the man that trusteth in Him. (Psalm 34:8)

"*Sap*" is what makes a tree grow straight and tall; its roots grow deep.

> And he shall be like a tree planted by the rivers of water, that bringeth forth his fruit in his season;

his leaf also shall not wither, and whatsoever he doeth shall prosper. (Psalm 1:3)

"*Sup*" is like the evening meal of supper.

Behold, I stand at the door, and knock; if any man hear my voice, and open the door, I will come in to him, and will sup with him, and he with me. (Revelation 3:20)

Come on now! Listen up! Ask Jesus into your heart and life and have a good taste!

"*Sip*." Start feasting on His Word, the Scriptures, and receive inner strength! "*Sap*" and you will have a continual feast with Jesus, Lord and Maker of all, for He is the One who will "*sup*" with you and you with Him! Jesus is our God! Jesus is awesome!

Do you remember in summer when as a child playing outside when the evening was cooling down? You were playing so hard and then you heard a voice calling, "Come home! It's suppertime!"

You ran as fast as you could to the door of your home to reach the table to perhaps be the first one there to get that "freshly fried drumstick" of the chicken or some other choices you knew Mom had prepared—and the feast was on!

Jesus wants to be first at the table of your heart, where He will feast with you continually!

And for all you prodigals out there who have left the Lord's kingdom for eyes on the ways of this world, Father God, Jesus, will run to meet you when you start heading His way but will stop at your heart's door until you ask Him to "come in"!

And He said, "A certain man had two sons: And the younger of them said to his father, Father, give me the portion of property that is coming to me. And he divided unto them his living. And not many days after the younger son gathered all

68

together, and took his journey into a far country, and there wasted his substance with riotous living. And when he had spent all, there arose a mighty famine in that land; and he began to be in want. And he went and joined himself to a citizen of that country; and he sent him into his fields to feed swine. And he would have filled his belly with the husks that the swine did eat; and no man gave unto him. And when he came to himself, he said, 'How many hired servants of my father's have bread enough and to spare, and I perish with hunger! I will arise and go to my father, and will say unto Him, "Father, I have sinned against heaven, and before thee. And am no more worthy to be called Thy son; make me as one of thy hired servants."' And he arose, and came to his Father. But when he was yet a great way off, his Father saw him, and had compassion, and ran, and fell on his neck, and kissed him. But The Father said to His servants, 'Bring forth the best robe, and put it on him; and put a ring on his hand, and shoes on his feet; And bring hither the fatted calf, and kill it; and let us eat, and be merry; For this my son was dead, and is alive again; he was lost, and is found.' And they began to be merry." (Luke 15:11–24)

Prodigal! Jesus loves you and wants you to come home!

CHAPTER 10

GETTING MARRIED

Don and I had only dated for a couple of months, but after I accepted the Lord, there seemed to be more of a closeness and bonding with him. I remembered my prayer at Christmastime and knew after sitting beside him in church that he could be the answer to that prayer. When he began to talk of marriage, he told me that he had also prayed. He had prayed for a woman "with children" because he had polio when fifteen years old and it wouldn't be possible for him to father a child. Don loves children and certainly proved it by the attention given to my girls. My girls seemed to be happy with all the activities we were already doing as a family. My mom and dad were elated! Being country, they liked Don's knowledge of the great outdoors but mainly that the girls and I would be provided for. So, it was time to talk with Don's family.

Don's real dad passed away when Don was only twelve years old, and his mom married Ralph when Don was approximately twenty years old. I had met quite a few of Don's family that spring at Easter when at a dinner at Don's brother's house, Ray with wife Loretta. I was talking with Don's mom and told her about my three daughters and was reaching in my purse to show her a picture.

She said, "You—have three girls!"

I thought Don had already told her, and when I met Ralph, his remark was, "Oh, you're the ole mother hen with chickens."

Now to me, coming from the country and knowing how much a mother hen protects her chicks under her wings, I took this as a compliment. But the way he looked at Don when saying this, he seemed to be saying, "Boy, do you know what you are getting into?"

When we arrived at Don's mother's house, Aunt Jean was also there, so there were the two matriarchs of the family. Don came right to the point and stated that we were planning on getting married and if they or anyone else in the family had any objections, he would like to know about it now so as to not have any interference after we were married! Aunt Jean quoted from the Scriptures:

> Whosoever shall put away his wife, except it be
> for fornication, and shall marry another, com-
> mits adultery. (Matthew 19:9)

She looked at me, and I told her about visiting my pastor and the divorce I had was because of adultery. They already knew Don's divorced situation. Mom and Aunt Jean both gave us their blessing!

I accepted an engagement ring sometime in May. We had gone to the city to pick up a set of table and chairs and had borrowed Les S's pickup truck. Don had a friend that was giving him the furniture and when I saw it thought how unusual that there were only five chairs. Most table sets came with either four or six chairs. But then, of course, the five chairs were perfect for the three girls, Don, and I! A beautiful evening, the windows rolled down, and the aroma of cow manure from a bed of truck was strong. As I admired my new ring, I thought to myself, *Yep! My good-looking city dude gone country!*

Daughters were the first to see my ring, and then I went over to show Granny Alta. She was very excited, threw her hands up in the air, and shouted, "O, I prayed for this!"

When the girls at the bank saw the ring, I noticed they were very amazed!

One of them said sort of offish, "Well! You're the first to get one of these! Don had told me in the eleven years after his divorce he had dated quite a few, and living in a small town when I had started to date Don, others had told me of his 'Don Juan reputation'!"

The saying is "Love them and leave them." I again started to think of rejection! I talked with friend, Bev, about this and told her if Don and I weren't married by a certain time, I had better break off the engagement. I didn't want to be led on—if that is what was happening.

One morning, on the way to work, I stopped by the cabinet shop.

Don approached me, grinning, and said, "There is a doctor down the street that wants some of your blood!"

How romantic! This is how he proposed! In the 1960s, everyone getting married had to get a blood test then wait three days for the results before marriage could take place. Don's sister, Mary, was visiting from California and was leaving in a couple of days. She had told her brother that he either got married while she was there, or he would have to wait until she visited again.

We got the blood test, signed the necessary papers at the courthouse and also wavering rights of three-day waiting and planned the ceremony. Since Mary was the instigator prompting the action, we asked her to be matron of honor. Bob Ingersoll was asked to be best man. Bev went with me to the city to buy a new dress, and Loren, her husband, came to the ceremony as "big daddy"! We called daughter Kim, who was at a church camp in Augusta, Kansas, to tell her what was happening and were concerned but knew Marge was there to help her understand. She was having good spiritual guidance. Jacque and Kris went to Loren and Bev's home for the weekend. A surprise reception was given us at Bob and Donna's home with Sherry helping. Pastor McGinnis, who worked part-time at the cabinet shop and also pastor of a little church in town on the corner of Pearl Street, married us there on July 17, 1969.

CHAPTER 11

BAPTIZED IN WATER

Being baptized in water is a birth announcement and funeral at the same time. A person is announcing their stand they have taken for Jesus and telling everybody that they want to be known as a follower of Jesus; and the water is the burial ground to represent dying to self and the things of this ole world.

> Know ye not, that so many of us were baptized into Jesus Christ were baptized into his death? Therefore, we are buried with Him by baptism into death: that like as Christ was raised up from the dead by the glory of the Father, even so we also should walk in newness of life. (Romans 6:3–4)

Jesus went to the cross, taking all our sins and nailing them there. Jesus died on the cruel cross, and they took him down and placed His body in a tomb. He arose again on the third day—the resurrection day!

Water baptism announces: We have asked for forgiveness of sins and accepted Jesus.

We go under the water to represent death.

We come up out of the water to symbolize newness of life.

Come on now! Listen up! Now is the time to start following Jesus, be baptized, *and tell others we are burying our old life and resurrected into the life of Jesus Christ!*

> In the days of Noah while the ark was being built. In it only a few people, eight in all, were saved through water, and this water symbolizes baptism that now saves you also—not the removal of dirt from the body but the pledge of a good conscience toward God. It saves you by the resurrection of Jesus Christ. (1 Peter 3:20–21)

> Water baptism saves us in the sense that it is an obedient expression of our repentance, our faith in Christ and our commitment to come out of the world. It is our confession and pledge that we belong to Christ and have died and risen with Him. (Donald C. Stamps, writer of study notes, *The Full Life Study Bible*)

The reference to Noah and the ark in the above verse, I thought about how the ark represents our Jesus. And, fellow believers, we are ever so safe in this ark! The water is a symbol of the Holy Spirit and holds up the ark in the water. The ark floats! Oh! How sweet this water is! What a wonderful Savior we have! With all this in mind, *the water could be a representation of Jesus's Spirit holding us up in this ole world!*

CHAPTER 12

BAPTIZED IN LOVE

The Holy Spirit of love will hold us up in this ole world. Our heavenly Father is God of love! He gave us His Son and His Spirit!

"Not by might, nor by power, but by My Spirit," saith the Lord of hosts. (Zechariah 4:6)

Dear family and friends! When first attending the full-gospel church, I hadn't read or studied the book of Acts in the Bible. Up to this point in my life, I thought of Jesus in heaven sitting at the right hand of the Father from where He will come to judge humanity. Our daughters came home from children's church singing choruses. One of the songs was

> Silver and gold have I none, Such as I have give I thee,
> In the Name of Jesus Christ of Nazareth, Rise Up and Walk!
> Walking and Leaping and Praising God!
> Walking and Leaping and Praising God!
> In the Name of Jesus Christ, Rise Up and Walk!

This song is taken from

> One day Peter and John were going up to the
> temple at the time of prayer—at three in the
> afternoon. Now a man crippled from birth was
> being carried to the temple gate called Beautiful,
> where he was put every day to beg from those
> going into the temple courts. When he saw
> Peter and John about to enter, he asked them for
> money. Peter looked straight at him, as did John.
> Then Peter said, "Look at us!" So the man gave
> them his attention, expecting to get something
> from them. Then Peter said, *"Silver or gold I do
> not have, but what I have I give you. In the name of
> Jesus Christ of Nazareth, rise up and walk."* (Acts
> 3:1–6)

> Taking him by the right hand, he helped him up,
> and instantly the man's feet and ankles became
> strong. He jumped to his feet and began to walk.
> Then he went with them into the temple courts,
> *walking and leaping, and praising God.* When all
> the people saw him *walking and praising God,*
> they recognized him as the same man who used
> to sit begging at the temple gate called Beautiful,
> and they were filled with wonder and amazement
> at what had happened to him. (Acts 3:7–10)

I knew Jesus did mighty miracles when He walked the earth—
but these men did this miracle after Jesus ascended into heaven! I
opened the book of Acts!

> In my former book, Theophilus, I wrote about
> all that Jesus began to do and teach until the day
> he was taken up to heaven, after giving instruc-
> tions through the Holy Spirit to the apostles

He had chosen. After His suffering, He showed himself to these men and gave many convincing proofs that He was alive. He appeared to them over a period of forty days and spoke about the Kingdom of God. On one occasion, while He was eating with them, He gave them this command: "Do not leave Jerusalem, but wait for the gift my Father promised, which you heard Me speak about. For John baptized with water, but in a few days you will be baptized with the Holy Spirit." (Acts 1:1–5 NIV)

When they therefore were come together, they asked of Him, saying, "Lord, wilt Thou at this time restore again the Kingdom to Israel?" And He said unto them, "It is not for you to know the times or the seasons, which the Father hath put in His own power. But ye shall receive power, after that the Holy Ghost is come upon you: and ye shall be witnesses unto Me Both in Jerusalem, and in all Judea, and in Samaria, and unto the uttermost part of the earth." (Acts 1:6–8 KJV)

As I typed the words "the uttermost part of the earth" above, I couldn't help but think of this full-gospel church and the one who is the pastor now. Pastor Roy, for the last two or three years, has taken a group of people to Panama, ministering in the remote areas there; and Pastor Luis lives in New Zealand, and has many trips to Mozambique and China, Bill and Pam Garfield with Natalie in Russia. Yes, the message is reaching the uttermost part of the earth"!

Come on now! Listen up! This is the time to pay close attention! Read further in Acts 1:9–11:

After He said this, He was taken up before their very eyes, and a cloud hid Him from their sight. They were looking intently up into the sky as He was going, when suddenly two men dressed in white stood beside them. Men of Galilee, they said, "Why do you stand here looking into the sky? This same Jesus, Who has been taken from you into Heaven, will come back in the same way you have seen Him go into Heaven."

Dear ones! Verses 9 through 11 tell us of Jesus ascending into heaven, and the Apostle Peter tells us in Acts 2:33:

Exalted to the right hand of God, He has received from the Father the promised Holy Spirit and has poured out what you now see and hear.

This is just part of the first chapters of Acts. Pentecost occurs on the calendar the seventh Sunday after Easter, the day we celebrate our Lord Jesus's resurrection. These next verses tell us what happened after Jesus ascended into heaven and sits by the Father! The disciples are waiting in Jerusalem because according to Acts 1:4, *Jesus commanded them to do so*! Jesus would not have told them to do this unless it is extremely important! Why so important? Read again Acts 1:8 KJV: "*But you shall receive power!*"

Come on now! Listen up! Now is the time to look further on in Acts 1:8 because it tells you what power—*after that the Holy Ghost is come upon you.*"

Now, dear ones! Jesus wants His followers to have His Spirit, the Holy Ghost. Read again the next phrase of Acts 1:8: "*and you shall be witnesses.*" *Whom* are we to be witnesses *for*?

"*Unto me both*" Jesus and the Holy Spirit—*for* Jesus and the Holy Spirit telling others that Jesus saves, Jesus keeps, and Jesus satisfies! The Holy Spirit will *always* honor Jesus!

The Holy Spirit in us for honoring Jesus in the world witnessing!
The Holy Spirit gives power to witness about Jesus!

The Holy Spirit gives power to tell others about the availability of salvation. Telling everyone you can about the Savior, who died on a cruel cross for our sins, was buried in a tomb but rose again, and then the glorious resurrection morning!

What a message! And we, as believers, need to tell this story again, again, and again! To tell everyone! Telling *all* people everywhere to give them the opportunity to believe *and accept Jesus*! That hell is not their eternity but by *believing in Jesus, heaven will be their eternal home*!

Love is the power! Our God is God of love and wants to immerse us with Himself!

Immersed in love to receive power!

"Baptism of love" and "baptism in love" = ONE!

Jesus tells us in John 10:30: *"I and the Father are ONE."*

Deuteronomy 6:4: *"Hear, O Israel: The Lord our God, the Lord is ONE."*

Our Father God, Jesus, and Holy Ghost are ONE!

Jesus prayed that we would be ONE like He and the Father are ONE!

> That they all may be ONE; as thou, Father, art in Me, and I in Thee, that they also may be ONE in us; *that the world may believe that Thou hast sent Me.* (John 17:21)

To have this oneness, to be at one with Jesus—having a right relationship with God, our Father. "In the beginning God created" Adam and Eve. God walked in the cool of the day to visit with them. You know the rest of this story! But since creation and time began, our Creator has wanted fellowship with mankind.

Scripture tells us in the Old Testament that our God was trying to reach the hearts of mankind through the words and deeds of the prophets and mighty miracles given throughout the history of Israel. In the New Testament is recorded the life of Jesus, God's only Son, Who did mighty miracles when He walked this earth. And the book of Acts tells us the facts about the Holy Ghost given to each and every believer so the mighty miracles Jesus did will continue through us. The greatest miracle is witnessing so another person is "born again"!

Here are three more scriptures telling us about the Spirit of our God:

> For I will pour water upon him that is thirsty, and floods upon the dry ground: I will pour My Spirit upon thy seed, and My blessing upon thine offspring. (Isaiah 44:3)

> And it shall come to pass afterward, that I will pour out My Spirit upon all flesh: and your sons and your daughters shall prophesy; your old men shall dream dreams, your young men shall see visions. (Joel 2:28)

> But this is that which was spoken by the prophet Joel; And it shall come to pass *in the last days, saith God, "I will pour out of My Spirit upon all flesh*: and your sons and your daughters shall prophesy, and your young men shall see visions, and your old men shall dream dreams." (Acts 2:16–17)

Dear ones, *the first outpouring was on Pentecost after Jesus ascended into heaven and today is still being poured out on believers in Jesus Christ*!

In 1975, Don and I had the privilege to travel to Israel. Oh, it was so marvelous to be in the land where Jesus walked. Jerusalem, the garden of Gethsemane, River Jordan, Sea of Galilee are all sights to behold! We also were able to take a side trip to Egypt where we saw the Great Pyramids. A tour guide told us the pyramids are so ancient historians have not agreed on the time of their construction. Their age is at such an early time frame; history records only that early Egyptians built these mammoth structures.

The man driving our bus that day told us the mathematical equation used to build them is so complicated; the same sort of formula was being used to go into outer space and even the moon. He also told us there was evidence these huge mountains of stone blocks were once covered with a shiny substance like gold or silver. People who walked the earth then didn't use money or valuable metals; they probably just traded their wares with each other. When the moon shined on these shiny pyramids at the angles built, the reflection glistened brightly and formed a cross.

I believe our God was even telling those early Egyptians the only way back to Him would be through the cross!

Where are we to witness according to Acts 1:8?

> *In Jerusalem, and in all Judaea, and in Samaria, and unto the uttermost part of the earth.*

"In Jerusalem, and in all Judaea, and in Samaria" describes areas in Israel. The part of the scripture saying "uttermost part of the earth" pertains to areas of uttermost distance from Israel. Therefore, from our point of residence on this earth, we are to be witnesses in our town, our country, in the nations and uttermost parts of the earth from where we live. This pertains to everyone who is a believer, so everyone is to be a witness *everywhere*!

I've heard it said: "*We either are a missionary or we need one!*"

> Go ye into all the world, and preach the Gospel to every creature. He that believeth and is baptized shall be saved; but he that believeth not shall be damned. And these signs shall follow them that believe; In My Name shall they cast out devils; *they shall speak with new tongues*; They shall take up serpents; and if they drink any deadly thing, it shall not hurt them; they shall lay hands on the sick, and they shall recover. (Mark 16:15)

Come on now! Listen up! Now is the time to read verses from the second chapter of Acts!

> When the day of Pentecost was fully come, they were all with One accord *in one place. And sud-*

*denly there came a sound from Heaven as of a rush-
ing mighty wind, and it filled all the house where
they were sitting. And there appeared unto them
cloven tongues like as* of fire, and it sat upon each
of them. And they were all filled with the Holy
Ghost, and began to speak with other tongues, as
the Spirit gave them utterance. (Acts 2:1–4)

Wow! Way out wonder! Our God is awesome! Our Father loves
us so much He gave fulfillment of the Holy Ghost: "*all filled with the
Holy Ghost.*"

The scripture just quoted says, "filled with the Holy Ghost,"
and Jesus says in Acts 1:5, "baptized with the Holy Ghost."

Filled is full to capacity. Dear ones, *we can be filled to capacity
with love. Our God is love; therefore, God's Spirit is love, and we can be
filled with love when we seek the Holy Spirit's outpouring*!

Benefits of the love baptism:

- Filled to capacity with love
- Power to witness
- Speaking with tongues

Speaking in tongues is uttering what the Holy Spirit gives.
When uttering what the Holy Spirit gives, we have direct access to
the Father! What a benefit!

For he that speaks in an unknown tongue speaks
not unto men, but unto God: for no man under-
stands him; howbeit in the Spirit he speaks mysteries. (1 Corinthians 14:2)

*And what a relationship of love fulfilled between our Creator
Father God and mankind!*

This "spirit of love infilling" is a dynamic exultation of one's
being, and we know by the Word of God that our loving heavenly
Father gives good gifts to them that believe.

Which of you, if his son asks for bread, will give him a stone? Or if he asks for a fish, will give him a snake? If you, then, though you are evil, know how to give good gifts to your children, how much more will your Father in Heaven give good gifts to those who ask Him! (Matthew 7:9–11)

The Full Life Study Bible note by Donald C. Stamps

Matthew 7:11 Your Father Gives Good Gifts. Christ promises that the Father in Heaven will not disappoint His children. He loves us even more than a good earthly father loves his children, and He wants us to ask Him for whatever we need, promising to give us what is good. He desires to provide solutions for our problems and bread for our daily needs. And most of all, *He gives the Holy Spirit to His children as their Counselor and Helper* (Luke 11:13; John 14:16–18).

This "love baptism" makes us *feel so good and gives us confidence. But we must realize that we are to seek Jesus and not an experience!' Jesus is real! An experience may be false.*

"The love baptism" of Holy Spirit will always exult Jesus and the Word of God. Jesus is the Word of God. *An experience* will have self-exulting results and carnal nature puffed up. The Word of God says it like this in 1 Corinthians 13:1:

If I speak in the tongues of men and of angels, but have not love, I am only a resounding gong or a clanging cymbal.

Stories about country living really intrigue me. Reading in one of my devotionals, a story about cows really spoke to me with great importance of genuine time alone with my Lord.

The following is from *Streams in the Desert 366 Daily Devotional Readings* by L. B. Cowman, edited by James Reimann (pp.176–177):

> The cows that were ugly and gaunt ate up the seven sleek, fat cows…The thin heads of grain swallowed up the seven healthy, full heads. (GENESIS 41:4,7)

April 30

This dream should be a warning to each of us. Yes, it is possible for the best years of our life, the best *experiences* we have enjoyed, the best victories we have won, and the best service we have rendered, to be swallowed up by times of failure, defeat, dishonor, and uselessness in God's Kingdom. Some people whose lives offered exceptional promise and achievement have come to such an end. It is certainly terrible to imagine, but it is true *Yet it is never necessary.*

Samuel Dickey Gordon once said that the only safe assurance against such a tragedy is to have a *"fresh touch with God daily—or even hourly."* My blessed, fruitful, and victorious *experiences* of yesterday have no lingering value to me today. In fact, they can be "swallowed up" or reversed by today's failures, unless I see them as incentives to spur me on to even better and *richer experiences today.*

Maintaining this "fresh touch with God," by abiding in Christ, will be the only thing to keep the "ugly and gaunt…cows" and the "thin heads of grain" from consuming my life.

—*From Messages for the Morning Watch*

The love baptism will create intense desire for *more love*, therefore wanting more of Jesus and more of His Word.

There is an initial filling of the Holy Spirit, but we must refill every day possible!

Dear ones! Listen up! It's time to realize the last days are upon us. To stand against whatever is coming, we need all the "Holy Spirit power" and Word of God available to us.

> But you, dear friends, build yourselves up in your most holy faith and pray in the Holy Spirit. Keep yourselves in God's Love as you wait for the mercy of our Lord Jesus Christ to bring you to eternal life. (Jude 20–21)

The Full Life Study Bible notes by Donald C. Stamps

Jude 20 Build Yourselves Up. Believers must defend and propagate the faith and resist false teaching in four ways:

1. By building ourselves up in our most holy faith. The holy faith is the NT revelation handed down by Christ and the apostles (v.3). This requires study of God's Word and a determined effort to know the truth and teachings of Scripture (cf. Ac 2:42; 20:27; 2Ti 2:15; Heb 5:12).
2. By praying in the Spirit. We must pray by the enabling power of the Holy Spirit, i.e., by looking to the Spirit to inspire, guide, energize, sustain and help us to do battle in our praying (see Ro 8:26, note; cf. Gal 4:6; Eph 6:18). Praying in the Spirit includes both praying with one's mind and praying with one's spirit (see 1Co 14:15; note).

3. By remaining in the sphere of God's Love for us. This involves faithful obedience to God and His Word (John 15:9–10).
4. By longing and waiting for our Lord's return and the eternal glory that will accompany His return (see John 14:2, note).

I trust from the preceding scriptures and information given that you are convinced the baptism of Holy Spirit is for us today! The way we received salvation was to ask—ask Jesus into your heart and accept Him. The Holy Spirit is received the same way. We ask! Ask the Father, in Jesus's name, to receive the gift of the Holy Spirit!

Father, in Jesus's name, I ask that everyone reading these writings will seek to be filled by Your Holy Spirit and that they will know You and the power of Your love! Increase in each a truer knowledge of You and what Your will is for their lives and Your kingdom ways established in their hearts and lives. May they go forth and proclaim the good news of the gospel until Your Spirit fills the earth as the waters covers the sea. Amen!

> Peter replied, "Repent and be baptized, every one of you, in the name of Jesus Christ for the forgiveness of your sins. And you will receive the gift of the Holy Spirit. The promise is for you and your children and for all who are far off—for all whom the Lord our God will call." With many other words he warned them; and he pleaded with them, "Save yourselves from this corrupt generation." Those who accepted his message were baptized, and about three thousand were added to their number that day. (Acts 2:38–40)

Dear ones, come on *now*! Listen up! It is time to be filled with the Holy Spirit! Our Lord wants to fill you with the same Holy Spirit that generates His Being! *Wow!* Way out wonder! Yes, this is Truth! The Bible, the Word of God, is Truth! And Scripture tells us:

> Don't you know that you yourselves are God's temple and that God's Spirit lives within you? (1 Corinthians 3:16)

> Do you not know that your body is a temple of the Holy Spirit, Who is in you, Whom you have received from God? You are not your own; you were bought at a price. Therefore, honor God with your body. (1 Corinthians 6:19–20)

> For we are the temple of the Living God. As God has said, "I will live with them and walk among them, and I will be their God, and they will be my people." (2 Corinthians 6:16b)

I believe everyone reading these words will want the reality of having their temple—their being—filled with the Holy Ghost. To receive the fullness of the baptism of love, just simply *ask!*

Ask the Baptizer, who is Jesus, and He will fill you with so much love, joy, and peace that these precious attributes will overflow out of you to all those around you, and you yourself will be so immersed in love that you will know for sure the reality of His presence.

If you have repented of all sins and forgiven all those that have wronged you, ask Jesus for the reality of this cleansing that can only come through repentance. Then get a mental picture of Jesus hanging on the cross where He shed His precious blood for the remission of those sins. Now, realize that Jesus is hanging on that cross for you and *for you alone*, then begin to *thank Him for forgiving you and giving you salvation.* Say, "Thank *You*, Jesus! Hallelujah (which means praise the Lord)! Keep thanking and praising Jesus *from your heart*, and I know His pleasure will be to give you His precious gift of the baptism of love. Jesus loves *you so much*! Our Lord wants to fill you with all the fullness of His love, joy, and peace. And remember, Jesus has promised never, never to leave you or forsake you. You may have this fullness for all eternity!

> Never will I leave you; never will I forsake you. (Hebrews 13:5b)

Yes, you can have the assurance that Jesus's presence, the Holy Spirit, is inside you forever!

> Fear not, little flock; for it is your Father's good pleasure to give you The Kingdom. (Luke 12:32 KJV)

> Repent, then, and turn to God, so that your sins may be wiped out, *that times of refreshing may come from The Lord.* (Acts 3:19)

The Full Life Study Bible (NIV) study notes by Donald C. Stamps

> *Acts 3:19 Times of Refreshing.* Throughout this present age and until Christ's return, God will send "times of refreshing" (i.e., the outpouring of the Holy Spirit) to all who repent and are converted. Although perilous times will come toward the end of this age and a great falling away from the faith will occur (2Th 2:3; 2Ti 3:1), God still promises to send revival and times of refreshing on the faithful. Christ's presence, spiritual blessings, miracles and outpourings of the Spirit will come on the remnant who faithfully seek Him and overcome the world, the sinful nature and satan's dominion (cf. 26:18).

In the daily devotional readings *Streams in the Desert*, the daily devotional of April 20 illustrates so beautifully the Holy Spirit power available to us all:

> Not by might nor by power, but by My Spirit, says the Lord Almighty. (Zechariah 4:6)

> Once as I walked along the road on a steep hill, I caught sight of a boy on a bicycle near the bottom, He was pedaling uphill against the wind and was obviously working tremendously hard. just as he was exerting the greatest effort and painfully doing the best he could do, a streetcar, also going up the hill, approached him. It was not traveling too fast for the boy to grab hold of a rail at the rear, and I am sure you can guess the result. He went up the hill as effortlessly as a bird gliding through the sky. This thought then flashed through my mind: "I am like that boy on the bicycle in my weariness and weakness. I am pedaling up hill against all kinds of opposition and am almost worn out with the task. But nearby there is great power available—The strength of the Lord Jesus. All I must do is get in touch with Him and maintain communication with Him. And even if I grab hold with only one little finger of faith, it will be enough to make His power mine to accomplish the act of service that now overwhelms me." Seeing this boy on his bicycle helped me to set aside my weariness and to recognize this great truth. (*The Life of Fuller Purpose*)

Abandoned

Utterly abandoned to the Holy Ghost!
Seeking all His fullness, whatever the cost;
Cutting all the moorings, launching in the deep
Of His mighty power—strong to save and keep.
Utterly abandoned to the Holy Ghost!
Oh! The sinking, sinking, until self is lost!
Until the emptied vessel lies broken at His feet;
Waiting till His filling shall make the work complete.
Utterly abandoned to the will of God;
Seeking for no other path than my Master trod;
Leaving ease and pleasure, making Him my choice,
Waiting for His guidance, listening for His voice.
Utterly abandoned! No will of my own;
For time and for eternity, His, and His alone;
All my plans and purposes lost in His sweet will,
Having nothing, yet in Him all things possessing
still.
Utterly abandoned! It's so sweet to be
Captive in His bonds of Love, yet wondrously free;
Free from sin's entanglements, free from doubt
and fear,
Free from every worry, burden, grief, or care.
Utterly abandoned! Oh, the rest is sweet,
As I tarry, waiting, at His blessed feet;
Waiting for the coming of the Guest divine,
Who my inmost being will perfectly refine.
Lo! He comes and fills me, Holy Spirit sweet!
I, in Him, am satisfied! I, in Him, complete!
And the light within my soul will nevermore
grow dim
While I keep my covenant—abandoned unto
Him!

—Author unknown

CHAPTER 13

GETTING ACQUAINTED

Don lived in a big two-story duplex on the west side of town. The upstairs was rented out, and when we married, he gave notice to the occupants to move. We stayed at the little duplex where I lived until this was accomplished. Don asked me to have the girls call him dad, I think, because he so wanted to be a dad, but now know it is also our Lord's divine order for a family. Don said he would like for me to be a stay-at-home mom for the girls, so I gave up my job. To compensate what my salary was, I would can produce from a garden especially going to Dad and Mom's farm, picking fruits and veggies in season. I loved doing this. No problem.

I also agreed to helping at the cabinet shop and doing errands as needed. At times I was given the job of going to the city for supplies. It took a while for me to gain confidence driving in city traffic, and some of the neighborhoods of some of the suppliers were quite scary, but this ole farm gal was determined to please my husband. I loved him and was happy with what our lives had become. He is everything I hoped for, and the girls were happy too!

I was busy remodeling upstairs of our home for the girls. The living room of the old duplex was Kim's room, the kitchen Jacque's, and the bedroom for Kris's room. We tore out old cabinets, painted and papered, and had all the carpeting replaced. Don let each girl pick out their carpet, and that was the color of their room. Kim's was blue, Jacque's purple, and Kris's was pink. Kim wanted a canopy bed with white ruffles above and blue bedspread beneath. She had the outside entrance in her room with a small balcony outside the door with steps leading down to the ground. We kept a big padlock on that door! At twelve years of age, she looked like eighteen!

Jacque saw a picture in a magazine of a room she liked, showed it to Daddy Don, and he built it for her. The bed was in a corner and scallops made of white paneling made a frame above the bed and short purple curtains swayed below this frame. A matching purple quilt was made by a seamstress.

I bought two pink bedspreads and made a swag designed like a crown above Kris's bed. She had dolls and stuffed animals and loves dogs. Don bought her a dachshund puppy. He was so little he really did look like a "weenie"! We asked her what she would name her new companion. Kris quickly said, "Choo Choo because he is long like a train."

We had other dogs for pets. Kim had a white French poodle that was called Peppe. I have a picture of her giving him a bath in the utility room sink. Jacque liked St. Bernard dogs, and when we moved to the north edge of town in 1975, Don bought her one for a present. The dog's registered name was Bannetta Suzanne, and Jacque called her Bandit Sue.

She was huge and so tall that when allowed in the house and standing close to the kitchen table, she would knock everything off it by wagging her tail. Bandit had eight puppies for us, and when they were old enough, before we could give them all away, our backyard looked like a cow lot! She was quite a pet.

The year Jacque was eight and Kris was six, Don made them a playhouse in the backyard. It was a building approximately six by eight feet with two small windows, and Jacque wanted a Dutch door so she could lock the bottom half and look out the top. The girls also had a long rope tied to a tree and, standing on top of a tall stack of a barbeque pit, would swing off it. This gave them and their friends lots of enjoyment.

In my spare time, I still liked to sew. The girls went every year to church camp, and I made them lots of culottes with matching T-shirts. The neck and arm bands had to be stretched as you were sewing them on. I sewed matching outfits for Kris and one of her dolls and one year, for Jacque, made a pair of knickerbockers to go skiing in. She wore a bright pair of socks with them, and I could easily spot her on the ski slope. When Kim was sixteen, I made her a pale yellow formal. She wore this in a beauty pageant and was the runner-up in the contest.

To also help clothe three girls, when in the city, I would stop at the Goodwill stores for bargains. This is a used clothing place, and clothes were donated; the public could buy, and proceeds helped needy people. A lot of the dresses were from name-brand places and could be purchased for fifty cents or a dollar. One time Don was hauling trash to the city dump and noticed a coat lying on a mound of junk. He asked the caretaker if the coat belonged to anyone, and "no, it was discarded." I sent it to the cleaners, and it came back like brand-new! It was brown suede with fleece lining.

Kim wore this to school, and one of her friends asked her, "Where do you buy your clothes?"

She told them, "The dress came from the Goodwill store and the coat from the city dump!" She told me, "Mom, they didn't believe me!"

Just before we were married, Don had purchased a camper from his friend Bill, who with brother Bob had a welding shop in town. This camper was built by them on the back of the frame of a Cadillac hearse. The cab was nice with the dashboard having all the looks of a stylish car. They had installed bucket seats, and between these was a door to crawl through going back into the camper. We had a bed in the back, bed over the cab, and stove and refrigerator and a booth to dine on. And there was a door on one side to get in and out. This was a very genius invention, but we looked like a "Sherman tank" going down the road. It even had a horn like a train whistle and a hole in the floor covered only with a loose board.

For an out-of-town getaway, the girls, Don, and I took a short trip to St. Louis. Oh! What fun we had! We spent a day at the zoo, another day at the most beautiful gardens that had a clock made with flowers, and headed for downtown to see the "Archway to the West." It was dark, so we decided to spend the night in a parking lot to be there next morning to go up in the arch. We slept late and woke up to voices outside. I peeked out a window and saw a group of people dressed in very fine apparel, pointing fingers at us and laughing! They had never seen such a sight as our "Beverly Hillbillish wagon"! We were parked practically at the door of a very distinguished bank!

On I-70, heading west back to Kansas, smoke started coming up through the hole in the floor. I looked back and saw sparks flying up as well. I hollered at the girls to grab the Kool-Aid to douse the fire. Don was a fireman, and he didn't seem to be too concerned; he just kept on driving his family home.

We were a very active family! The summer months we went boating and waterskiing at the city lake and swimming at Bill and Ernie's pool. In winter we had snowmobiles and went ice skating at Les's pond. Les had wood gathered for a bonfire to roast hotdogs and marshmallows, and Pat made the hot chocolate. One year during Christmas vacation from school, Les and Pat and two boys, Paul and Mark, our two girls, Jacque and Kris, Don, and I all made a trip to Mexico in our '68 Chevrolet cab-over camper. The eight of us traveled down the highway, talking and laughing and playing games as we went. New Year's Eve we were across the border—lots of excitement there! And yes, we were still friends when we arrived safely back home.

Every year the first week in February, we would head for the ski slopes of Colorado with a group from church. Usually a caravan of vehicles would communicate as we traveled with CB radios. Don's handle was Donald Duck, and mine was Lady Duck. We would leave Sunday night after church, drive all night to be first in line at the chairlift to go up the mountain. CB radios helped to keep us awake for nighttime traveling. After skiing on those gorgeous white slopes, what could be more refreshing and relaxing than the devotionals and singing around a warm fireplace back at the lodge!

When coming home from one of these mountaintop experiences, we stopped in Littleton and picked up sister-in-law Hazel.

She wanted to visit family back in Kansas, so she decided to travel back with us; and after staying a week or two with Dad and Mom L, Jim, her husband, would come to take her home. We were traveling 1-70 in Western Kansas when one of those snow-blowing storms hit. It was a blizzard, for sure, and we knew the highway would soon be shut down; and when this happens, most people have to stay in service stations or school gymnasiums. Several pheasant hunting seasons, Don had stayed with friends that lived north of a town we were very close to. The snow was drifting so badly and the wind blowing so hard we could barely see the road. It definitely was a blinding snowstorm. We turned off I-70, and for some reason, north and south roads don't drift as bad as the east and west roads. We made it to shelter at Buel and Ruth's beautiful home. Another family—a minister, wife, and two small children—had arrived safely several hours before us. The house was so warm, and so was the hospitality.

The storm was so severe and snow so deep that before the roads were cleared off to travel on, we were kept there three days. Buel had hired hands that kept livestock fed and other chores, so he and Don had a great time talking about the old-time West. Buel's ancestors had homesteaded here and sure had lots of interesting stories. The girls were entertained by their teenage daughter, who was a champion horse rider. The two teenage boys really enjoy getting out of a vehicle that was stored in a shed for such a time. It was a tractor with a cab, but instead of wheels, it had tracks for traction like a caterpillar. That machine could go anywhere in those mounds of snow. Everyone had fun making tracks in the new fresh fallen snow. It was cold, but we had plenty of warm winter gear along.

This family was well prepared food wise and had plenty of groceries stored in. Hazel and I helped Ruth with the cooking, and every meal was quite a spread of morsels with items from beef grown on the ranch to delicious homemade rolls. In between meals, the women would sit by a huge fireplace—the backside in kitchen and the front in the living room. Looking into the fire and watching the flames, we could see into the other room. The little children of the other guests would play games on the floor nearby. The women would read or visit about our families, and Hazel crocheted on an afghan that she later would send to this family in appreciation for sheltering us.

The second day there was Sunday. We gathered chairs in a circle for all, and what a message of God's love and protection from a storm. Instead of a collection plate passed, each one in the circle told of their love of Jesus! What a change in *my life* to when I sat in a circle in a state institution.

The girls were in a contest for perfect Sunday school attendance back home, and papers were given to each one. They indeed had attended services with a minister of the gospel present too, and we were all so blessed how our Lord helped us weather the storm.

Another trip to Colorado was made one year in the fall for a deer hunt. Dave and Georgiea took their horses, and we usually stopped in a Western Kansas town where Georgiea's parents lived. Pastor George and Maxine were wonderful hosts, and knowing Don's sweet tooth, Maxine made him a fresh coconut cream pie! I feasted too! In the mountains, Dave and Don went hunting, and Georgiea and I went to the lodge to do our favorite thing—a good long chit-chat about anything and everything! We were sisters! It was getting late in the day, so we decided to try and locate our husbands. Driving down the mountain, we spotted them on horseback coming out of the woods. They seemed very excited as they jumped off the horses and asked Georgiea and I to take the horses back to the barn so they could take our vehicle to go to town.

"What's your hurry?" we asked.

They replied, "We shot two deer and left them on the mountain. We don't have our hunting license and need to get to town quickly before store closes to purchase license!"

The evening was very cold, and it started to sleet snow and be windy. Georgiea and I rode the horses approximately a mile to the barn, took the saddles off, wiped down the horses because they were wet, and fed and watered them—and we were freezing and fuming!

We took the deer back across state line to Kansas; they had to be tagged. We tied the deer to the top of our vehicles and traveled at night to keep them cool. In the basement of the cabinet shop, Don had a butcher come and dress the deer. Georgiea and I took the hunks of meat back to our home and ground those deer up into hamburger meat. We were grinding our teeth as well, trying not to open mouths with sarcasm to our guys, but we were and still hope to be dutiful wives for our husbands!

Our full-gospel church has summer camps for children and teens and also family camps. The summer months are busy ones for our husbands with their respective jobs, so Georgiea and I decided to go to Woodston Camp in Western Kansas. We had sold the "old hearse" and bought a camper that was in excellent condition from friends Leo and Violet.

We loaded up and headed west on a Sunday night after church. Georgiea sponsored our pastor's daughters, Laurie and Cherie; and they, the girls, and I started traveling. Marge wanted to come, but as a pastor's wife, she had lots of duties.

It was such a beautiful night! The moon shone so brightly that you hardly needed the headlights on. The girls in the back finally fell asleep, and Georgiea and I were keeping awake by talking and listening to an eight-track tape. I pulled off the main road to drive the last forty or fifty miles to the camp. Georgia and I remarked, "We sure hope nothing happens because this stretch of the road is so desolate, and the shoulders are not wide enough to pull over on."

A song on the eight-track was stuck on a song "Lord Keep Your Hand upon Me," and played it over and over again and was getting ever so faint to hear, so I pulled it out of the player thinking the tape had broken. It was a warm night and we had the windows halfway down and I thought the windshield was fogging over, so I kept wiping at them. The moon was shining so bright I didn't notice the headlights going dim. We turned into the driveway of the camp and could hardly see the road.

Georgiea spotted the tent her parents were in and said, "Let's pull up in front of the door to the tent, and they will be surprised when they see us in the morning!"

Not wanting to wake them, I turned the ignition key off, and the camper coasted up beside the tent. Georgiea and I went to the back to sleep for a while.

The next morning, Georgiea's family was surprised, and while visiting, Exie, Georgiea's brother, said he would move our camper for us so the folks could get in and out of the tent better. He soon came and said the camper wouldn't start. Pastor George and Exie looked under the hood and found a wire completely broken in two between the generator and battery; with no power to the engine, it was impossible for the camper to travel those last miles there. Our Lord had indeed "kept His hand upon us"!

Pastor Vic's wife, Marge, did get to come to camp a few days later. A man who had started to attend church had a plane and was a pilot; he flew Pastor Vic and Marge there. The guys stayed for a couple of hours, but Marge had packed three dresses and undergarments, each one rolled up ever so tightly in one of those small 13L x 8W x 8H cosmetic satchels with a mirror in the lid. The little suitcase was unbeknown to Pastor Vic, and he was very surprised when she expressed desire to stay longer, but Marge assured him that she had everything needed. There were already seven of us in the camper, and we gladly made room for one more. Kim slept in a sleeping bag on the floor; Laurie, Cherie, Jacque, and Kris had the bed over the cab, sleeping across the bed; and Marge, Georgiea, and I slept crossways on the back bed of the camper. Marge stayed the rest of the week, and we all went home together in the camper after Pastor George and Exie repaired the broken wire.

The services for family camp were held in a huge old barn fondly called the "tabernacle." When seated inside, you could see outside through the cracks between the boards—but what a meeting we always had! That old barn was the "most beautiful tabernacle ever" because the Holy Spirit ministered to each one there in such a refreshing way! We sang songs: "Give Me That Old-Time Religion," "The Old Rugged Cross," "There Is Power in the Blood," "I'll Fly Away"! Miracles happened! Our joy complete, and we were all together in *one* accord!

Come on now! Listen up! Now is the time to believe the gospel.

The old-time religion happened over two thousand years ago on an old rugged cross. The power is in the blood Jesus shed to take away all our sins. Jesus so willingly gave His life, His blood for our redemption. The blood of Jesus gives power over the enemy.

> They overcame him by the blood of the Lamb
> and by the word of their testimony. (Revelation
> 12:11)

Dear ones! Listen up! The Israelites were in bondage in Egypt for over four hundred years. Before the great Exodus from Egypt, the Lord, through Moses, commanded blood from a lamb to be placed at the top and sides of the entry door to their homes. The Lord protected the Israelites when seeing the blood but killed the firstborn of the Egyptians. The people were to commemorate for generations a festival to the Lord—a lasting ordinance, the Passover. (This story is recorded in chapters 11 and 12 of Exodus.)

Come on now! Listen up! *Now is the time to apply the blood of Jesus Christ, the Lamb of God, over the doorway of your heart!*

I remember getting the worse scolding as a child when I left a gate open. Dad sternly said to me, "A gate is to keep good things in and bad things out!"

This is what I want over the door of my heart—a gate to keep all harm out! The blood applied on the top and sides of the doors of the Israelites in Egypt so many years ago *formed a cross!*

The Israelites in early Egypt had only until midnight—one night—to apply the blood!

Dear ones, we don't know how soon the midnight hour is coming for us!

We all need to apply the blood!

Earl and Sharon, a couple where we attend church in East Texas, sing this song:

The Blood Is Still There

> One dark night in Egypt
> A fearful time had come
> One little Hebrew boy

Who was his father's firstborn son
With the angel of death passing low
It was hard to fall asleep
One little lamb stood in his mind
As he lay there counting sheep

He wondered why the young lamb had to die
Why his blood was on the door
Through the wind and rain it had still remained
But he wanted to be sure
So he called out to his earthly father
With a trembling voice so scared
Crying, "Father, will you please look and see
If the blood is still there?"

Chorus:
And he said, "Son, now don't you worry
For the blood is there to stay
Wind may blow and the rain may fall
But it won't just wash away
The blood will stand the raging storm
It's been applied with loving care
Safe secure, you can rest assured
That the blood is still there."

Looking over the damage
Satan's storm had left behind
A flood of endless questions
And doubt had filled my mind
The fear that gripped my troubled soul
Brought me back to my knees in prayer
Crying. "Father, will you please look and see
If the blood is still there?"

(Sing chorus again.)

CHAPTER 14

FALLING

Busy, busy, busy! I love to keep busy! But dear ones, we can be "too busy"!

After Don and I were married, I had a wonderful time establishing my new home. I couldn't do enough to show how grateful this "newfound life" was to me! I kept busy cleaning house, preparing meals, canning fruits and vegetables, sewing clothes, running errands for Don and my girls, helping at the shop, and basically, I was going places, doing things, and helping people. All the while, I had my eyes "on things and other people." I looked to the ways of others and wanted to be just like them.

Don had told me his fondness for pear honey. I found a recipe and told him if he brought the pears home, I would can the pear honey. He loves to pick and eat fruit. Strawberries and blackberries are among the favorites. He has blackberry patches, some only known to him, and loves to be out in these areas when the berries are in season. Yes, I did go with him a few times because he loves others to be with him, enjoying what he enjoys doing. One day, Don's sister Mary, our friend John, Don, and I were in the blackberry patch. This was a very hot, sticky kind of day, thorny bushes everywhere, and always looking at the ground for a sneaky snake. We had lots of water with us to drink, and after filling buckets with berries, we started throwing water on each other. The coolness of the water was so refreshing, and to this day, John and Bonnie call my sister-in-law "Blackberry Mary"!

Someone did give Don pears, approximately three or four bushels of them. He brought the pears home and told me of an invite to go hunting down in the Ozarks, a very heavily wooded area good for any critter that gets in front of the gun. My thought on a man's hobbies: when they get away from all the pressures of their jobs and regular routine, they come home refreshed, and dispositions are so much better! Now Don had been at his cabinet shop day in and day out for weeks. He had just picked up bushels of pears, and I readily agreed going on the overnight hunting trip with the guys was a good idea. I was going to be canning those pears!

I started peeling pears, and there can't be a thicker skin on any fruit than of those I peeled that night. I peeled pears, cooked pears, canned pears—all night long! Yes, I did think of hubby that night; in fact, quite often! But I haven't peeled or canned "pear of honey" since. Don still loves it but either buys it, or he encourages someone else to can it for him. (Thank you, Pat!)

I finally told Don that we are a partnership. He picks the berries, and I bake the pies; and should he bring home pears, he does the peeling, and I can do the canning.

Taking the girls to their school every morning and picking them up in the afternoons is a mom's job. The school was very close to the cabinet shop, so I would stop to see if anything was needed, or Don would call me ahead of time to pick up supplies. I used to tell Don he made more sawdust than anything else at the shop, and the girls thought so too! It was one of their jobs to sweep the sawdust up for an after-school job. He paid them to teach the ole routine of work and pay. Entering the shop one day, I could see my husband was a little under pressure. He tells me of a set of cabinets that needed stained out so he could lacquer them and allow to dry overnight. This just had to be done that evening in order for them to be at the job site on time. I guess it's my country upbringing, my thinking being "see a job to do—fill it!" I tell hubby that I will gladly help him. In fact, I kept a one-piece coverall at the shop to protect the clothes I was wearing to put on when needed.

I took the girls home first. They had homework and piano practicing to do. I knew supper was taken care of, for I usually prepared a big meal at noon and we ate leftovers in the evening and I went back to the shop to do my job. I was on my knees putting stain on a bottom cabinet when I heard voices at the front of the shop in the entryway. I looked up, and there was Carl, caretaker at the lake, showing Don a large fish. Said it was a carp and they were coming into the shallows of the lake near the banks to lay their eggs. Don got so excited! I could hardly believe how quickly his disposition changed. He loves to shoot these fish with a bow and arrow when they come in like this.

He yells back to me, "Hon, I'm going out to the lake with Carl for a while. I need to go now before it gets dark."

Now I had canned carp too! About an hour in the pressure cooker, it comes out looking like salmon and taste like it as well. But that evening, as I was sitting on the floor of the shop looking at the stain that had built up under my fingernails, salmon didn't appeal to my taste buds! I think my insides became a pressure cooker too! I did finish the job—I told the man I would do it—but those coveralls sure disappeared from the cabinet shop.

The decision was made after this for me to be that stay-at-home mom for the girls. Don could arrange time at the shop with hired help to get a job out on time.

The girls were also having quite a time in making the adjustment to this new family-life style. Besides schoolwork and sweeping sawdust, they were asked to keep their rooms clean, take care of any pets we had, practice piano, and wash and dry the dishes. We didn't have a dishwasher. I taught them at an early age to do their own laundry. If they wanted to change clothes ever so often, they could keep them neat and clean. In season, there was a lawn to mow and leaves to rake.

My parents were elderly and needed more of my attention, and I had a friend, Janie, who was only four years younger than me but considered my little sister. Janie had cancer and was quite critical.

When I was a junior in high school, I worked at a hamburger and ice cream drive-up restaurant after school until nine or ten at night. My parents living five miles out in the country came to town each night to pick me up. When they drove up out front, I looked out the window and saw how tired they looked. They were used to hours like "getting up and going to bed with the chickens," or early to bed and early to rise.

One of my first customers in the afternoon was Lily. There was only one house in between the drive-up and her home. Lily's husband had died when the youngest of her children was a baby, and she was telling me about Jane and Bill who were now about eleven and seven years of age. Older daughter Donna was married and away from home, and Clay, older son, was in the Air Force. There was a problem making sure Jane and Bill arrived at school on time each morning because she worked at the hospital from six in the morning until two in the afternoon. Lily said she had to phone from work each morning and let the phone ring and ring for the kids to answer and then wasn't sure they ate breakfast or dressed properly. I told Lily my situation of Dad and Mom having to come to town each night.

Lily had an idea! She had a back room with a door that faced the drive-up, and this could be my room "for free" if I would see the children to school each day. I accepted her offer. Jane, Bill, and I walked approximately eight blocks each morning, and Lily was home from work in the afternoon when school was dismissed. When I got off from work at night, I walked to my room across our neighbor's backyard. A family lived here that I knew and didn't care that I took those steps across their property.

I became very close to Lily. She was a very spunky and jovial person. Being with that family, Donna was an older sister, Clay is an older brother, and I consider Bill my younger brother. That school year I only saw Dad and Mom on Sundays when they stopped to pick me up for church, and I would go out to the farm for the afternoon.

When told of the seriousness of Janie's illness, I wanted to see her as much as possible. I wanted to be at home with my girls and also help Don. I still did errands and probably went to the city once a week for supplies for the shop. I had to consider my parents' age and failing health, and we were involved in a lot of activity at the church. Don and I taught a junior boy's Sunday school class. I thought this was great for Don because he now had a household of the female gender, and being with the boys was more masculine.

Sundays were the one day of the week we could spend any time together as a family. Don worked at the cabinet shop the other six days. In the summer months, we spent most Sunday afternoons at the lake, boating and skiing. I packed a picnic lunch, and we left for the lake as soon as church was over. We returned three or four hours later to shower and change clothes and be in church for the evening service. Why did I do this? I wanted Don to have a release from the pressures of business, and I wanted the girls to have happy grow-ing-up years like I did! We were so busy!

The people at church were such dedicated role models to live up to. I so wanted to be like them but felt inside of me I just wasn't making the grade!

There was Sister Agnus—what a prayer warrior she was! One evening after a service, I was just walking by where she was talking with some other ladies and heard her say, "It takes a lot more prayer to raise kids these days!"

She and Brother M had one daughter, Donna, married to Dan, and they were in the ministry. I knew if Sister Agnus had prayed and her child was in the kingdom, I really better start praying for my three daughters. I did, but being so busy, I was so tired at night and fell asleep before praying very long! And besides, I *could never be like* those ladies at church because none of them had ever been married before! I started feeling so guilty!

I loved to cook and invite people over for a meal. I had been in some of the homes of people at church and felt much was required with a variety of food. I invited Jack and Martha to come for an eve-ning meal. With Don's schedule, he was only home at noon for one hour, always having to be back at the shop by one o'clock to oversee the hired help; and besides, I wanted this to be a family time where the children would be home from school. I talked with hubby to decide what evening would be best, and I proceeded to get ready for our party.

First, I had to clean house. All the homes I had been to of the people at church were spotlessly clean! Why, I even heard Sister

Wilma say she always scrubbed the kitchen floor on her hands and knees because she could get the dirt out of the corners better than using a mop with a long handle. So I cleaned and polished the floors, windows, light fixtures, and especially the bathrooms that really had to shine! The dusting had to wait until the very day because when company came, no spot of dust should be seen anywhere. All the while doing this, I would be thinking of what foods to prepare. It just had to be a seven-course dinner, so resting from the cleaning, I would be looking up recipes knowing everything had to be homemade!

And then there were the interruptions. Don could call from the shop for me to go pick up some supplies he just had to have, Mom could call and tell of some need on the farm or just call to chat (to see how things were with us), and I felt the need most days to visit Janie. Dying with cancer is a horrible sight to see. I remembered what brother Mel had to go through, and I hurt because of missing my brother, and I would hurt for Janie.

The day of the dinner party with Jack and Martha and family, I was up early to start preparing food. Homemade rolls and pies had to be fresh. I usually made pies the day before because if they didn't turn out just right, I could get up earlier to make them right. Lemon and coconut were favorites, and pudding had to be firm but not too firm—never runny!

I fixed a baked ham but also some other kind of meat because everyone may not be able to eat pork. I also fixed meatballs, had a recipe from Mary, Sister Wilma's daughter, that everyone just loved! You always have to eat sweet potatoes with ham; they just go together. My dad grew the best, so they were really homemade! I prepared macaroni and cheese, a favorite of the girls, green beans (home-canned), corn that had been picked from Dad's garden—cut off the cob and freshly frozen—and made salads. Had to have a variety here: fresh lettuce salad and the jelled ones, fruit (had to have fruit somewhere), and cranberries with nuts—salad that taste so good with meat.

Oh, yeah, chocolate! Some desert had to have chocolate in it, most likely a cake. I always prepared sweet tea and tea without sugar. If I placed a sugar bowl on the table, grains of sugar would spill from the spoon to the glass on the clean, freshly ironed tablecloth!

The evening arrived! Everything came off the stove and oven at the correct time. The guests arrived right on time—but where was hubby! Don had told me he would be installing cabinets that day and would be at a newly constructed house where no telephone had been installed yet. It was time to eat, and I couldn't let food get cold. As politely as I could, I told guests where to sit at the table. Don usually sat at the head of the table with the guest of honor on the right or left of him. I would sit at the other end with the wife seated next to me and the children on either side on the table. The food, I thought, turned out nearly perfect, and the girls were showing good manners, but to look across the table at the empty chair, I felt so rejected! I knew Don was delayed because of circumstances that went out of control for him at the installation, and he would be very frustrated!

After the guests left that evening and Don arrived at home later, all I could do was listen to the sad tale of woes going on in his life that day. He is such a good man, and I am so grateful to him for all he was providing and doing for the girls and I. I ached for Don—and I ached inside of me! I was so tired, and the ache in both lives was such a hindrance of happiness and love on other days. What was happening? We both had planned this day to go so perfectly. Why was there an enemy wanting to destroy something so beautiful that we had together! What could we do to prevent this from happening in the future? I was so tired, and when asking myself these questions, I felt so discouraged about my life, and a deep battle started to rage inside of me.

CHAPTER 15

BREAKDOWN TWO

It is possible to let the enemy rob us of joy and for another spirit to take hold.

> Take us the foxes, the little foxes that spoil the vines. (Song of Solomon 2:15)

I was as busy as a bee but sure wasn't making honey. The busyness was all good, but the tiredness and frame of mind was not of the Lord! In everything I was doing, I did not take the time to acknowledge my Lord.

> Trust in The Lord with all thine heart; and lean not unto thine own understanding. In all thy ways acknowledge Him, and He shall direct thy paths. (Proverbs 3:5–6)

> Do not be anxious about anything, but in everything, by prayer and petition, with thanksgiving, present your requests to God. And the peace of God, which transcends all understanding, will guard your hearts and your minds in Christ Jesus. (Philippians 4:6)

> And He humbled thee, and suffered thee to hun-
> ger, and fed thee with manna, which thou knew-
> est not, neither did thy fathers know; that He
> might make thee know that man doth not live
> by bread only, but by every word that proceedeth
> out of the mouth of The Lord doth man live.
> (Deuteronomy 8:3)

> But be ye doers of the word, and not hearers only,
> deceiving own selves. (James 1:22)

Come on now! Listen up! Now is the time to hear the Word of
the Lord and *do it*!

Sitting in a church service and listening to the Word being
delivered and not applying the Word in our hearts and lives is being
deceived, and we know who the great deceiver is. The enemy wants
to get our hearts and minds so in tune with this ole world we miss
heaven. So much of the time, I would sit in church and let my mind
wander to what was happening in our lives, the things we were doing
as a family, and looking at my saintly sisters, wanting to be like them.
Yes, I know the scripture in John 10:28: "I give them eternal life, and
they shall never perish; no one can snatch them out of My Hand."

Dear ones! Listen up! *No one else* can snatch us out of the Lord's
hand, but we can snatch our *own selves out*!

> *Keep yourselves* in God's love as you wait for the
> mercy of our Lord Jesus Christ to bring you to
> eternal life. (Jude 21)

Don, the girls, and I had come home from the fiftieth anniversary celebration of in-laws Claude and Faye. It had been a gala
evening, and the girls and I were so happy to see loved ones in this
family. I am so thankful for the way this family kept me as a sister-
in-law and now included Don as close as being a brother-in-law too!
The nephews called him Uncle Had because of having an Uncle Don
on their side of the family.

The girls had gone to bed, and Don and I were sitting on the couch in the family room. I again was thankful for my "Hubby Don" and still so amazed what a good man he is and how good he was to me, but I couldn't keep my mind from thinking. I was wondering "why" and "what if" in so many ways. Why did the divorce happen? Why does Don love me? What if he rejects me? What if I can't get a good job to support the girls and me? Why does he think I'm so special? I remembered a song Chuck sang to me when we were first together—"You are my special angel sent from heaven above" and at the last of the marriage "Please release me, let me go. For I don't love you anymore."

Attending the party at the same house I had once called home brought back lots of memories, but I couldn't stay away from this function; these are my daughter's grandparents. I so wanted to have fellowship with this family; they are my daughter's blood relatives. I went to sleep in confusion, and we know who the "author of confusion" is.

After a very fretful sleep, I woke up in the enemy's camp of confusion. I was so out of it Don called Georgiea to pick up the girls so they wouldn't be in the house. Kim stayed with Dave and Georgiea and Jacque and Kris stayed with Pastor Vic and Marge and Don proceeded to take care of me himself. I again found myself in that deep, dark cave, and coming into contact with anyone, I fought them screaming!

Don called the doctor, and Dr. Robert said, "That woman needs to be in the state institution!"

Don said, "No way will I take her there. She has already been there!"

I was insanely mad! I ran to the kitchen screaming and grabbed a butcher knife and came at Don with it. He quickly grasped my wrist with one hand and took the knife from me with his other hand. I broke loose from his grip and ran screaming to the front door, thinking if I just got outside on the street, maybe a big truck would run over me and put me out of my misery.

The train tracks were a couple of blocks away. If I could lie down on the tracks, I knew a big locomotive could do away with me!

As I reached the door, Don caught up and grabbed me around the waist, and he said I was so strong it was all he could do to hold me. He was behind, and his arms were tightly around me; my legs shot up in the air like I was walking up the wall almost to the ceiling. I was fighting and reaching and grabbed hold of the board that is the trim around the doorway. The board came completely loose from the wall. Don said it was most unbelievable that someone my size had this much strength!

Clarence and Wilma from church came to pray for me. As they reached out to touch me, something was telling me, "Play dead!" I knew it wanted me dead anyway, so I quickly obliged and threw myself on the floor and didn't move a muscle until they left.

I thought there was a terrible odor in the house. It smelled like rotten eggs, sulfur, and something dead all rolled into one. When lying on the bed looking out the bedroom door into the dining room, it looked to me like green smoke drifting two or three feet above the floor. It was horrible!

The only way Don could get any sleep at night was to push the bed up against the shut bedroom door and make sure there was nothing in the room I could hurt myself with. Georgiea and Marge took turns staying with me in the daytime. They discovered reading Scripture to me would calm me down. There was peace. A very picturesque memory I have of Georgiea is when I saw her kneeling at the foot of my bed, looking up toward heaven, tears streaming down her face, and speaking in an unknown tongue! Even with my mind being the way it was, my heart knew she was praying for me!

When Don called his sister Lois, I know she and Frank immediately went to praying. They are prayer warriors! Lois had been attending a Bible study that was led by a Spirit-filled minister of the same denomination I grew up in. They were meeting in the home of Bob and Margaret, and Lois tells them of the circumstances Don and I were in. They all agreed to have a prayer meeting at our house. Pastor Joel, Lois, Bob, and Margaret came and said they were prepared to stay "however long it took" to see healing results in me.

The four determined warriors gathered in our family room with me lying on the couch.

There is a fireplace on one wall, and the couch was in front of it with a coffee table in between, leaving the back and both sides of the couch open to room area. When these determined people entered the room, each one found their corner to pray in. Reading Scriptures calmed me, but the soft, quiet voices praying were just as soothing. I started to relax and started to think, *What is wrong with me?*

I was very conscious of sound I heard—the noise of dishes and chatter in the kitchen—and was told Louise and Sherry were doing the dishes. This put me in mind of seeing my pastor's wife Marge, who came and gathered up dirty clothes and took it to her home to launder.

I questioned, "Why were these people having to do my work that I needed to be doing?"

Hearing the voices praying ever so softly, it seemed like the whole room was peaceful. The peace was all around and hovering over me. All at once, such a strong presence of peace stood directly above me, the side of the couch my head was on, and it felt like my brain was being touched by this peace! But I still had a gut feeling of something in the pit of my stomach, nausealike! I remembered what a minister counselor told me when at the state institution of what I should do when something bugged me. I said in a loud voice, "Get to hell, out of me!"

As I leaned over the side of the couch to vomit, the most horrible scream sounded out of my mouth; and from deep down inside of me, it did indeed feel like it came from the very pit of hell! Whatever it was, it was gone! I could feel peace flowing in me and around me. I sat up! I recognized Lois and was introduced to Pastor Joel, Bob, and Margaret who were now all exuberantly praising the Lord! They witnessed a miracle!

I was very conscious of the way I was dressed—an old house dress and with all these people here. My hair felt so dirty. It had not been washed in over two weeks. Sherry asked to do my hair, and she and I went to the kitchen sink. The scrubbing of my head, and I wanted it done ever so hard, felt so good! With that hair washing, I was hoping "cobwebs" were gone and the "spider was dead"!

Don was in the front room of the house and could hardly believe the change in me in such a few minutes of time. Pastor Vic and Marge came and visited with me about how I was feeling now! They knew and witnessed the previous days. Lois stayed for a few days with her brother and I, and we read scriptures together and sang choruses around the piano. The girls were extremely excited and enjoyed the happy atmosphere.

My dad and mom were astonished! They never heard of such a happening, but when a minister from their denomination was there, this really ministered to them. Most people around the town didn't believe at all! "Deliverance from demons" was unheard of! I'm sure we were the subject of a lot of "religious controversy."

But Pastor Vic, in the following Sunday night services, preached a message from the scripture Matthew 12:28:

> But if I drive out demons by the Spirit of God,
> then the Kingdom of God has come upon you.

There was a lot of speculation and questioning after my deliverance: What is a demon? How did demons originate? Where did the demon come from? How did the demon enter?

"Why, I thought those people were Christians. How could this have happened to them?"

"This is America. Demons aren't here—at least this is something I've never heard of before?"

"We better keep an eye on her. If it happens again, she belongs over at the state institution!"

"Was this possession or oppression?"

I was so enthralled over the countenance I was experiencing now I didn't notice the talk. I had such an exuberant feeling over what I had before the deliverance. I know who appeared so real to me that day! I know who my Deliverer is! His name is *Jesus*! I was rejoicing once again in the relationship with my Lord and Savior Jesus Christ! He is Lord of lords! He is King of kings! He is the Great I Am! He is the Truth, the Life, the Way! Praise His holy name forever! I was so blessed and didn't care what people were saying. I was in love with Jesus, and He loves me!

Come on now! Listen up! It's time to sing when the Spirit of God delivers:

> Jesus Loves me! This I know, For the Bible tells
> me so;
> Little ones to Him belong, They are weak, but
> He is strong.
>
> Chorus:
> Yes, Jesus loves me, Yes, Jesus loves me,
> Yes, Jesus loves me, The Bible tells me so.
>
> Jesus loves me! He Who died, Heaven's gate to
> open wide;
> He will wash away my sin, Let His little child
> come in.
> Jesus loves me! Loves me still, Though I'm very
> weak and ill;
> From His shining throne on high, Comes to
> watch me where I lie.
> Jesus loves me! He will stay Close beside me all
> the way,
> If I love Him, when I die He will take me home
> on high.
>
> Sing unto The LORD, O ye saints of His, and
> give thanks at the remembrance of His Holiness.
> (Psalm 30:4)

CHAPTER 17

SECOND HONEYMOON

A week or so after the deliverance, Don thought I still looked weak and frail from it all, so he decided we needed to take a trip. Granny Alta would stay with the girls, and since we like RV traveling, we loaded up the camper. It was in the fall of the year and warmer weather was south. We were going to Mexico! In fact, he drove that rig all the way to Monterrey, Mexico!

The colors inside the camper are as colorful as the ones in Mexico. We have a red refrigerator on red-brick linoleum, and I put a red spread on the bed (tongue twister).

On the red stove, I placed a bright-yellow tea kettle. It just seemed to fit, plus we needed it to heat water. On the wall was a little sign, saying, TO SHOW CHILDREN LOVE IS LOVE THEIR MOTHER! We were surrounded by brightness, and we were happy!

On a street corner in Monterrey, a little boy was selling newspapers from the States, and Don proceeded to buy one. Knowing the little guy spoke Spanish and wanting to find out how much the paper cost, Don bent down to his level, held up fingers indicating whether one or two, and looking into his big brown eyes, said, "Taco! Taco!"

The little one's big eyes kept getting bigger and bigger as Don persisted and kept saying, "Taco!"

I was laughing so hard I couldn't get it out of my mouth to tell Don he should say "Peso."

We rode donkeys up to the falls that are close to Monterrey. I asked the young man leading them what their names were. He said "Superman" and "Speedy Gonzales." Those critters walked so slowly, but then we were going up a mountain. The houses along the way had a roof with a pole on each corner for support. Looking in, I could see women preparing a meal or sweeping the dirt floor. What humble surroundings to a place they call home. They looked so content with what they were doing I decided they must know Jesus too! I believe the Lord's blessings of love, joy, peace that gives contentment and satisfaction when working are great virtues!

Come on now! Listen up! Now is the time to know the following scriptures:

> But godliness with contentment is great gain. (1 Timothy 6:6)

> The fear of The LORD tendeth to life: and he that hath it shall abide satisfied; he shall not be visited with evil. (Proverbs 19:23)

> I am not saying this because I am in need, for I have learned to be content whatever the circumstances. I know what it is to be in need, and I know what it is to have plenty. I have learned the secret of being content in any and every situation, whether well or hungry, whether living in plenty or in want. I can do everything through Him Who gives me strength. (Philippians 4:11–13)

Taking this trip reminded me of Don's and my first honeymoon. We were married in July, and the business is busiest in the summer, so we didn't take a trip until October. Don's sister Mary lived in California, so we flew to Los Angeles where Mary picked us up at the airport. For sightseeing the area, we could use her car. When Mary wasn't working, we wanted her to go with us touring; she is such a fun person to be with. We visited most all the usual tourist places of the area, even a fishing trip to Catalina.

But before we left our home in Kansas, the church we attended had quite a surprise for us. Not expecting "saintly people" to do something like this made it all the more surprising.

Don, the girls, and I had attended church on this October evening and were back home sitting around the table, talking in the kitchen. I heard scratching on the screen of the window over the sink and looked up to see two ladies waving and laughing at me that were at church earlier too! About this time, the front doorbell rings, and Don goes to answer, opens the door to people who also were previously at church. They started shouting, "Chivaree!" "Chivaree!"

At these events, it's customary for the groom to take the bride for a wheelbarrow ride; and of course, my "chariot" was waiting! My eager groom picked up quickly the enthusiasm of the group standing on our front porch and turns to me and says, "Come on, you're going for a ride!"

A sweet sister took me aside and said, "We couldn't find a wheelbarrow that has more of a flat bucket. All we brought for you to ride in is a garden cart! You better put on a pair of slacks!"

"Thank you, sister!"

When sitting in the bucket of that cart, my head would hit the back, and out the front my legs were sticking practically straight up! And we had to go all the way to the town square, which is five blocks there and back! There was quite a gathering around us, and most everyone was beating on a pan with a spoon or ringing a bell and shouting, "Newlyweds! Newlyweds!" and making quite a commotion. Doors of homes all along the route opened, and people would shout us their congratulations!

Now a lot of the dear, sweet ladies from church didn't go on that little walking spree that night. Before we left, they just politely and ever so innocently said, "We'll stay back and prepare snacks and drinks to eat when you return."

Now I'm a country gal and probably took part in my first chivaree when only five years old. When Vic and Flossie married, she never forgot that it was I who rang the cow bell so loud, and I knew of the tricks that were done, but ladies from church surely didn't do such things.

Yes, they did! The sheets were shortened, mirrors were wrote on with lipstick, salve on doorknobs, clear plastic wrap over the toilet seat, and for weeks we didn't know what was in the canned goods because all the labels were taken off. Those ladies had so much fun that night and the food brought in was delicious! We had quite a celebration, and I really love every one of those dear people!

"I love those dear hearts and gentle people that live in my hometown, for those dear hearts and gentle people will never ever let me down!"

A friend loves at all times. (Proverbs 17:17)

A cheerful heart is good medicine. (Proverbs 17:22)

CHAPTER 18

STINKIN' THINKIN'

After returning from Mexico, everything seemed to be smooth sailing on the sea of life. It was like life was "peachy keen" and "everything coming up roses." I enjoyed the new release my Lord had given me. I was in awe and still am for His deliverance. The power of God's love is so strong! At times I can't thank Him and praise Him enough!

I started searching Scripture about Jesus walking this earth, delivering others:

> And at even, when the sun did set, they brought unto Him all that were diseased, and them that were possessed with devils. (Mark 1:32 KJV)

> The whole town gathered at the door, and Jesus healed many who had various diseases. He also drove out many demons, but He would not let the demons speak because they *knew Who He Was*. (Mark 1:32 NIV)

You ask, how do the demons know who Jesus is? I believe according to Scriptures, demons are fallen angels.

How art thou fallen from heaven, O Lucifer.
(Isaiah 14:12)

The fallen angel is Lucifer, or Satan. Pride caused him to fall; he said in verse 13, "I will exalt my throne above the stars of God."

Pride goeth before destruction, and a haughty
spirit before a fall. (Proverbs 16:18)

Dear ones, Satan had a long fall that day, and he took a third of the angels with him. But at one time, they were in heaven enjoying all the benefits when with pride they fell.

Dear ones! Listen up! It's time to stand on *the Word*! If they recognized Jesus when He walked this earth, if you have Jesus in you, they will recognize you too! They will tempt you every step you take unless you stand on *the Word like Jesus did*!

Then Jesus was led by the Spirit into the desert to be tempted by the devil. After fasting forty days and forty nights, He was hungry. The tempter came to Him and said, "If you are the Son of God, tell these stones to become bread." Jesus answered, "*It is written*: 'Man does not live on bread alone, but on *Every Word That Comes From The Mouth Of God*.'" (Matthew 4:1–4)

Dear ones! Listen up! Before my deliverance, I let pride take hold of me! I was so proud of our new home, the lifestyle Don brought into my life—so proud to have a man of great integrity that wanted me for a wife, so proud of all the task and duties I was doing I neglected the most important *one* in my life! *We must constantly be on guard that our relationship with Jesus is number one.*

I know your deeds, that you are neither cold
nor hot. I wish you were either one or the other!
So, because you are lukewarm—neither hot nor

cold—I am about to spit you out of my mouth. (Revelation 3:15–16)

A question of great debate of my deliverance was depression, oppression, and possession.

> Depression: "an inability to concentrate, insomnia, and feelings of dejection and guilt."
> Oppression: "a feeling of being heavily weighed down either mentally or physically."
> Possession: "the state of being dominated by or as if by evil spirits or by an obsession."
> (*The American Heritage Dictionary*, Second College Edition)

I didn't realize the initials together of three words above spell out DOP! I wonder if this is where the term *dopehead* originated. The characteristics and meaning are there.

I don't know who wrote this, but I found this poem that has great meaning for me:

> Look around and be oppressed,
> Look inside and be depressed,
> Look to Jesus and be at rest.

Before the deliverance, I was looking to people, things, and pleasure, and yes, even work, and they dominated my thinking. If there is anyone or anything that stands between us and Jesus, it becomes an idol. Idol is "an image used as an object of worship." We must not let anyone or anything be in the way of a full view of Jesus at all times. Jesus must be number one and on top of all priority in our hearts at all times and in every place we journey in this life.

The first and second of the Ten Commandments our *Lord God* gave Moses are

1. You shall have no other gods before Me.

2. You shall not make for yourself an idol in the form of anything in Heaven above or on the earth beneath or in the waters below. You shall not bow down to them or worship them; for I, The LORD your GOD, am a jealous GOD, punishing the children for the sin of the fathers to the third and fourth generation of those who hate me, but showing love to a thousand generations of those who love Me and 'Keep My Commandments. (Exodus 20:4–6)

As I read in Scripture about Jesus casting out demons, the story I identify with is the story of the demon-possessed man. The description of his actions is closely associated with how I felt in the state institution and before my deliverance.

They sailed to the region of the Gerasenes, which is across the lake from Galilee. When Jesus stepped ashore, He was met by a demon-possessed man from the town. For a long time this man had not worn clothes or lived in a house, but had lived in the tombs. When he saw Jesus, he cried out and fell at His feet, shouting at the top of his voice, "What do you want with me, Jesus, Son of the Most High God? I beg You, don't torture me!" For Jesus had commanded the evil spirit to come out of the man. Many times it had seized him, and though he was chained hand and foot and kept under guard; he had broken his chains and had been driven by the demon into solitary places. Jesus asked him, "What is your name?" "Legion," he replied, because many demons had gone into him. And they begged him repeatedly not to order them to go into the Abyss. A large herd of pigs was feeding on the hillside. The demons begged Jesus to let them go in them, and He gave them permission. When the demons came out of the man, they went into the pigs, and the herd rushed down the steep bank into the lake and was drowned. When those tending the pigs saw what had happened, they ran off and reported this in the town and countryside, and the people went out to see what had happened. When they came to Jesus, they found the man from whom the demons had gone out, sitting at Jesus' feet, dressed and in his right mind; and they were afraid. Those who had seen it told the people how the demon-possessed man had been cured. Then all the people of the region of the Gerasenes asked Jesus to leave them, because they were overcome with fear. So He got into the boat and left. The man from whom the demons had gone out begged to go with Him, but Jesus sent him away, saying, *"Return home and tell how much God has done for you,"* So the man went away and told all over town how much Jesus had done for him. (Luke 8:26–39)

The words Jesus told the man to do, "Return home and tell how much God has done for you," is why I'm typing these words. *I want to tell others of all my Lord Jesus has done for me, and these writings are a means to do so.*

Come on now! Listen up! Now is the time to really believe *all Jesus can do for you!*

Jesus saves! Jesus keeps! Jesus satisfies!

Dear ones! My heart aches for my generation of people and future generations if our Lord should delay His coming. The newscast are full of such horrible disasters and wickedness I want to scream as loud as I can: *"Accept Jesus!"*

Come on now! Listen up! This is the time to really listen and *act on what you hear!*

> When an evil spirit comes out of a man, it goes through arid places seeking rest and does not find it. Then it says, "I will return to the house I left." When it arrives, it finds the house unoccupied, swept clean and put in order. Then it goes and takes with it seven other spirits more wicked than itself, and they go in and live there. And the final condition of that man is worse than the first. That is how it will be with *this wicked generation.* (Matthew 12:43)

This is what Donald C. Stamps wrote in his study notes, *The Full Life Study Bible NIV*:

> *Matthew 12:43 An evil spirit.* Vv.43–45 teach three important truths concerning demon-possession. (l) Evil spirits desire to return to one formerly possessed. (2) Evil spirits cannot return if that person's heart is occupied by the Holy Spirit (v.44; cf 1Co 6:19; 2Co 6:15–16, note). (3). A whole nation or society may seek the pleasure of evil to such extent that *the society itself can become demon-possessed* (cf. Rev 16:14).

Dear ones! Our children, our grandchildren and great-grandchildren are in great danger!

This generation needs to be so full of our Lord's Holy Spirit to give future generations a hope and a future!

Months after my deliverance, I was still so amazed at what had taken place. To be in such a state of confusion and instantly be set free—*Wow!* Way out wonder! I continued my study of Scripture. I read a chapter of Proverbs every day—one chapter for every day of the month—and the first of next month start reading it over again.

There is so much wisdom in this book, impossible to retain, so reading over and over again helps maybe to plant it a little deeper each time around.

I love the worship and praises of Psalms and reading Jesus's words of the gospels—the Apostle Paul and all his instructions to churches in his lifetime but also words of wisdom for us today and so much encouragement in the New Testament *for our future*! But because of my deliverance, I was still intrigued with the casting out of demons and evil spirits. I would read these scriptures and knew just how each one felt when Jesus delivered them. I was amazed about Jesus healing a boy with a demon.

> Jesus rebuked the demon, and it came out of the boy, and he was healed from that moment. (Matthew 17:18)

And I was so touched, as a mother of daughters myself, with this woman's story:

> In fact, as soon as she heard about Him, a woman whose little daughter was possessed by an evil spirit came and fell at His feet. The woman was a Greek, born in Syrian Phoenicia. She begged Jesus to drive the demon out of her daughter. "First let the children eat all they want," He told her, "for it is not right to take the children's bread and toss it to their dogs." "Yes, Lord," she replied, but even the dogs under the table eat the children's crumbs." Then He told her, "For such a reply, you may go; the demon has left your daughter." She went home and found child lying on the bed, the demon gone. (Mark 7:25–30)

And then the story of Mary Magdalene and other women recorded in the book of Luke 8:1–3:

> After this, Jesus traveled about from one town and village to another, proclaiming the good news of the Kingdom of God. The Twelve were with Him, and also some women who had been cured of evil spirits and diseases: Mary Magdalene from whom seven demons had come out; Joanna, the wife of Cuza, the manager of Herod's household; Susanna; and many others.

With my interest and curiosity so keen on deliverances, I regret to have to say my devotion to Scripture turned to other books. I started reading about other people's deliverances in books I purchased at Christian bookstores and became so caught up in every detail. Again, my neglect of reading and studying Scripture was my own denial.

By denying myself access to *the Word*, I again entered the realm of evil spirits.

CHAPTER 19

BREAKDOWN THREE

In 1973 I was attending a seminar in the city. An inspirational speaker had just finished his presentation in the conference room of the motel, and friends and I were in the restaurant having a noon meal. Another meeting would be starting soon. My head was swimming with thoughts given from the speaker, and I was caught up in a "spiritual high" as we sat there visiting. I knew the speaker would have the message at a church there in the city the next morning, so I asked Wilma H if she would fill in for me as Sunday school teacher of the junior boys. This was Saturday evening, and I wanted to stay in the city and attend church next morning. Don was on a hunting trip to Montana with Dave and Russell. The girls could spend the night with a girlfriend—they loved this!

Later on that afternoon, my thinking became fuzzy, and my speech, I know, was incoherent. Thinking rest would help, friend Margaret took me to her home, but insomnia had taken hold. I remember people gathering around in a circle with me in the center, praying, but my mind would not concentrate on the words. My mind could not hear or listen to "Words of Life"!

With Don still away on the hunting trip, Frank and Lois took me to their home. I know prayer was going up for me almost continually here, but my being couldn't enjoy the presence of peace that is an attribute of prayer. Bewildered by the darkness that again was within, I went to the kitchen and picked up a butcher knife to put an end to the torture I was feeling. Lois, with her soft voice, talked me out of this and calmly took the knife out of my hand. Why oh why was this happening again?

A few days later, when Don returned home from his trip, he and Pastor Vic came to pick me up, and I remember being in the car stopped by a train at a crossing. I was thinking, *If I could get out of this car and get under that train, this would all be over!*

The girls had once again been taken to the homes of Pastor Vic and Marge and Dave and Georgiea. Don was taking care of me in the home. At some point, Don, Pastor Vic, Marge, and Georgiea took me to an appointment with Pastor Ernie in the city. I remember once again being between my two precious sisters in the backseat of the car, peace on either side of me but not within. Pastor Ernie did pray for me, but I remember most sitting across his desk from him; he opened a Bible and showed it to me and said, "Woman, you need to make your stand on the promises of 'this Word.'"

Come on now! Listen up! It is time to make a stand for all times!

> The name of THE LORD is a strong tower, the righteous run to it *and are safe.* (Proverbs 18:10)

> For God has not given us the spirit of fear; but of *Power, and of Love, and of a sound mind.* (2 Timothy 1:7)

> There is no fear in Love; but *Perfect Love cast out fear,* because fear Has torment. He that fears is not made perfect in Love. (1 John 4:18)

I was having a difficult time comprehending the Word because so many negative thoughts were in my mind. I couldn't focus on what was being read, but the presence of the Word is so soothing! It was like my house was all cleaned up after my deliverance, but by me reading from the enemy's camp, it had gotten filthy, dirty! I now know if we are *not feeding and standing on God's Word, we will die spiritually.* I was just so thankful the enemy hadn't been able to get to the "basement of the house."

The Holy Spirit needs to control the body. The body—the old man or carnal nature—needs to die.

Dear ones! Come on now! Listen up! It is time to recognize reality! A person cannot live on one meal a week! One meal on Sunday morning will not sustain our spiritual being. *We need daily meals of the Bread of Life* just like the physical body needs a proper diet with lots of nutrition. Jesus tells us in John 6:48–51:

> *I am the bread of life.* Your forefathers ate the manna in the desert, yet they died. But here is the bread that comes down from heaven, which a man may eat and not die. I am the living bread that came down from heaven. If anyone eats of this bread, he will live forever. This bread is my flesh, which I will give for the life of the world.

To be healthy spiritually, physically, and emotionally, we need *daily meals in the Word of God!*

> When the evening was come, they brought unto Him many that were possessed with devils; and He cast out the spirits *with His Word*, and healed all that were sick; That it might be fulfilled which was spoken by Esaias the prophet, saying He Himself took our infirmities, and bare our sicknesses. (Matthew 8:16–17 KJV)

> This is my comfort and consolation in my affliction: that *Your Word has revived me and given me life.* (Psalm 119:50 AMP)

Come on now! Listen up! It's time we all put good thoughts into our minds!

> Finally, brethren, whatsoever things are true, whatsoever things are honest, whatsoever things are just, whatsoever things are pure, whatsoever things are lovely, whatsoever things are of good report; if there be any virtue, and if there be any praise, *think on these things.* (Philippians 4:8 KJV)

Daily we need to submit to God by Scripture reading and praying. *Our minds should never become a battleground. Submit to God by saying yes. Resist the enemy by saying no.*

> *Submit yourselves, then, to God.* Resist the devil, and he will flee from you. Come near to God and He will *come near to you.* (James 4:7–8 NIV)

> Above all, my brothers, do not swear—either by heaven or by earth or by any oath, *but let your "Yes" be Yes, and your "No" be No, so that you may not fall under condemnation.* (James 5:12 ESV)

Dear ones! Listen up! Come on now! It is time to ask ourselves, "What is a sound mind?"

> For God hath not given us the spirit of fear; but of power, and of love, and of a sound mind. (2 Timothy 1:7 KJV)

Our hearts pump blood to the rest of our body. It is very important that the blood reaches the brain. The same principle applies to our spiritual beings. *We have applied the blood of Jesus to the doorpost of our hearts; let heart flow reach our minds! This is the only way to "resist fear and have power, love, and a sound mind."*

A sound mind is the sound you! The sound you is within, producing the fruits of the Spirit. Fruit begets more fruit of the same kind. Love begets love. Joy begets joy. Peace begets peace. All the fruits of the Spirit will beget their own kind but also listed in sequence one following the other to produce a sound mind.

> But the fruit of the Spirit is love, joy, peace, patience, kindness, goodness, faithfulness, gentleness and *self-control*. Against such things there is no law. Those who belong to Christ Jesus have crucified the sinful nature with its passions and desires. *Since we live by the Spirit, let us keep in step with the Spirit.* (Galatians 5:22–25)

Let us again review the scripture found in Philippians 4:4–9:

> Rejoice in the Lord always. I will say it again: Rejoice! Let your gentleness be evident to all. The Lord is near. Do not be anxious about anything, *but in everything, by prayer and petition, with thanksgiving, present your requests to God.* And the peace of God, which transcends all understanding, will "*guard*" *your hearts and your minds in Christ Jesus.* Finally, brothers, whatever is true, whatever is noble, whatever is right, whatever is pure, whatever is lovely, whatever is admirable—if anything is excellent or praiseworthy—*think about such things.* Whatever you have learned or received or heard from me, or seen in me—*put into practice.* And the God of Peace will be with you.

If anything is disturbing my peace, I need to do a "*checkup from the neck up.*" *If anxious about anything—pray*!

> Casting all your anxieties on Him, because He cares for you. (1 Peter 5:7)

When I said, "My foot slippeth"; Thy Mercy,
O Lord, held me up. In the multitude of my
thoughts within me Thy comforts delight my
soul. (Psalm 94:18–19 KJV)

Dear ones! After the third nervous breakdown, the above scripture became very meaningful. I did not want to ever be found in the enemy's camp again, and *putting into practice by thinking on the Word of God became my healing.* I needed to keep grace and mercy flowing from the throne of grace and mercy to my heart by praying and thinking on the Word of God and flowing into the hearts of others by praying for them.

Don took care of me at home for a few days with others coming in the daytime to stay with me. All those wonderful ladies from church—Georgiea, Pat, Marge, Louise—such precious "sisters in the Lord," they fed me, led me to the bathroom, bathed me, cooked meals, and cleaned house; and so precious—read scriptures and sang worship songs.

One day, Don took me to the home of John and Bonnie. John was away at work, and Georgiea came out to be with Bonnie. They both read scriptures to me. Bonnie was giving a bath to her little girls, Jennie and Tammy, and when finished with them asked if I would like a bath.

"Well, yes! That would feel good!"

When I walked into the bathroom, I saw her pouring oil in the water.

I cried out, "No, no! Don't put that in the water!"

This was alarming to me, for Mom always said "oil and water don't mix!"

Bonnie could tell this upset me. She drained the tub and ran fresh water. I still didn't have it all together.

I liked going for rides in the car, and on one of these drives, Don took me by the home of Bob and Donna. We were standing on the steps when she opened the door, and I heard her exclaim, "Oh! I prayed to God they would bring you to me!" She was looking at me, and I felt right at home. I stayed two weeks!

Donna talked to me even though I had nothing to say. She helped me put puzzles together, play card games, and pick out walnuts. Sherry came to bathe me and wash my hair. I know by their efforts they were trying to get my mind to function again.

One evening, Bob was sitting in his chair, reading; Donna and I were on the couch, looking at a photo album; and Bobby, their son, was playing records on a player. It was lively music, and one of the songs was a "shodish," the tune of an old-time folk dance that I did as a child. I jumped up off the couch and started to dance:

> One, two, three hop; one and two and three hop,
> One hop, two hop, three hop, four hop.

And around the room I went! Bob, Donna, and Bobby laughed and clapped their hands to the timing of the music, and we played that record over and over again.

Praise the Lord for people who open their hearts and minister!

From this moment on, my climb to reality and upward out of the cellar of darkness was steadfast but slow. Until my mind could once again concentrate on the Word of God for myself, I depended on others. Being around people with an upbeat attitude, or positive thinkers, was the big boost toward my healing. I learned that a lot of the times *how something is said—or the spirit that is behind what is said—is extremely important.* The old saying "action speaks louder than words" is so true. *A person's countenance speaks volumes!*

> Those who look to Him are radiant; their faces
> are never covered with shame. (Psalm 34:5)

> A cheerful look brings joy to the heart and good
> news gives health to the bones. (Proverbs 15:30)

A cheerful heart is good medicine, but a crushed spirit dries up the bones. (Proverbs 17:22)

Then you will look and be radiant, your heart will throb and swell with joy. (Isaiah 60:5a)

CHAPTER 20

OFF THE FENCE, ON THE FENCE

I'm free! I'm free! I am "off the fence of offence!" When an offence comes our way, we either let it bother us, or we let it run off of us like water off a duck's back. We either forget what has been said to us, or we dwell on it until it can be like making a mountain out of a molehill. The fence is the offence, and we make the choice to accept it or reject it *in our thoughts*! We get off the fence on one side or the other.

My daddy would say, "When you sit straddling a fence, you then decide which side you are getting off on." On one side is freedom, and the other side is where the big, bad bull lives! He was mean! His name was Curly because of the wavy, curly hair on his back, and he was so protective of his domain. The only place to straddle the fence was sitting on the gate as the rest of the fence was barbed wire—a long stretch of wire with sharp points. I respected these sharp points; I received many a scratch when crawling in or out between the wires.

One day, when in second year of high school, my friends Pat, Helen, Joe Ann, Karen, and I were at the farm. Wanting to show them my ability to jump a fence, I backed up to make a running jump. I cleared the fence, but the points of the barbed wire cut into the upper part of my leg and left a gash—deep, wide, and bleeding.

I was humiliated, and this hurt worse than the cut! I went to the house, cleaned the wound, taped it shut, and went walking slowly on to the pond with my friends.

With these same friends at ballgames, I would chant with them a cheerleading yell that ended with these words: "Be calm, be cool, and be collected!" This is what I want to be if and when an offense happens—be calm, cool, and collected. In other words, remain calm, do not become angry, and keep my composure. *Jesus did!*

> A man's wisdom gives him patience; it is to his glory to overlook an offence. (Proverbs 19:11)

> Son of man, say to the house of Israel, 'This is what you are saying; "Our offenses and sins weigh us down, and we are wasting away because of them. How then can we live?" (Ezekiel 33:10)

Dear ones! Listen up! Now is the time to get rid of all offences!

When we sit on the fence of offence, we have set ourselves up as a judge. We judge the person that has put the hurting in our hearts, which is offence, and then bitterness and resentments take root. Our hearts are hardened, and countenance is one of sadness and defeat.

To break this hardness, we must forgive and pray for the one that hurt us. Jesus did!

> Then said Jesus, "Father, forgive them; for they know not what they do." (Luke 23:34)

> Judge not, and ye shall not be judged; condemn not, and ye shall not be condemned; forgive, and ye shall be forgiven. (Luke 6:37)

I lived for years in the offence received by the rejection of my first husband. Every time *I would think* about it, the offence became buried a little deeper inside of me. There was an ache that *thinking about it* caused depression and death to life. When depressed, I wasn't enjoying the abundant life *Jesus has made available.*

> The thief comes not but for to steal, and to kill, and to destroy; I am come that they might have life, and that they might have it more abundantly. (John 10:10)

When I started to pray for my ex-husband, the ache would go away. But when I would *think about it, think about how hurt I had been, and the ache would return.* This went on for years.

I would give the situation to *my Lord* and *think about it until the ache returned.* Send and receive! Send and receive! Finally, I got the picture of a young child playing a game of catch the ball with their sad. I could see a little boy standing a ways from a man and saying, "Throw me the ball, Daddy!" I finally realized that is what I had been doing—playing a game of catch with my Father. I threw the burden to my Father, and in a sense, when I started *to think* about the hurt, my Father had no choice but to send it back to me—*my thinking demanded it!* I was asking and receiving, asking and receiving the hurt over and over again. I finally realized what I was doing and released the whole situation to *my Lord God. What freedom and peace on this side of the fence! Release to the Lord for relief! Praise and thanksgiving are ways of keeping our mind on our Lord and Savior.*

> Give thanks in all circumstances, for this is the will of God in Christ Jesus for you. (1 Thessalonians 5:18)

> Thou will keep him in perfect peace, whose mind is stayed on Thee. (Isaiah 26:3)

> Glorifying and praising God for all they had heard and seen, as it had been told them. (Luke 2:20)

I often wondered about the older brother in the story of the prodigal son. The older brother lived at the Father's house. This older son had *everything that belonged to the father*, and because of a party and an old dead calf, he became angry!

Now on the farm growing up, a lot of butchering was done. The animal was slaughtered, skinned, and hung by a single-tree high up in a tree so the dogs on the ground couldn't reach it. It probably hung overnight and the next day brought down, cut up in sizes needed, and then hung in the smokehouse for the winter. All a messy process!

Why did the older brother become so jealous and angry over the killing of a calf? And why did he become so angry when he heard the sound of music of a party?

I remember going to a neighborhood gathering when on the farm of my childhood. My family had gone to the home of Roy and Pauline, whose property joined ours to the north. All the neighbors were there that lived up and down our road, so we had quite a gathering. Country cooking can't be beat! The best cooks are "down to earth," for they know how to prepare food that comes out of God's earth. The music that evening was loud and lively, but we were out in the country, and the sound went out into the fields and timber. Pauline had invited some of her family and friends from the city. One of them played a steel guitar, and I was so fascinated with this sound. Hawaiian and country all rolled into one instrument and with a fiddle player, side guitars, and drums, we were rockin'! Not the hard rock that is heard today, but it has the sound that sways with the evening breeze. What can I say—it's country!

At this gathering, the neighbors shared their interest; the men talked of crops planted or harvested, and the women talked of gardens that produced food for the table and beautiful flower gardens. Flowers are to share with others, so there usually was an exchanging of seeds or a promise to supply. The visiting was of genuine interest in each other! There was a heartfelt purpose to help that neighbor if a need was found out, and as a child, I loved to sit and listen to these adult conversations. Oh, how I loved these gatherings! They seemed to rejuvenate, and folks went back to their homes refreshed!

The older brother in the story from Scripture had to be jealous and bitter. When he heard the music from the party and found out his brother had come home, *the first thoughts in his mind* had to be envy. He was so envious he goes accusingly to the Father and basically says, "Why not me! Why aren't I the honored one?"

He had pride! Envy with pride will produce such *negative thinking*, it will wound and kill one's spirit.

I used to sit in church and look at the pianist and think, *Why couldn't I have that talent?* But I didn't want to take the time to practice playing the piano so I could. I would look at the pastor's wife and think, *Why couldn't I be like her?* But I was not spending time in the Word to "can up the goods" so my spirit could be rejuvenated. Oh, I perhaps looked sweet on the outside to others, but inside I was like "dead men's bones." During dry times, we need to soak up the "Water of the Word" to fill our reservoir or well. We need to keep full to have a supply of the Water of the Word to water someone else's garden. This is what "filled believers" did for me in assisting to gain my healing after my second and third breakdowns. I now know the only way to overcome "dryness of spirit" is to go "take a washing" *in the Word*. I love a song Ron and Shirley sing called "Washed By the Water of the Word":

Washed By the Word

Do you know what it is
not to have one guilty feeling
Not to wonder where you're going
when you die
Not condemned by the past,
not afraid of what tomorrow
holds in store
And to know the reason why
Well that's just how it is
When you go down in the water
For by faith you believe in what you've heard
It's not by anything you've done

But by the gift of God's own Son
When you're washed by the water of The Word

Chorus:
Are you washed by the water
Washed by the water of The Word
Are you washed by the water
Washed by the water of The Word
It's just like being born again
With a whole new life to live
Never having to look back on what you've been
For according to The Lord
you just started your existence
For as he's Concerned there never was a sin
So when God looks on you
He no longer sees a sinner
But a saint who's been washed white as snow
It's no impossible dream
You can start all over clean
When you're washed by the Water of The Word.

Donald C. Stamps, in *The Full Life Study Bible*, says this in his footnotes:

> Luke 15:28 BECAME ANGRY. The "older son"
> represents those who have a form of religion and
> outwardly keep God's commands, but inwardly
> they are separated from Him and His purposes
> for The Kingdom. (vv.28–30)

Dear ones! Listen up! It's time we let *Jesus in our lives "inside and out."*

Our Lord God knows our every desire of the heart and every thought anyway! We cannot hide from *our Lord God; He is everywhere*! There was a time in my life when I finally realized this, became convicted, and decided to *open my heart's door* so *Jesus the Word* could flow more freely in my heart and life. I wouldn't trade the world if I could for what *Jesus* has placed in my heart today. I have found *this side of the fence* to be full of "green pastures and fresh water."

> Delight yourself in THE LORD; HE will give the desires of your heart. (Psalm 37:4)

> THE LORD knows the thoughts of man, and they are vanity. (Psalm 94:11)

> THE LORD is my shepherd; I shall not want. He maketh me to lie down in green pastures: He leadeth me beside still waters. He restoreth my soul: He leadeth me in the paths of righteousness for His Name's Sake. Yea, though I walk through valley of the shadow of death, I will fear no evil: for Thou art with me; Thy rod and Thy staff they comfort me. Thou preparest a table before me in the presence of mine enemies: Thou anoints my head with oil; my cup runneth over. Surely goodness and mercy shall follow me all the days of my life: and I will dwell in the house of THE LORD FOREVER. (Psalm 23)

The pasture south of my folk's house was a huge play area for me. All I had to do was crawl though the barbed wire fence; but if Daddy had the electric wire on, I climbed over the gate. In the spring, the grass was thick and green and so much fun to run barefoot on or do cartwheels and somersaults. On the way to the pond was the gas well that supplied fuel for our lights at night. Around this well were lots of little rocks, and since they were on the way to the pond, I learned to run over them with my bare feet. I chased ducks and geese that were heading for a swim. I liked to walk around the pond to see how many frogs I could scare up and watch them jump in. The pond had a deep and shallow end with the spillway that overflowed when Willis and I tried to "dam up the works."

Daddy built steps over the barbed wire fence that led to the neighbor's house. This let the pasture be more accessible for Willis and me to play together, and since this family lived the closest to us, the easier to go a borrowing. The pasture was home to the cows, and I had to watch very carefully my steps so as not to step in what the cows left behind.

If Curly the bull was in with the cows, Daddy gave strict orders not to play in the pasture: "When going to the neighbor's house, walk down driveway to mailbox and walk the road to their home."

If the cattle were at the far end of the pasture, I would take the short way over the steps and run as fast as I could before the bull looked up from his grazing; and yes, I've been chased several times by a bull!

One day Willis's older brother and sister, Wesley and Rosie, were with Willis and me around the pond. We had cane poles with corks floating, and we were fishing. I fell in the deep end, and Wesley reached down and pulled me up out of the water by pulling on my hair. Ouch! But I was glad he was there!

When it rained, we country kids liked to run and play and let the water soak to the skin. We were just as frisky as a calf out of its stall. One day, Willis and I were feeling our oats, jumping and leaping in the rain, when all at once the ground lit up around us. It was a light so bright it momentarily blinded my eyes, and I thought to be lifted up in the air with an electric shock going through me—the shock I knew from holding my daddy's hand at the electric fence, but the light that blinded my eyes scared me to pieces! I started running toward home just as fast as my legs would go. I did a quick glance over my shoulder to see about Willis; he was at the steps heading toward his home. I was halfway to the house when I heard the loudest *boom*. The sound was so loud I thought a train had blown its whistle directly behind me! I was so thankful to see my daddy waiting for me at the gate with arms opened wide. I jumped up and felt the safety of my father's arms. *Lightning indeed travels faster than sound.*

It was my growing-up years on the farm from which I learned to respect fences. A fence served as an enclosure and also a means of defense and protection, but a fence can be the dividing line between good and evil. Just like Daddy said, "Keep that gate shut!" The gate needs to be closed to "keep good things in and bad things out"!

Dear ones! Listen up! Now is the time for us all to stay on the good side of the fence!

For years, I had the gate open to my mind and let the stinkin' thinkin' in. I allowed negative thoughts to override the positive ones! My thoughts allowed the enemy to set up camp in me. I should have *thought of my mind to be a fence dividing good and evil.*

It is like the enemy is shooting arrows of stinkin' thinkin,' and in my case, at times the arrows came constant. Now I know the enemy does not know what we are thinking; he only knows when he hits a bull's eye! The devil can't tell if the arrow penetrated in until I accepted the thought, *started dwelling on the temptation and by my actions.*

This is where I needed to have more of the *Word of our Lord* to rightly discern *the truth.*

> For the Word of God is quick, and powerful, and sharper than any two-edged sword, piercing even to the dividing asunder of soul and spirit, and of the joints and marrow, and is a discerner of the thoughts and intents of the heart. (Hebrews 4:12)

The Word of God is our defense to determine good and evil as well as truth and untruth. Knowing scriptures is our fence to keep good things in and bad things out. We need to keep our fence strong to stand against any stampede of the enemy. We need to be stayed on this fence, *the Word,* and stay off the fence of offence. Extra stressful times call for greater indulgence in the Word and prayer. There is strength in the tightness of a fence and the solid foundation and straightness of a fence post, no looseness. We need to keep tight our knowledge of scriptures and prayer links strong. Yes, this fence we need to stay on. *I like to think the Word of God is the post that holds the fence up, and prayers are the links between the post. Both are absolutely necessary and needed to keep our fence and defense strong.*

Over the years, I have collected old farm tools that remind me of growing up on the farm. I have on our back deck a cream separator like the one daddy used after milking. He poured the milk into the bowl of the separator and let me turn the handle. To see cream come out of one spout and whey the other was the result of the cranking. Daddy really liked cream in his coffee but sold most of the cream to the creamery in town. I have corn shucks that was worn on the hand to help shuck corn from the field. At one time, Daddy was a champion at corn shucking. I have an old-time corn-shelling box with the date of 1907 on it. This is like the one Daddy kept outside the grain bin in the barn to shell corn to feed the chickens, ducks, and geese. My job here was to put the ear of corn in the bowl, pointed end first, so the ear of corn would go down in the part that could separate the kernels from the cob. Daddy turned the handle because it was a little harder to turn than the cream separator. I also have old hoes, rakes, shovels, weed-cutting devices, and even a push lawnmower, but a tool I treasure a lot is my PHD (post hole digger)! I do not have a college degree, only my PHD! And a PHD (post hole digger) is used to dig a hole, put the post in the ground to build a fence. The fence, the Word of God, is so useful for abundant life and needed for complete victory our Lord wants us to have.

The state institution where I was a resident when having my first nervous breakdown was outside the town where I graduated from high school. I now tell people that my degrees of education are from OHS for high school and OSH for state hospital, sort of like when a person says they attended the "school of hard knocks"—this saying meaning they have their degree by going through so many trials of their lives. But you know, *all the degrees in this world will not graduate a person to heaven!*

The Apostle Paul was a very learned man, and he says it like this in 1 Corinthians 2:2 KJV:

> For I determined not to know any thing among
> you, save Jesus Christ, and Him crucified.

We can have all the knowledge this ole world has to offer, but if Peace—Jesus Christ—does not abide within, a person is doomed! *Only Jesus Christ within will graduate us to heaven!*

> Do not let your hearts be troubled. Trust in God; trust also in Me. In My Father's house are many rooms; if it were not so, I would have told you. I am going there to prepare a place for you. And if I go and prepare a place for you, I will come back and take you to be with me that you also may be where I am. You know the way to the place where I am going. (John 14:1–4)

> Peace I leave with you; My Peace I give you. I do not give to you as the world gives. Do not let your hearts be troubled and do not be afraid. (John 14:27)

It is not knowledge gained but Who we acknowledge that makes us whole and bound for heaven!

> Trust in the Lord with all your heart and lean not on your own understanding; in all your ways *acknowledge Him* and He shall direct your paths. *Do not be wise in your own eyes; fear The Lord and shun evil.* (Proverbs 3:5–7)

The Apostle Paul also says he "counts all things but loss." Listen to what he says in Philippians 3:8–11 KJV:

> Yea doubtless, and I count all things but loss for the excellency of the knowledge of Christ Jesus My Lord; for Whom I have suffered the loss of all things, and do count them but dung, that I may win Christ.

And in verse 9:

> And be found in Him, not having mine own righteousness, which is of the law, but that which is through the faith of Christ, the righteousness which is of God by faith; That I may know Him, and the power of His resurrection, and the fellowship of His sufferings, being made conformable unto His death; If by any means I might attain unto the resurrection of the dead.

Life in the Spirit Study Bible's notes by Donald C. Stamps

> *Philippians 3:8–11 that I may win Christ.* These verses show the apostle's heart and the essence of faith. Paul's greatest longing was to know Christ Jesus more intimately, to experience His personal fellowship and nearness in greater measure. His pursuit involved the following:
>
> 1. To know Christ intimately as a person as well as to know His ways, nature and character as revealed in the Word of God. True knowledge of Christ involves listening to His Word, following His Spirit, responding to His dealings with us in faith, truth and obedience, and identifying with His concerns and purposes.
> 2. To be found in Christ (v.9), i.e., to be united in close fellowship with Christ and be a partaker of His righteousness (1:10–11; 1Cor. 1:30, note; see article on *Biblical Words for Salvation, p. 1736).*
> 3. To know the power of the resurrection of Christ (v.10),i.e., to experience fully His life and the power of the Spirit who raised Jesus

from the dead (cf. Rom.8:11) so as to minister the gospel with power and life, and finally in the end to experience his own resurrection from the dead (v.11; Eph 1:18–10).

4. To share in Christ's sufferings by self-denial, crucifixion of the old self, and suffering for the sake of Christ and His cause (cf. 1:29; Acts 9:16; Rom 6:5–6; 1Cor 15:31; 2Cor 4:10; Gal 2:20; Col 1:24; 1Pet 4:13).

In 3:9—righteousness which is of God. The righteousness of believers consists first of all in being forgiven, justified and accepted by God as a gift received through faith (see Rom 4:5, note).

1. However, *God's Word states that our righteousness is also Christ Jesus Himself, living within our hearts* (cf. 1:20–21; Rom 8:10; 1Cor 1:30; Gal 2:20; Eph 3:17; Col 3:4); in the OT the Messiah is referred to as the "righteous Branch" and "THE LORD OUR RIGHTEOUSNESS" (see Jer 23:5–6 and note). Thus the righteousness we have is not of ourselves but of Jesus, in whom we put our faith (1Cor1:30, note; Gal 2:20, note). Through this indwelling, we become in Him "the righteousness of God" (see 2Cor 5:21 and note).

2. The ground for our salvation and our only hope of righteousness is the sacrificial death and shed blood of Christ (Rom 3:24; 4:25; 5:9; 8:3–4; 1Cor 15:3; Gal 1:4; 2:20; Eph 1:7; Heb 9:14; 1Pet 1:18–19; 1John 4:10) and His resurrection life within our hearts (Rom 4:25; 5:9–10; 8:10–11; Gal 2:20; Col 3:1–3; see Rom 4:22, note).

At the grain bin in the barn, Daddy had nailed tin on the floor and halfway up the sides. When the bin was empty, I would look in through the door and watch mice eating the left-behind grain kernels.

Mom said, "When the cat's away, the mice will play."

I would go find the barn cats and put them in with the mice and watch the cats have a banquet. When the bin was full of wheat or oats, the door to the grain bin was kept shut. A definite "do not open"! The inside of the door also had tin nailed to it. If a mouse got in somewhere, he could only nibble around the edge of the grain. That mouse may have touched on the edges, but he sure couldn't get to the full of the bin.

My mind—the fence "Word of God"; get off the fence on the good side. I need to keep the bin full of the good so bad cannot enter.

> Thou will keep him in perfect peace, whose mind
> is stayed on Thee: Because he trusts in Thee.
> (Isaiah 26:3)

> And be not conformed to this world: but be ye
> transformed by the renewing of your mind, that
> ye may prove what is that good, and acceptable,
> and perfect, will of God. (Romans 12:2)

Dear ones! Listen up! Now is the time to share a scripture I've already shared. Sometimes it helps my mind to have something run through it one more time!

> When an evil spirit comes out of a man, it goes
> through arid places seeking rest and does not find
> it. Then it says, "I will return to the house I left."
> (Matthew 12:43)

When it arrives, it finds the house unoccupied, swept clean, and put in order. Then it goes and takes with it seven other spirits more wicked than itself, and they go in and live there.

And the final condition of that man is worse than the first. That is how it will be with this wicked generation.

Dear ones! The scripture above talks about seven demons. We had the Scripture previously in these writings telling about the "man among the tombs" that had Legion because there were many demons in him. When I had the second breakdown and was so miraculously delivered, I was told they thought I had one demon, "a spirit of condemnation." The horrible visions I saw, the way it took my mind, and I believed the insane way it had me thinking: I am so concerned to think something more devilish could enter my being.

With all my heart, soul, and mind, I want to concentrate on my Lord God Jesus Christ. The Word is the only power to keep me full and keep me free! I need to stand on God's Word!

Therefore, there is now no condemnation for those who are *In Christ Jesus*. (Romans 8:1)

The Full Life Study Bible study notes written by Donald C. Stamps

Romans 8:1 Those who are in Christ Jesus.
Paul has just shown that life without the grace of Christ is defeat, misery and bondage to sin. Now in ch. 8, Paul tells us that spiritual life, freedom from condemnation, victory over sin and fellowship with God come through union with Christ by the indwelling Holy Spirit. By receiving and following the Spirit, we are delivered from sin's power and are led onward to final glorification in Christ.

This experience is the normal Christian life under the full provision of the Gospel.

He brought me to the banqueting table, his banner over me is LOVE. (Song of Solomon 2:4)

CHAPTER 21

KEEP YOURSELVES

Though I walk in the midst of trouble, *You preserve my life.* (Psalm 138:7a NIV)

But *keep your spiritual fervor, serving The Lord.*
(Romans 12:11)

When on the farm growing up, Mom did a lot of canning of vegetables and fruits. She did this to *preserve*, or keep them from spoiling and for future use. Some veggies had to be placed in the pressure cooker for a while and others in hot water baths. After the process, they are used to keep life flowing—to keep someone from hunger!

Come on now! Listen up! Now is the time to persevere!

To remain constant in our purpose of serving our Lord, we need to maintain our spiritual fervor; and to maintain, we need to *remain in our Lord God's Word*!

Dear ones! After I asked Jesus into my heart, after being baptized in His love, I didn't *retain* because I didn't *remain in God's Word to maintain*!

I didn't have "the canned goods"! There wasn't enough Scripture in me like Jesus saying, "*It Is Written! Not enough stored up to 'bring life!'" I became like dead.*

I read a story about Smith Wigglesworth: He was aroused from a sound sleep, thought he saw the enemy at the foot of his bed; he looked straight at the devil and said, "Oh! It's just you." And Smith Wigglesworth rolled over and went back to sleep. (Smith Wigglesworth was a circuit rider preacher in the 1800s.)

Dear ones! He had faith! *He knew the Word, believed the Word, and stood!*

To be as down and out, as I was in having three breakdowns, I allowed the enemy to place thoughts in my head like kernels of popcorn popping! The Word of God is the source needed to overcome the enemy. *The Word Is Jesus!*

Read the Word to be healthy, and practice the Word to be more *like Jesus.*

> I want more of Jesus, More and More and More,
> I want more of Jesus then I ever had before,
> I want more of His Great Love,
> So Rich and Full and Free,
> I want more of Jesus, so I'll give Him more of me.

Yes, more reading His Word, more studying and practicing His Word.

On Sunday evening of Memorial weekend in May 1996, as Don and I were driving home from the church service, we could tell we were going to have "one of those Kansas storms"—the sky with clouds so dark and the wind blowing so strong debris and dry grasses were crossing the pathway of our car. We hurried into the house for protection. Our usual routine after evening services is to have a snack before going to bed. To be comfortable, I changed into my nightclothes with duster on and went to the kitchen to dish up ice cream. Don loves homemade ice cream, and we usually have this in the freezer. I dished some up, and since Don was still back in our bedroom, changing clothes, I decided to start eating.

As I was eating, I was thinking about the church services we had just attended. The sweetness of the Holy Spirit had ministered, and I was sitting there feeling very blessed! As I ate the ice cream, a song we sang that evening came to mind. I started to think on these words and starting singing the words to the tune "All in My Mind":

> The name of The Lord is A Strong Tower,
> The Righteous run into it and are safe!
> The name of The Lord is A Strong Tower,
> The Righteous run into it and are safe!

Eating the ice cream and singing this chorus over and over in my mind, I was looking out the window and noticed how the wind was blowing the trees. They were not just swaying back and forth but seemed to be going round and round, a circular motion. All at once, a tree limb came through the ceiling about five feet above and away from me. I looked at it, stunned to see such an object in my kitchen. The branch of the tree had come through so quickly it was like a knife going through paper! I couldn't move! I looked up at it and yelled at Don whom I heard coming through the living room, "Don, I think we have a problem!" And I proceeded to sit at the kitchen table, cool as a cucumber, eating the ice cream.

Coming through the doorway into the kitchen and in answer to my comment about having a problem, Don said as he looked at the tree branch, "Yes, I think we do!"

I thought the way the wind was blowing in the circular motion that a branch came off of a tree and shot through the roof of the house, like a 'torpedo out of a submarine!' But Don opened the backdoor out of the kitchen leading into the yard, looked out, and saw a huge tree had come down. The one between the house and garage and one of the branches had indeed gone through the roof and ceiling of our kitchen. We were told later the storm was called a "microburst."

When the roof was torn off to repair the damage, five rafters were found broken directly above where I was sitting at the kitchen table.

Dear ones! Listen up! It wasn't me that held up the tree that kept it from crashing down on my head. It was *the Word of God in me! Jesus is the Word!*

> The Name of THE LORD is a strong tower; the
> righteous run into it, and is safe. (Proverbs 18:10)

Dear ones! Listen up! The only way anyone can be righteous, having a right relationship with our Lord God, is by the shed blood of Jesus, the Lamb of God, who loves me and gave Himself for me. Won't you join me now and enter His kingdom? Jesus loves *you* too and wants *you* for *His own*!

There is the story about a woman walking down the street of a large city. A thief snatched her purse, and the only Scripture that came to the lady's mind was, "I'm covered with feathers! You can't have my purse!" She yelled this at the thief, and he turned (probably to see if she really was covered with feathers), dropped the purse, and ran away. This may be humorous, but point being *the Word used is strong*!

> Surely He will save you from the fowler's snare
> and from the deadly pestilence. He will 'cover
> you with His feathers,' and under His Wings you
> will find refuge. (Psalm 91:3–4)

> When the enemy shall come in like a flood,
> the "Spirit of The Lord" shall lift up a standard
> against him. (Isaiah 59:19)

> *Submit yourselves*, then, to God. Resist the devil,
> and he will flee from you. Come near to God,
> and He will come near to you. (James 4:7–8)

The power of the Word will destroy the bondages on our lives.

Come on now! Listen up! Now is the time to submit to our Lord Jesus Christ so the Spirit of the Lord will lift up a standard *when you use the Word!*

Dear ones! It is for each one, our choosing *to keep ourselves in the Word.*

When Jacque and Kris were about fourteen and twelve years of age, I was taking them to piano lessons every Saturday morning in a town approximately twenty miles north of our town. On the way home, both girls were lying down, one beside me in the driver's seat and the other in the back. They were probably resting because of a slumber party the night before with their girlfriends as we had a lot of these back then. Anyway, to their way of thinking, Saturday mornings were for sleeping in.

Approaching a small incline north of our town, I noticed I was traveling every bit of the speed limit, if not a little more, so I eased my foot off the accelerator a little. As we crested the hill, I could see a car pulled up to a stop sign on a side road. I thought they would stay stopped, so I kept on with my speed as I had the right-of-way, and the speed limit was at least sixty-five miles per hour. All at once, I saw the car leave the stop sign and pull into the highway. The car was now in our pathway, and we were heading to hit them broadside. I will never forget the look of horror on a young teenage girl's face as she saw our vehicle aimed to where she was sitting in the front passenger's seat of that car.

Dear ones! Listen up! It is time to hear about a *one-word prayer*!

At this instant, my mind didn't come up with a scripture; but quickly I said the word *Jesus*! As I was speaking, I immediately laid my right hand and pressed hard downward on my daughter lying in the front seat. I didn't want her to be sitting up and go through the windshield!

With my left hand, I reached for the emergency brake down on the left side by the door, and at the same time, my right foot flew off the accelerator to the brake. Yes, I did take my hand off the steering wheel when reaching to pull on the emergency brake, so when my left hand came back to the steering wheel, it felt like it was locked in place. I then threw by body on top of my daughter while my right foot was pressing on the brake as hard as I could. As I think about this moment, it seems as though the speaking, the hand and foot motion all happened in a split-second of time.

It felt like that ole '65 Plymouth station wagon had turned into an airplane coming in for a landing. The thrush of a sudden stop and tires squealing on pavement was like we were at the airport breaking to a complete stop.

I checked on daughter in backseat first because I heard the sound of her body falling to the floor with a thud. She was okay, so I told her to stay put and the same for daughter in the front. I didn't want them to sit up until I looked out the window to see what had happened at the other car.

I looked out the front windshield and saw only two passengers in the other car. Two teenage girls were sitting erect in the front seat with expressions of unbelievable fright on both. Everything seemed okay with the car; I didn't hear any hissing or smell gasoline; I told Jacque and Kris they could sit up but not to leave the car. I went to check on the girls in other car. They were scared to pieces, but I assured them if no one was hurt in the accident, it would all be okay. Other cars were now stopping from both directions, and people were coming to see if they could help. Both vehicles ended up on the right side of the road, so someone started directing traffic around us. I looked at the damage done to the cars. The left front bumper of our car had come to rest and dented in the right rear door of their car. No one in either car had received a scratch!

> JESUS, JESUS, JESUS, there's just something about that NAME,
> MASTER, SAVIOR, JESUS, like the fragrance after the rain,
> JESUS, JESUS, JESUS, let all Heaven and earth proclaim,
> Kings and Kingdoms will All pass away,
> But there's something about THAT NAME!

> I am the vine; you are the branches. If a man *remains in Me and I in him,* he will bear much fruit; apart from Me you can do nothing. If anyone does not remain in Me, he is like a branch that is thrown away and withers; such branches are picked up, thrown into the fire and burned. *If you remain in Me and My words remain in you,* ask whatever you wish, and it will be given you. This is to My Father's Glory, that you bear much fruit, showing yourselves to be My Disciples. (John 15:5–8)

CHAPTER 22

LOOKING FORWARD

After my deliverance from depression and offences, I felt as free as a child again. The meaning of the words *look up* is "to search for and find," like when you seek a word in a dictionary and find your source. *Look* means "to turn one's eyes on and see," and *forward* means "onward, to be gaining or winning." I was advanced from defeat to gaining "new life" every day. I was changed and charged, renewed and regenerated with hope in my heart that can only be credited to my Lord God and Savior Jesus Christ.

Jesus is my source and strength.

> Thy Word is a lamp unto my feet and a light
> unto my path. (Psalm 119:105)

With the lamp light of the Word, I am moving onward and upward. Every day is a new challenge, for I am blessed with the One who said,

> Never will I leave you; Never will I forsake you.
> (Hebrews 13:5)

My Lord God's presence is the security I needed to move forward.

A special time of day to *look forward* to living in the country is when the mailman comes. My sister and I every weekday and

156

Saturdays would watch for the truck that would pull up to our mailbox at the end of the driveway, then we would race to see who could get there first. She did let me win some of the time, for my sister could outrun anything on the farm including our brothers. If a catalog or newspaper was in the mailbox, they were searched through to see if any article of clothing or any useful items for the home was needed and any information of interest in our closest town and county.

I really *looked forward*_to the evenings when the chores were done, supper over and dishes done, and the family gathered on the front porch in the fading light of a summer evening. The porch faced the west, and the sun setting gave a red-orange-purple glow to the horizon. Brother Mel played a harmonica, and he would prompt me to sing a song he taught me:

> K K Katie, beautiful Katie,
> You're the only beautiful G G G Girl that I adore,
> When the M M M Moon shines, over the cow shed,
> I'll be waiting at the K K K Kitchen door!

Another song my sister and I sang was

> I was born in Kansas, I was bred in Kansas
> And when I get married, I'll be wed in Kansas
> There's a true, blue guy who promised he would wait
> He's my sunflower from the sunflower state.

After a few songs and listening to family members discussing their day, I would begin to get sleepy and I *looked forward* to the best time of all. I would crawl up, for he would be waiting, on my daddy's lap. Daddy always wore bib overalls, and when I laid my head on his chest, I wondered sometimes which was ticking the loudest in my ear—his heart or the watch in his bib coverall's pocket. Daddy always had a treasure in one of those pockets—a penny or piece of gum—and I would search to find which pocket it was in.

Daddy would carry me to bed, and the last thing I would remember at night would be of him turning off the gas lamp in the living room which shone into my bedroom. The red wick that glowed kept getting dimmer and dimmer and dimmer. I slept. The next sound I would hear was the rooster crowing!

> It is of the Lord's mercies that we are not consumed, because His compassions fail not. They are new every morning: Great is Thy faithfulness. (Lamentations 3:22–23)

I am amazed that my life has come so full circle, for today what I *look forward* to the most is still to crawl up in my Father's lap. The physical touch isn't the same, but the sweet, protective spirit is! The arms around letting me know I am loved is the same! The treasure out of His pocket is beyond all imaginations, and the promises are so real and true! Everywhere I read in His Word is an expression of His love, and the hope He gives for today, tomorrow, and for all eternity is beyond comprehension. Peace! How do you explain peace to a world where there is no peace? I can only say, "*Ask Jesus!*"

Come on now! Listen up! It's time to ask Jesus to supply you with His peace!

> The mind of sinful man is death, but the mind controlled by the Spirit is life and peace. (Romans 8:6)

Come *on now*! Give Jesus control of your heart and life so He can give you His peace.

I can remember a last time battling depression. We have a basement family room with recliner chairs and television. I curled up with my blanket in one of these chairs, all set to have my pity party. I can't remember why or for what reason depression hit; I just didn't care and shut the door to be in the dark. Depression doesn't have to have a rhyme or reason. I turned on the television and snuggled down—mad at the world, mad at anybody and everybody, and most of all, mad at myself. Depression is really anger on the inside of a person.

The show on television was about a young girl that lived in the country with her aunt and uncle, and she was sitting up in her bed, having a crying fit about her hair. The time period was the late 1800s. This young teenager hated the color of her red hair and had bought a bottle of black shoe polish, or in those days a stove blackening from the peddler wagon. She thought this would dye her hair black. It didn't. It turned her red hair to green, and she was in a stupor!

The staunch, largely built auntie comes walking through the room carrying a basket of laundry. The young girl cries out to her, "Auntie, don't you ever despair?"

"*Never,*" replies Auntie. "*Because to despair is to turn ones back on God!*"

I came up out of that chair and knew immediately that I needed some time with Jesus!

I repented, asked *my Lord* to forgive me because to think that for even a moment I would turn my back on all He has done gave me unbearable shame. But this is what is so wonderful about *our Father God; He is always available! And anything unbearable to us He gladly bears.*

> If we confess our sins, He is faithful and just and
> will forgive us our sins and purify us from all
> unrighteousness. (1 John 1:9)

Anything at all that disturbs our peace within, we need to quickly seek Jesus for restoration. We need a right relationship, not religion, and Jesus as our Deliverer!

> Feeling, Faith and Fact, three men walking on a
> wall,
> When Feeling took an awful fall,
> Now Faith was so close to Feeling,

That he then fell down too,
But Fact remained, brought Faith up
And Faith brought Feeling too!
(Author unknown)

So then faith comes by hearing, and hearing by
the Word of God. (Romans 10:17)

Coming out of depression, I had to learn to "accentuate the positive." If depression was inside of me, then I needed to look beyond myself. The first *one* to look to is *Jesus*! My mind needed to turn to thoughts of Jesus the Word. To do this, I needed to be reading and studying scriptures; when not doing this, meditate on what I learned.

Hence, good thoughts!

As I was coming out of the third nervous breakdown, I was so impressed to stay in the Word. I was very leery of reading anything contrary to my *Lord God's Word*. My sister-in-law, Lois, gave me a little paperback book called "Prison to Praise" by Merlin Carothers. The book isn't about a prison with bars but about a prison of circumstances—and how to be set free, the concept being to *"Praise our Lord God in everything!"*

To appoint unto them that mourn in Zion, to
give unto them beauty for ashes, *the oil of joy for
mourning, the garment of praise for the spirit of
heaviness*; that they might be called trees of righteousness, the planting of THE LORD, that He
might be glorified. (Isaiah 61:3)

In reading the scripture above, I saw the word *garment*. We need to put garments on our outer body ourselves, and yes, inner garments are also put in place by self. I read the scripture in Psalm where David *commanded his soul to bless the Lord*!

BLESS THE LORD, O my soul: and all that is within
me, BLESS HIS HOLY NAME. (Psalm 103:1)

Both scriptures above are choruses put to music, and I would sing these tunes around the house and quite a bit of the time just in myself. While cleaning my home and doing menial tasks, Scripture songs and praise music kept my thoughts on *the positive*. I would also put praise music on the stereo while working around the house. I would be by myself, just *the Lord God* and me. I would get so happy my feet would even want to dance. I did sometimes, but after all, I had a house to clean while keeping my *inside house full so nothing else could possibly enter*!

> Rejoice evermore. Pray without ceasing. In every thing give thanks: for this is the will of God in Christ Jesus concerning you. Quench not the Spirit. Abstain from all appearance of evil. And the Very God Of Peace sanctify you wholly; and I pray God your whole spirit and soul and body be preserved blameless unto the coming of Our Lord Jesus Christ. (1 Thessalonians 5:16–23)

Dear ones! Listen up! It's time to be sure *the Lord God is first*!

I found at this time in my life not ever wanting to have another nervous breakdown. *All scriptures are for today!* From Genesis to Revelation, every chapter and verse needed to be applied to my life. After all, this is *God's Word*!

When I applied the first principle of putting my *Lord God* first, loving others came easier and, lastly, myself. JOY—*Jesus, others, yourself.*

> Hear, O Israel: The Lord Our God Is One Lord: and you shall love The Lord Your God with all your heart, and with all your soul, and with all your might. (Deuteronomy 6:4–5)

By applying *His Word* to my heart and life, not only did I attain *peace*, but my *love for others* became more meaningful. I love to read the "love chapter" of 1 Corinthians 13 and 1 John 4:

If I speak in the tongues of men and of angels, but have not love, I am only a resounding gong or a clanging cymbal. If I have the gift of prophecy and can fathom all mysteries and all knowledge, and if I have a faith that can move mountains, but have not love, I am nothing. If I give all I possess to the poor and surrender my body to the flames, but have not love, I gain nothing.

Love is patient, love is kind. It does not envy, it does not boast, it is not proud. It is not rude, it is not self-seeking, it is not easily angered and it keeps no record of wrongs. Love does not delight in evil but rejoices with the truth. It always protects, always trusts, always hopes, and always perseveres.

Love never fails. But where there are prophecies they will cease; where there are tongues they will be stilled; where there is knowledge it will pass away. For we know in part and we prophesy in part but when perfection comes the imperfect disappears. When I was a child, I talked like a child, I thought like a child, I reasoned like a child. When I became a man, I put childish ways behind me. Now we see but a poor reflection as in a mirror; then we shall see face to face. Now I know in part; then I shall know fully, even as I am fully known.

And now these three remain: faith, hope, love. But the greatest of these is LOVE. (1 Corinthians 13)

Dear Friends, let us love one another, for love comes from God. Everyone who loves has been born of God and knows God. Whoever does not love does not know God, because *God Is Love*! (1 John 4:7)

"And love does not notice when others do wrong." When I'm prais-ing my Lord God, I'm accentuating the positive.

> Shout for joy to the Lord, all the earth. Worship the Lord with gladness; come before Him with joyful songs. Know that the Lord is God. It is He Who made us, and we are His; we are His people, the sheep of His pasture. Enter His gates with thanksgiving and His courts with praise; give thanks to Him and praise His name. For the Lord is good and His love endures forever; His faithfulness continues through all generations. (Psalm 100 NIV)

Yielding to the Lord God in praise is to enter His presence—I can now have a forward look!

> You have made known to me the path of life; You will fill me with joy. (Psalm 16:11)

In Your presence, with eternal pleasures at Your right hand.

You may be wondering if I ever look back on the darkness of my past especially the nervous breakdowns. Yes, especially when seeing a person with a sad countenance. I see sadness and pain in their eyes, walking with heads down and not looking up or forward. The look of hopelessness on faces is when I think a lot about the darkness I was in, but I can't forget about that individual I have seen. I pray for them (you know, praying can be said without opening your mouth) and pray that if I don't have the opportunity to share Jesus, someone will soon come into their lives who will share Jesus, and I cannot let my mind dwell on my past.

> Forget the former things; do not dwell on the past. (Isaiah 43:18)

Daddy used to put salt licks out in the barnyard for the cattle. They were mounted on a pole sticking up out of the ground and were for the cattle to lick to put more nutrients in them. They then wanted to drink water, and yes, I licked them too! I liked the taste of salt, but these blocks of salt were harder than a rock! There is a story in Scripture that tells of a woman who looked back:

> But Lot's wife looked back, and she became a pillar of salt. (Genesis 19:26)

Dear ones! I don't like to look back when driving out of my driveway! These breakdowns I have been telling about happened over forty years ago. The Israelites wandered in the wilderness for forty years heading for the Promised Land.

> And I have promised to bring you up out of your misery in Egypt into the land of the Canaanites, Hittites, Amorites, Perizzites, Hivites and Jebusites—a land flowing with milk and honey. (Exodus 3:17)

> Blessed is the man who perseveres under trial, because when he has stood the test, he will receive the crown of life that God has promised to those who love Him. (James 1:12)

> Listen, my brother: Has not God chosen those who are poor in eyes of the world to be rich in faith and to inherit the kingdom He promised those who love Him? (James 2:5)

Dear ones! Listen up! It is time everyone reading this knows for sure the security of *looking forward to the Promised Land!*

But in keeping with *His Promise* we are "*looking forward*" to a new Heaven and a new earth, the home of righteousness. (2 Peter 3:13)

Do not be afraid of what you are about to suffer. I tell you, the devil will put some of you in prison to test you, and you will suffer persecution for ten days. *Be faithful*, even to the point of death and I will give you the crown of life. (Revelation 2:10)

Yes, I am *looking forward* to an eternity with Jesus in that Promised Land called heaven!

CHAPTER 23

MARRIAGE TRIANGLE

S ometime after going through the nervous breakdowns, I asked Don, "Why did you put up with me?" There were times I was so out of it like coming at him with a butcher knife, kicking him in the shins, and the horrible depressed state that I was in.

Don calmly looked at me and said, "I don't know. I guess you will have to ask the good Lord that one?"

His answer stunned me at first; we wives like to hear the sweet talk like "I love you so much, honey" or "I just couldn't live without you." But Don's answer sure made me start thinking about my prayer life.

I remembered going to my knees beside my bed at Christmas time in 1968, asking God for a Christian husband and daddy for my girls. Oh! I knew now how very, very much *our Lord* had granted my request. My husband Don was like the Scripture:

> Blessed is the man who does not walk in the counsel of the wicked or stand in the way of sinners or sit in the seat of mockers. But his delight is in the law of THE LORD, and on his law he meditates day and night. He is like a tree planted by streams of water, which yields its fruit in season and whose leaf does not wither. Whatever he does prospers. (Psalm 1:1–3)

Our Lord had abundantly answered my prayer, but how much was I the Christian wife? I had to be honest with myself. I needed to search the Scriptures:

> THE LORD GOD said, "It is not good for the man to be alone. I will make a helper suitable for him." (Genesis 2:18)

I remember watching my dad and mom working out in the garden together. It was work, but this is when I would see them so happy. Most of the time Daddy would be working in the field, cleaning the hen house, or feeding farm animals; and Mom was in the house getting meals, patching coveralls, and sewing or doing the bookkeeping. Mom was so sharp with a pencil. She always figured the income tax. One year they were called before the tax board. Mom worked on the books for weeks, and when they went before the IRS, Mom's figures were right! She only had an eighth-grade education, and this is why she insisted all her kids were going to graduate from high school. But the place I saw Dad and Mom together was in the garden *helping one another.*

The hayfield is a place I remember the whole family worked in. The old stationary hay baler was parked in the center of the field—not so far to gather in the hay from all sides. Daddy stood by the chute to feed the hay in with a pitchfork, Mom sat on a hay bale on one side of the baler, tying the wire, and my sister Vernita sat on a hay bale on the other side of the baler, poking the wire through to Mom. I stood at the end of the baler to catch a block that was used to separate the bale of hay and carried this block back to my daddy. He placed the block in the baler at an appropriate time to make the bales of hay while also feeding loose hay into the hopper. My brothers Lawrence and Melbourne were raking and gathering up the hay in the field to bring to the ole stationary baler, and my other brother, Eldon, along with neighbor boy, Leonard, stacked the bales on a wagon to haul back to the barn and lift up into the haymow.

Everyone was working together to get a job accomplished that was so needed. The hay that the cows ate for their food gave us meat and milk. When the ole baler broke down, everyone was sad; but the baler got fixed, and the work resumed. It wasn't the extreme heat of the day or the way the hay would stick to a sweaty body I remember the most, *it was the togetherness! We were together as a family.*

Don and I had our family times too, but mostly in the great outdoors swimming, waterskiing, and fishing is what we did for family togetherness. These were the activities we did in the "hot ole summertime." We were united with each other and had fun!

These times were not without challenges. I had to learn to drive a boat so precisely when Don was waterskiing so he didn't get wet! I had to watch the speed and run that boat at such a steady pace with no jerking so he didn't fall! He actually would stand on the boat dock, holding on to the handles of the rope; when ready, he would signal me in the driver's seat by yelling, "Hit it!" And I would push forward on the throttle until just the right speed, circle the lake, all the while watching for other boats and skiers down and at the precise spot would make the turn heading for the dock. Approaching the dock would swing in close but not too close and not too far ahead as there were swimmers there. I would then turn that boat to the left at just the right angle. I looked ahead to make sure nothing was in front of the boat, all the while keeping the correct speed. After doing all this, I would give a quick glance back toward the dock to see my husband sitting there high and dry.

I have found the only way I enjoyed fishing with Don is in a boat. When we first married, he would ask the family to go on outings at ponds or lakes to fish. We carried all the fishing gear, and he has boxes of lures, hooks, and fishing line—"you never know what you might need"—and a fishing pole for every kind of fish there is, for you never knew what kind of fish might be biting.

We piled all this paraphernalia on the bank of the ole fishin' hole. After we all had the correct bait or lure on our hooks, we cast the line out into the water and waited for the fish to bite. Don was real good, getting everyone's fishing pole ready for fishing; but as we sat there waiting for the fish to bite, I looked around for my husband, and he was nowhere in sight. He was either down or up the bank from us or across the water on the other bank. I decided that sometimes a man just needs his peace and quiet, and *for together time,* we'll "fish from boat."

Don is a perfectionist with his cabinet building, and as with any artist, another person doesn't always get the picture. When building cabinets, everything has to be made with the correct measurement in order to fit a precise place. Cabinet building to Don is him being an artist at work. He loves his work. The finished product shows his expertise, and the satisfaction comes with a "job well done." I have found the best way to be a helpmate to my husband with the business is to be the bookkeeper. I enjoy this, and after all, someone has to make sure bills are paid on time; and with all the government regulations and taxes due dates, this job would be impossible for me without a good accountant. Garry and Sally, I appreciate you so much!

> Husbands, love your wives just as Christ also loved the church and gave Himself up for her. (Ephesians 5:25)

When I asked Don his reason for hanging in there—the years of my severe depression and breakdowns—he said, "I needed to ask *our Lord*"; I got the picture—he kept his cool and patience *by praying!* He had talked to *our Lord* about me and the whole scenario. I got a picture in my mind of Don in a corner praying! All the circumstances and terrible things that happened had him backed into a corner, and with his back to the wall, he prayed—and he said these prayers to *the Most High God!*

If my Christian husband was praying for me, then I, as a Christian wife, should be praying for him. *I should be in my corner praying for him!* If he is in his corner and I am in a corner opposite him, *the Most High God is above all!*

To my way of thinking, this formed a *triangle.* Our Father God is the most high point and husband in one corner and wife in the other corner.

Scripture says the husband is to "love their wives as Christ loved." The husband represents Jesus. Our Father God is at the highest point then the Holy Spirit needs represented to make complete triangle. *Father, Son, and Holy Spirit are one!* A triangle is *one complete unit* with the husband *one* with his *Lord God* and *one* with his wife, and the wife is *one* with her *Lord God* and *one* with her husband.

The triangle reminds me of a tepee, the name Indians called their dwelling. A dwelling is an abode or "*your abiding*," and this is "*our home.*"

> *Abide* in Me, and I will *abide* in you. No branch can bear fruit by itself; it must *abide* in the Vine. Neither can you bear fruit unless you *abide* in Me. I am the Vine; you are the branches. If a man *abides* in Me and I in him, he will bear much fruit; apart from Me you can do nothing. (John 15:4)

GOD
Father

Philippians 4:19
"And my God shall supply
all your needs according to
His riches in glory in Christ
Jesus."

Son
Jesus
Husbands

Holy Spirit

Wives

Ephesians 5:25
"Husbands love your wives just
as Christ also loved the Church
and gave Himself up for her."

Galatians 5:22
"But the fruit of the Spiritis love,
joy, peace, patience, kindness,
goodness, self-control against
such things there is no law."

Abide–Abode
= Dwelling
= Tepee

If you *abide* in Me and My Words *abide* in you,
you shall ask what you will and it shall be done
unto you. By this is My Father glorified that
you bear much fruit and so prove to be My disciples. Just as the Father has loved Me, I have
also loved you; *abide* in My Love. If you keep

My Commandments, you will *abide* in My Love.
(John 15:7–10)

The reasoning behind me asking Don why he put up with me,
I was thinking why didn't he leave me? His answer told me that *our
Lord the solid rock is solid rock. Both our lives are built on Jesus; our
marriage is built on Jesus—the only foundation for life.*

> Therefore, everyone who hears these words of
> mine and puts them into practice is like a wise
> man who built his house on the rock. The rain
> came down, the streams rose, and the winds blew
> and beat against that house; yet it did not fall,
> because it had its foundation on the rock. But
> everyone who hears these words of mine and
> does not put them into practice is like a foolish
> man who built his house on sand. The rain came
> down, the streams rose, and the winds blew and
> beat against that house, and it fell with a great
> crash. (Matthew 7:24–27)

Someone may ask if I have moments of frustration in thinking,
'I want out! How can I escape this man? Honest answer is yes—*and
this is when I head for the prayer corner.* There is a particular instance
that comes to mind.

Several years prior to 2001, brother Eldon and wife Peggy and
sister Vernita and husband Reed told the rest of the family to save up
their dollars (used to be pennies) for their fiftieth anniversary.' They
wanted everyone to go on a cruise with them. Both couples were
married in 1951—sis in February and brother in August—and they
didn't want to celebrate fifty years in some reception hall eating cake
and drinking punch. A cruise to Alaska was in the planning. The trip
was scheduled for first of August 2001.

My bachelor brother, Lawrence, now at the age of seventy-five
years, fell on the ice and fractured a hip. His surgery took place on
January 1, 2001. Since I am the relative living closest to him, a lot of

overseeing his care was mine. I wouldn't want anyone else to do this anyway as he has done so much for me. After the hospital, he was in a rehab facility to receive therapy.

In our home at this time was a granddaughter that had come to live with Don and I to attend our church's academy, thinking the close attention at a private school would help her make the grade. It did! And in 2005, we witnessed her high school graduation. But the school term ending in May 2001 was quite a challenge for all concerned.

The first few months of 2001, I kept busy with my brother and granddaughter as well as keeping up with the home, church and school activities, and cabinet shop business.

It was also in May of that year daughter Kris told me of a lump on her breast, and I urged her to see a doctor as soon as possible. The appointment was made for June. The result was cancer, and the mastectomy was scheduled for the last of July 2001.

The end of May 2001, on Memorial weekend, my dear friend Barb had seizures that broke both shoulders. She had surgery on both shoulders that required no usage of her arms. This enervated her for weeks! Lee, her husband, took excellent care of her as well as daughter Vicki, but I wanted to be with Barb as much as possible as she is very dear to me. We don't know why she had the seizures; she did not have symptoms before and has not had one since. We are *praising our Lord!*

With all the circumstances happening to people close to me, Don and I were still planning a cruise to Alaska for August. I was looking forward to just being with family, but Don was a little reluctant because he is a land lubber. He didn't think there would be anything he liked to do on a ship, confined for seven days, and wanted to be able to fish on land in Alaska. Consequently, I called the cruise director, and she provided me with phone numbers in Anchorage to see about renting a motor home. This I did and scheduled stops for two weeks touring Alaska. Hubby said this may be a one and only trip, and he wanted to see as much of "this great state" as possible.

Kris's surgery was the 27th of July 2001, and Jacque, Don, and I headed for Oklahoma City. The operation took hours! The first surgeon did the removal, and the plastic surgeon came in to do the rest of the procedure, requiring skin from her abdomen. As I sat in the hospital waiting room that day, praying and doing my crocheting, I didn't see any possible way to make the cruise. Kris would be needing lots of care after having such a serious operation. Jacque had assured me on her intent to stay as long as needed, but I was the mother and really wanted to be the one with my youngest girl. I was thankful that I purchased insurance on booking the cruise—a family emergency would give us a refund—but if we were going on this cruise, we had to be at the Kansas City airport in three days!

I shall never forget the first moment seeing Kris after this surgery. Walking into the recovery unit of intensive care, she has tubes, needles, and every medical machine possible hooked up to her. I leaned over her in the bed, and she opened her eyes to look at me and says in a very weak but positive voice, "Mom, I'm okay. You're going on that cruise!"

If my daughter after going through such a humongous ordeal could be so positive that everything was okay, and the first words I hear out of her mouth was to think of someone else's situation, I needed to listen to the desire on Kris's heart. Jacque stayed with Kris. Don and I stayed one more day at the hospital and the next day left for home where we finished packing. The third day, we were at KCI boarding a plane flying to Seattle.

I want to acknowledge *our great merciful and gracious Lord!* At this writing, daughter Kris has been cancer-free for over twenty years. Don and I are *believing for a healthy eternity for her and our other children and all their families. All praise be to our Lord God and Savior Jesus Christ—forever!*

The plane flying from Kansas City to Seattle was nonstop, and about midway, approximately thirty-three thousand feet in the air, this little episode took place. Don came back from the aerial potty, leaned over, and told me he is bleeding when urinating. I looked at him in disarray and at this moment was wishing to be strong enough *to stand up, take my husband by the throat and shoulders, shaking him, shouting as loud as I could, "Why did you not tell me before leaving KCI you need medical attention!* But I said to him as sweetly as I could, "Don, this could be serious. You need to see a doctor as soon as possible!"

He said, "I didn't tell you before leaving. I knew you would have canceled the trip."

I turned to my right and looked out the window, watching the clouds, thinking if I could only drift serenely by like they were and maybe even hitch a ride on a big fluffy one. I knew Don's symptoms could be an indication of a lot of serious illnesses. *I would not let my mind go there!* I prayed a *prayer of release* and started *looking forward* to seeing my family. There were forty-two family members having reservations for this cruise, some of the nieces and nephews I hadn't seen in years. Then I realized two of my nephews are doctors! Dr. Dan is a radiologist, and Dr. Bill is an MD! Bill had stayed with us once on his way to college in Hawaii, surfboard and all! Don would surely consider telling Bill his situation.

With this on my mind, I turned to Don and asked him about talking to Bill.

He said, "Yes, on one condition—that Bill or I would not say anything at all to other family members on the cruise."

"Fair enough," I told Don. "Bill is a doctor, and I'm sure we can place our confidence in him."

Bill prescribed an antibiotic that he picked up on our first port of call in Alaska. We all had a very memorable time aboard ship and the three ports we stopped at. I know Don was miserable with his ailment, but he never let on.

We picked up the rented motor home in Anchorage. Bill called in another prescription to a drug store there, and Don and I headed the camper north to Denali Park. We were one of the few that summer to have a clear view of Mt. McKinley. We traveled on up to Fairbanks and from there flew to Barrow, the northernmost point of Alaska on the Arctic Ocean. Standing on this shore, we could look over these waters and see the coast of Russia. Back in Fairbanks, we traveled south to Valdez where Don did his salmon fishing. He caught three really nice ones. From Valdez, we boarded a ferry— camper and all—that took us back out to sea, arriving at Homer where we went deep-sea fishing.

From Homer, we again headed north to Anchorage. We were amazed at the beauty of *our Lord's* creation in Alaska and the wildlife we witnessed along the highway. A blessing to Don was the fact his dad worked in Alaska during Don's childhood. Traveling along the Alaskan Highway and seeing the Valdez Pipeline was special. We boarded our plane in Anchorage and flew home to Kansas City. As soon as possible, I called a urologist and made an appointment, and he was given priority. It was determined Don had a stone in the bladder that had to be removed surgically.

The day of the surgery, Don's sister, Lois, and Pastor Roy waited with me. I was doing some crocheting, and the yarn became so tangled everyone in the waiting room was helping to untie the knots. I looked up from where I was sitting toward the double doors going into the surgical unit, and they burst wide open. There was my husband, sitting up on a gurney, still with a surgical hat on, grinning like a cat that swallowed the canary. They wheeled him on down to a room and helped him get into a bed. In the room was the door to the bathroom and a lavatory on the opposite wall from the bed. The nurse came in and instructed Don as soon as the urine sample was clear, he could go home. They brought Don a meal. He was famished, and he laid back to rest awhile. He soon got up and went into the bathroom, brought the bottle he was supposed to have a sample in out empty, and headed to the lavatory, filled the sample bottle with water from the lavatory, and sat down on the edge of the bed.

The nurse came in and said, "Well, Mr. Hadlock, I see the sample is clear. You can go home!"

What does a wife do at this point?

Marriage is a commitment. I vowed to *our Lord* on our wedding day to be true to my husband and love him. At times, this is only possible for both spouses when inside *the triangle of love! Our God of love is the head. Husbands and wives, to be like Jesus, need to be filled and yielded to the Holy Spirit—this is my goal I need to keep striving for!*

I told my daughter Kris that we need to love our husbands like they were a little boy and they would become a man.

She was silent for a moment and then asked very seriously, "Mom, how long will this take?"

I told her, "I don't know, Kris. My husband is over seventy-five years old, and I'm still working on this one too!"

CHAPTER 24

THE FASTED LIFE

"On a clear day you can see forever!" This saying seems to indicate that it is "smooth sailing ahead." On the right side of the fence and looking forward, there seemed to be no obstacles in the way. When I felt something in my life wasn't what it should be, I learned to follow:

> If we confess our sins, He is faithful and just and will forgive us our sins and purify us from all unrighteousness. (1 John 1:9)

And if a burden was there for another individual, the scripture found in 1 Peter 5:7: "Cast all your anxiety on Him because He cares for you."

Not only knowing the Word but doing the Word gave me freedom from anxiety and stress. If the problem was me, after praying, I would keep looking forward; and if someone else, I would think of them as being alongside of me and after praying for them watching *our Lord* unravel the problem.

Come on now! Listen up! Now is the time to give problems *to the Lord!*

> *"Fix" these Words of Mine in your hearts and minds;*
> *tie them as symbols on your hands and bind them on*

your foreheads. Teach them to your children, talking about them when you sit at home and when you walk along the road, when you lie down and when you get up. Write them on the doorframes of your houses and on your gates, so that your days and the days of your children may be many in the land that The Lord swore to give your forefathers, as many as the days that the Heavens are above the earth."
(Deuteronomy 11:18–21)

Let us "fix" our eyes on Jesus, the author and perfecter of our faith, Who for the joy set before Him endured the cross, scorning its shame, and sat down at the right hand of the Throne of God. Consider Him Who endured such opposition from sinful men, so that 'you will not grow weary and lost heart.
(Hebrews 12:2)

The previous scriptures have the message for all those wanting and needing *a fix!*

When my children were teenagers, as a mother, it was heart wrenching seeing them walk so close to the edge. I did as a teenager, and so did my children as they too wanted to be accepted. The cries of the wild with a wolf howling off in the distance can prick and wound a mother's heart. At times, there aren't words to say to them, for your words can be taken very offensively. It seemed to be the same attitude when they were two-years old and we asked them if they would like our help to put their clothes on.

"I can do this myself," they would say.

This was a learning experience with two-year-olds, and we would let them dress themselves. But to recognize situations in those teenage years as learning experiences is difficult indeed.

When attitudes and dispositions were upsetting our household, I had nowhere else to go but *to the Lord.* The girls didn't always want to take orders from Don; he was their stepdad. Matt, wanting to be a man like his dad, went through many a trial and didn't want orders.

He wanted to be on equal basis with Don. Many conflicts arose. I leaned on Don a lot, but he was feeling himself a failure as a dad. It was these years of my life that I learned about *prayer and fasting*!

> While they were worshiping the LORD and fasting, the Holy Spirit said, "Set apart for Me Barnabas and Saul for the work to which I have called them." So after they had *fasted and prayed*, they placed their hands on them and sent them off. (Acts 13:2–3)

> Paul and Barnabas appointed elders for them in each church and, with *prayer and fasting*, committed them to The LORD, in whom they had put their trust. (Acts 14:23)

> I humbled my soul with *fasting*. (Psalm 35:13)

> *When you fast*, do not look somber as the hypocrites do, for they disfigure their faces to show men they are *fasting*. I tell you the truth; they have received their reward in full. But when you fast, put oil on your head and wash your face, so that it will not be obvious to men that you are fasting, but only to your Father, who is unseen; and your Father, who sees what is done in secret, will reward you. (Matthew 6:16–18)

I took these previous scriptures very seriously. Don didn't know a lot of the time when I fasted. His hours in the business, being self-employed, would bring him home lots of time after the supper hour, and I guess he thought I had already had my meal. Other times he did know, and I had to assure him I was okay without eating.

When I fasted, I always drank water—more than usual. And when I got older, I drank apple juice in the morning, cranberry juice at noon, and goat's milk in the evening. I added the goat's milk because it eliminated some cramping in my legs that I developed on a previous fast. If a goat is fed good feed, the milk tastes so good! I found a source in the country and really enjoyed my weekly visits with Vince and Becky. Goat's milk has less fat and digests better.

I didn't fast any more often than perhaps the spring and fall, but there was a time when our church had a corporate fast the first three days of every month. I thought a lot of strongholds were broken, and it sure gave a close connection among members.

Most of the time I would fast three days. I think only twice did I do a five-day fast. The third day was the day of exuberant victory! I felt closeness to my LORD like no other day, and this was worth all the sacrifice of food. No one else knew I was fasting, so I was in a secret place with just my LORD and me. The time usually spent in eating a meal was spent in feasting in the Word. I never regretted not eating food with my mouth, for the spiritual food was always more refreshing and strengthening. Just like Jesus rose the third day, I felt like the third day of fasting was like coming out of a tomb! In my being, there was definitely a newness of life.

My age in years: I'm now over eighty. They say a woman that shares her age will tell anything! Well, my life has now been made an open book. Anyway, the reasoning behind this thought could be my age, for in recent years I've not fasted as much because I have felt more impressed to live a *fasted life*.

Come on now! Listen up! Now is the time to cleanse soul, mind, and body!

I found that when reading Scripture—*the Word of God*—my mind would be cleansed and my soul refreshed. Drinking water cleansed, refreshed, and restored my body. I drank the spiritual water for the spirit and the earthly water for the body. *After fasting* it seemed like my whole body came together; my insides connected! I felt so good! Life is definitely worth the living!

Before doing a fast, hints were given me about giving up red meat and caffeine but come off the caffeine slowly to avoid a possible headache. I did this, and fasting did wonders for me the way I think *our Lord* intended it to.

Our Lord's Word says in Matthew 6:16 *"When you fast..."* indicated to me that He fully expected us as his disciples at some time or other *to fast*!

Drinking coffee I had done since childhood. Don never drank it, so I was putting a pot of coffee on every morning just for me. Being country, I couldn't go for too much of this instant stuff. I quit the coffee drinking and drank fresh frozen orange juice every morning. I did this for several months and found I had more energy in the afternoons. I didn't have that sluggish down-and-out feeling or the midday droops when I quit drinking the morning coffee. I got to thinking back at the state institution, and for months after coming home from there, I took medication (drugs!). These gave me the same effect as caffeine in a diminished way, of course, and I thought to need another dose of medicine or the latter—another cup of coffee! Caffeine is a drug!

When I cleansed my body with fasting and after the fast started eating and drinking the way I always did, I recognized the effects. I had been delivered from stinkin' thinkin' by thinking on *the Word of God*, the best food there is. *My body needed to be delivered from junk food by eating and drinking good nourishing food and water! Wow!* Way out wonder! I knew the saying "You become what you eat!" I needed to eat good food—like eat your vegetables! I also try to eat foods as much as possible this day and age that do not contain artificial preservatives. In my grandparents' and parents' time, the meat and produce was preserved by salt. Salt was a cure all. An example of the effects of preservatives in food, I think, is shown in the last two generations of my own family. My mom started her monthly periods when eighteen years of age, my sister was sixteen, and I was twelve. Mine could have happened prematurely because of an appendectomy. Today, I have heard of a girl as young as ten years having to ride that monthly white horse.

Come on now! Listen up! My physical body needed attention to maintain, to retain being healthy, to *sustain my whole being*!

> Even to your old age and gray hairs I am He; I am
> He Who will *sustain* you. I have made you and I

will carry you; I will *sustain* you and I will rescue you. (Isaiah 46:4)

The Son is the radiance of God's Glory and the exact representation of His being, *sustaining* all things by His powerful word. After He had provided purification for sins, He sat down at the right hand of the Majesty in Heaven. (Hebrews 1:3)

In the fall of 2002, Don was diagnosed with lymphoma. He did the chemo, and when the hair started to come out, his sister Mary shaved his head. I liked his shiny bald head, and we kept it shaved for several years. Don's attitude through all of this was very optimistic, for he was looking forward to *our Lord* healing him. In these last years' visits with the oncologist, Dr. L, Don has had excellent blood test results. Don claims his healing and gives thanks and praise to *our Lord*!

I watching the chemo zap Don's body, so I started looking for ways to put more nutrients in him. We watched *The 700 Club* on television; Pat Robertson talks about "good food for one's whole being!" The middle-of-the-week show is called "Skinny Wednesday!" From this show, I ordered a recipe for a protein drink that Don and I have drank every morning for almost twenty years. Don is over eighty-five years old, and well, you know my age. We have more energy and strength, more "intestinal fortitude" than before starting the intake of this protein drink. Here is a copy of this recipe:

Pat's Age-Defying Shake

6–8 ounces of orange juice (water, other fruit juices can be substituted).
5 tablespoons soy protein isolate
5 tablespoons whey protein isolate
2 tablespoons natural apple cider vinegar
1 tablespoon flaxseed oil

1 tablespoon safflower oil
2 tablespoons (or more) soy lecithin
1 teaspoon MSM powder
1 teaspoon glutamine powder
5–6 frozen strawberries

In a blender, combine ingredients

Don and I like to add a few blueberries, strawberries, and one banana to each drink. We also like a homemade oatmeal-raisins cookie or a piece of homemade cinnamon-nut bread. Don was leery of this being enough for breakfast as he had always been a big breakfast eater. We both found this drink so satisfying our bodies are content until noon or next meal, and our energy level *sustained*!

We also take vitamins as a food supplement. The food today isn't grown on that good ole country dirt quite like my daddy's garden. The fertilizer he used came out of the chicken house or barnyard mixed thoroughly with the dirt, and the animals were fed grain produced from the soil without additives—a good healthy combination! What came out of the soil goes right back in with nothing added to it!

I buy food products in a health-food store some, but this is quite expensive, so I don't indulge buying too much there. Don really has a sweet tooth, so it's difficult to refrain from desserts, and I still like a good piece of smooth chocolate with nuts. In fellowships, I will drink an occasional cup of coffee or hot tea, but I'm not addicted to them—addicted meaning the craving or feeling "I just have to have the caffeine." Don and I both get plenty of exercise in outdoor fresh country air. He is an avid fisherman out in God's great creation, and I like to play in the dirt in my flower garden and ride a bicycle—and yes, a good ole time gathering of a fish fry is a family favorite!

For the Kingdom of God is not a matter of eating and drinking, But of righteousness, peace and joy in the Holy Spirit. (Romans 14:17)

One of my young 'uns was out on the edge, and I had entered a time of prayer and fasting. I say "on the edge" like meaning "sittin' on a fence." On one side is good, and the other side not so good—the story of good and evil again. "On the edge" is like the good, at the top side of the edge, and "over the edge" is the downside of heading toward evil. I love the story in Scripture about the sheep that wandered off:

> What do you think? If a man owns a hundred sheep, and one of them wanders away, will he not leave the ninety-nine on the hills and go to look for the one that wandered off? And if he finds it, I tell you the truth, he is happier about that one sheep than about the ninety-nine that did not wander off. In the same way your Father in Heaven is not willing that any of these little ones should be lost. (Matthew 18:12–14)

It was the third day of fasting, and I was searching Scriptures for comfort. I had prayed a prayer of release to *my Lord*. A prayer of release is releasing a situation or problem to *the Lord*; and by not thinking about the situation or problem, I am making sure it stays in the Father's hands. I learned by trial and error that prayer is not a game of catch with our Father. For years, I had been guilty of praying about something and giving it to my Father but didn't receive peace because of catching myself up into the problem again by worry and fretting. It was a release-and-catch scenario!

I was reading Scripture to keep my mind off the situation of my child being tempted to be out in the world. All at once, this verse seemed to illuminate before me: Proverbs 11:21: "But the seed of the righteous shall be delivered."

Dear ones! Listen up! The Bible is the only book that is alive! Scripture has the only words that can restore life! That day I was rejuvenated about my child. In the above verse, the seed is my child. The only way I am righteous is by the blood of the Lamb Jesus! My child was being delivered! My child was coming home! And I started to rejoice for the marvelous breakthrough I had received. Oh! They hadn't arrived home yet, but I knew they were coming. I think it was weeks or several months before I actually saw them come through the door of home but kept rejoicing and praising *my Lord* that He was searching for the lost sheep, and they would be safe in His arms!

By the way, I still refer to my adult children as my kids! My parents called me the baby of the family when I was in my forties, and our Father in heaven doesn't have any grandchildren or great-grandchildren. We are all our Father's children, and the only way to enter His family is through the gate of the fold one by one!

> We all, like sheep, have gone astray, each of us has turned to his own way, and The Lord has laid on Him the iniquity of us all. (Isaiah 53:6)

The Full Life Study Bible by Donald C. Stamps study notes

> Isaiah 53:6 WE ALL, LIKE SHEEP, HAVE GONE ASTRAY. Every person at one time or another has preferred following his or her own selfish and sinful way to obeying God's righteous commands; we are all guilty, and therefore *we all need Christ to die in our place.*

Matt was about twelve years of age when the pastor of our church called for a corporate fast. I thought a growing boy needed all the nourishment possible, and Don, Matt, and I decided not to be fasting food, but for a week, we would fast television. For seven days our home was more peaceful, and I believe there was a better aroma.

Dear ones! Listen up! Now is the time to be more protective of our ears!

> Thorns and snares are in the way of the "froward": he that keeps his soul shall be far from them. (Proverbs 22:5 KJV)

185

In the paths of the wicked lie thorns and snares,
but he who guards his soul stays far from them.
(Proverbs 22:5 NIV)

And the Peace of God, which transcends all
understanding, will *"guard your hearts and your
minds in Christ Jesus."* (Philippians 4:7)

The word *froward* means "stubbornly, contrary, disobedient,
and obstinate." I was delivered in my second breakdown of *froward*
and *wicked* thoughts. I was free, and my "house was clean," but I
allowed the wicked airways of this ole world to enter, and I had the
third breakdown. The third breakdown taught me that *I am the
responsible one to guard my heart and mind in Christ Jesus*!

Dear ones! The same principle applies in our homes. I had to
stand in my home and come against any television program, CDs,
DVDs, anything that came in the mailbox—magazines and books
of ill-repute and cursing from others mouths and say, *"This is not
allowed in my home!"*

Television and computer Internet will not take us to heaven. In
fact, the influences from these modern-day devices will take a person
in the direction they really don't want to go. With the brain waves
so relaxed and not dwelling on God's Word and heeding His commands, what we see and hear over these airwaves can take an individual down the wrong road, which can eventually lead straight to
hell! Even though most of the programs or shows are make believe,
the subconscious mind, while listening and watching, accepts them
as fact. People can be in such a trance with television and Internet;
watching it is really a form of hypnotism.

Come on now! Listen up! It is time to realize the spirit that
attaches itself to some of this hearing and viewing from these media
screens is so sneaky and appears so innocent that a person does not
realize anything has entered their being until drastic signs are notice-
able. *Depression* starts out mildly but becomes "a deep pit of with-
drawal from life itself." *Offences* like watching arguments on soap
operas which can cause one to think offenses against one's own mate.

Apathy starts out with such a relaxed state of mind and ends up not caring about anyone else or even oneself. A person can become like a baby again—eat, sleep, and get fatter! They have been given the name "couch potatoes." A little card with this saying was given to me years ago:

> The Lord gave you two ends, one for sitting and
> one for thinking. Your success depends on which
> you use. Heads you win, tails you lose.

The "eat-sleep mode" and "self-seeking entertainment" is not the victorious living our Lord intends for us to have. Jesus came so we could have abundant life (John 10:10)—not death! Not DOA—dead on arrival! Depression, offences, and apathy puts one in such a state of mind that we become like a walking zombie.

Dear ones! I have been in all these modes of being, and what kind of person would I be if I did not warn others of these sneak attacks and where they can come from? It is like Eve in the garden of Eden looking at a beautiful piece of fruit and the horrible lasting results of biting into that fruit! A television show or website is equally as alluring, also with lasting side effects; and if a television show happens to be good entertainment, what about those enticing commercials?

Questions to ponder: What kind of people have we become if every evening we feel the need to sit around and be entertained? Does this type of thinking advance the kingdom of God? And Who do you suppose is behind this lax type of thinking? What enemy out there does not want to see the coming of our Lord Jesus again?' What will happen to this enemy when Jesus returns? Now, do you understand why the enemy wants to keep people in a state of apathy? How do you suppose the enemy can keep people from reading the Word of God and doing the Word of God? Do you realize that *people are being seduced by the entertainment media*?

After my third breakdown, I was determined not to ever have another. Enough was enough. I sure didn't want to take up residency behind bars in a state institution. The frame of mind that caused me to have nervous breakdowns is in the past. With the help of our Lord, I know I will never have another. The help our Lord has given me is His Word. If we are not continually fed with God's Word, we will starve spiritually. Read the Word. Study the Word. Stand on the Word. After the third breakdown, there was a fight inside of me to keep my mind on positive thinking which after this breakdown I came to realize the only positive thinking in this ole world is *to think the Word of God*. This brought victorious living and the abundant life for me.

Dear ones! That third breakdown happened over fifty years ago. The world is so much more demonic today, and if you and I are able to cope and rise above devilish schemes, *what about our children*?

In March 1975, Don and I had the marvelous privilege to visit Israel, the Holy Land! We were so excited to be in the land where *our Lord God Jesus Christ* had actually walked this earth. I can now visualize when reading stories in Scripture the place and area they happened. I love and treasure this good thinking!

One of the places visited cut deep into my heart, for the tour guide said, "This is where children were sacrificed." I just could not think that any parent could do such a thing. We were from America, and I had not heard of such happenings. I spent my childhood in the peace of good ole country surroundings and knowing I was cherished by my parents and siblings. What a grotesque thought that children were sacrificed.

After returning from our trip to Israel, I found a verse in *Full Life Study Bible* study notes by Donald C. Stamps:

> They sacrificed their sons and their daughters to
> demons. (Psalm 106:37)

Those who served idols in OT times were, in actuality, dealing with demons; for behind all false religions are demonic manifestations, powers, and influence. Likewise, when a believer in Christ conforms to the world and adopts its ungodly customs and ways, he or she is in reality submitting to demonic influences. *Today some in the church unknowingly sacrifice their children to demons by allowing them to be influenced by the ungodliness and immorality of the world through the entertainment media, unbelieving companions, or instruction contrary to biblical truth.*

> *Great peace* have they which love Thy law; and nothing shall offend them. (Psalm 119:165)

> Thou wilt keep him in *perfect peace*, whose mind is stayed on Thee; because he trusteth in Thee. (Isaiah 26:3)

> For to be carnally minded is death; but to be spiritually minded is *life and peace*. (Romans 8:6)

> Dear Heavenly Father,

> I come to You in the name of Jesus, thanking You and praising You for who You are! Thank You for giving us Your Word. Help us to apply Your Word to our hearts and minds that we do not sin against You. Help us to save the children by our influencing their young minds with thoughts of You, Lord, for Jesus as our Lord is the Word. Jesus is the Truth. Help us all to have our minds stayed on You.

> In Jesus's name, amen.

CHAPTER 25

DAUGHTERS

The greatest joy I have on this earth, are my children. Each one is unique in their own way, and I've so enjoyed seeing each of them blossom into adulthood. Flowers on this earth bloom for such a short time and bring beauty to their surroundings, and I am so thankful to *our Lord* that each child of mine knows Jesus and will bloom forever!

> I have no greater joy than to hear that my children are walking in the Truth. (3 John 1:4)

In the spring of 1972, Don and I planned a family vacation to Florida. This was in March, and the girls had to be taken out of school, so a lot of homework was done while traveling in the car. We planned the trip at this time because business at the cabinet shop wasn't extremely busy and no winter road conditions. On the way, we spent a weekend in New Orleans, touring and seeing the sights of this city along the Mississippi River. When arriving in Sarasota, Florida, we stayed in the home of Claude and Kathy and children Mic, Chuckie, and Shannan. Shalaine came later when they lived in Hawaii. I am so grateful for the hospitality my in-laws of Chuck's family have always extended. What a blessing! We had so much fun! Their home was across the street from the Ringling Circus Museum, and with Sarasota being on the Gulf of Mexico, we were ecstatic with excitement on things to see. The area has so much to offer with the white sandy beaches and warm sunny days. Fishing and scuba diving was also a plus, and of course, we spent time at Disney World and Cypress Gardens.

We spent a part of most every day at the beach. The girls loved lying on a raft, waiting for a wave to carry them back to shore. Building sand castles and burying one another in the sand was unique entertainment for us. The girls also loved to feed the seagulls some of their snacks. We were having so much fun that at the end of two weeks, none of us were ready to head back to Kansas—not even Don. He especially was enjoying his family in these surroundings. We were all so excited when Don came up with a plan that so surprised us.

Don flew home to take care of business and left the girls and me to look for a rental house. While back home, he would also get school records to enroll the girls to finish their school term in Florida. We felt like it was a miracle when we found a lady wanting to rent her home for a few months so she could leave to take care of a sister recuperating from an illness. Not only was this a furnished home but was completely stocked with kitchen utensils, bed linens, towels, washcloths, etc. The house had three bedrooms, and each of us had our own bed. What a find! And it was in a very nice neighborhood. We were really having a dream vacation—extended!

The full-gospel church we attended accepted us as family, and Kim turned twelve the time we were there and started attending the youth group of Christ's Ambassadors. Jacque and Kris enjoyed their Sunday school classes, and we were all blessed with the worship and praise singing.

We could see the grade school that Jacque and Kris enrolled in from our front yard. There was a huge pond across the street to the southwest, and the school was on the other side. The two girls would walk around the edge of these waters, feeding the ducks that swam here some of their breakfast on the way to school every morning. I was one of the parents that went on a school field trip where we rode a bus to an Everglades Park for a day. It was great fun having a picnic and putting pieces of bread on our heads to have gorgeous colorful birds perch there and eat with us.

Kim was in junior high, and I took her to a bus stop every morning where she boarded a bus with her cousin Sherry. The last class of the day was gym and was usually an outdoor activity. This particular time of the year, they were giving lessons on sailing at Bradenton Beach. As soon as Jacque and Kris came home from their school and so Kim wouldn't have to ride the school bus home, we would head for this beach and watch those bright, colorful sails glide over the blue waters of the gulf. Kim was really intrigued with learning this adventurous sport. After class was dismissed, the girls and I headed for the beach where we spent the remainder of the afternoon. What a life!

When Don returned, he adapted to this lifestyle like a duck takes to water and started looking for a place to establish a cabinet shop. We looked at several buildings and other homes, knowing the one we lived in was temporary. We were also much in prayer about making such a move. We loved the area, and all the activities we so greatly enjoyed; but more than anything, we wanted our Lord's will. After over three months of deliberating about this, we decided it best to head north to our home in Kansas. This was definitely the right decision. We traveled home by way of Indiana where we visited my dear friend from first grade on, Ed and Pat G. and family. Love ya, Pat!

A friend loves at all times. (Proverbs 17:17)

Upon Kim's graduation from eighth grade, Don and I decided a neat gift for her would be a sailboat so she could utilize what she learned in Florida. When we picked the boat up at the sports store where our order had been placed, the shipping box was still around it. We surprised Kim with it, and since she was the only one that could identify all the parts, I said, "Let's go to the lake and open up this box to make sure everything needed is enclosed." We had a ski boat that proper identification numbers were displayed on, but this little two-passenger sailboat was new, and it takes a while to acquire these numbers by mail coming from the state offices, so Don thought it best to ask a ranger if it was okay to set the boat in the water. I think it was the way the question was presented because Don asked the man if he would turn his head while we set the boat up at the dock.

The official replied, "I don't turn my head for anybody!"

We were driving the cabinet shop truck to be able to haul the length of the boat. Don didn't want to take it off the truck to store away until the identification numbers arrived unless we had assurance that all connecting parts were inside this box. It was decided to set the boat up by one of the boat docks—not attempt sailing, just identify all the mechanisms for this skiff. We all helped unwrap this pride and joy and carried the lightweight plastic and sails to the dock. Don and Kim figured out perfectly where everything fit. The sails went up beautifully. The last part to make sure of a fit was the rudder. The wind was blowing against us from the lake side. Not thinking anything could happen with the wind from this direction and wanting to make sure the rudder fit, Don got in the back of the boat and placed it in the post. He must have turned the rudder to just the right angle for *swissh*—Don was a first-time sailor practically out in the middle of the lake.

We were all taken so by surprise (especially Don), but it was such a funny sight that the girls and I started laughing. We laughed until we cried. When Kim could get her composure from laughing, she started shouting instructions to Don which way to turn the rudder in order to get back to dock. To all of our amazements, the boat was still upright and was coming to shore. I was watching those sails and my husband almost conquering the situation with coming into dock when all at once I hear the sound of marching boots. I turn to see three rangers coming down the dock, walking with a heavy gait and very stern determined looks on their faces. I again turned to face the waters just in time to see our pretty little sailboat capsize a few feet from the dock. Don, an excellent swimmer, just pushes the boat into the dock. The whole family, including Don, was still laughing almost hysterically. But the serious-faced officials never even cracked a smile while writing out a ticket for my husband. What party poops!

Arise, shine, for your light has come, and the
Glory of The Lord rises upon you. (Isaiah 60:1)

On the farm, a rooster was my alarm clock; but when my children needed rousing out of bed, they would hear me call, "*Arise and shine*—time to get up!"

In August 1975, our family moved to the north edge of town. Each girl had their own room, and Don and I gave them a choice of what type of bed they would like. Kris chose a waterbed, and I thought it gave a person the feeling of sleeping on a raft afloat in the ocean. It seemed to roll like the tide coming in and out. She seemed to enjoy it, and one morning, thinking she was enjoying it a little too much, I walked into her room to see why she hadn't responded to the wakeup call. We didn't have central air in the house, so her bedroom window was open. It faced the south, and a gentle breeze was blowing in. I glanced out the window, and as I did, I noticed writing on the screen with fingernail polish. I started to turn to Kris and ream her out for painting on the window screen, but before I did, I realize what the writing said. It simply said, "Hi! God!"

I practically melted in my tracks. Here was a young girl, looking out her window into the starlit night, so in tune with her Creator she could simply tell Him hi.

And a little child will lead them. (Isaiah 11:6)

Jacque chose for her room an antique bed. We purchased an old iron bed stead and painted it white. It had brass knobs on each corner to polish. She really enjoyed her room and had lots of girlfriends to spend the night. A frequent sleepover friend was Tammy, and she and Jacque were kindred spirits for sure! I would hear them chattering long into the night.

Our church had been on a ski outing in Colorado, and since we caravanned there and back, Jacque and Tammy had returned to our home before Don and I. When I walked into the kitchen, I noticed on a little antique chalkboard that hangs by my old-time wall phone these written words: YOU ARE GOD'S GIFT TO ME! This saying is still there on the same chalkboard now for over forty years. I take chalk now and then and copy over it.

> Every good and perfect gift is from above,
> coming down from the Father of the Heavenly
> Lights, Who does not change like shifting shad-
> ows. (James 1:17)

Kim still had her canopy bed for her room, so she designed a dresser with a kneehole in the center. Don built it for her. It looked more like a long desk, and she enjoyed sitting there. Kim, being the oldest, has always been a good example for her younger siblings. When she was a young teenager, Kim penned these words: Be patient with me, my Love; I'm learning more about You, others, and myself every day!"

We had the saying framed and placed it on a wall in her room.

> Love is patient, love is kind. It does not envy, it
> does not boast, it is not proud. (1 Corinthians
> 13:4)

My daughters are beautiful! Reminds me of Scripture about Job's daughters:

> Nowhere in all the land were there found women
> as beautiful as Job's daughters. (Job 42:15)

I would tell my daughters, "Beauty is only skin deep! If you are ugly on the inside, you are ugly on the outside." They are beautiful inside and out—so much so as a mother I could not stand to see my girls put on a swimsuit and go to a public pool. Don and I talked and decided to build a swimming pool in our own backyard. This not only kept my daughters home more, but you should see all the gatherings we have poolside.

We have an open invitation to our church family and put up a sign in pool house:

ALL MEMBERS AND PROSPECTIVE MEMBERS OF
OUR LORD'S FAMILY ARE WELCOME!

The girls were not allowed to date until sixteen, and never were they to sit in a parked car out in the driveway. I kept snack food on hand, even frozen hamburger patties they could quickly fry, for them and their friends. They could have a rip-roaring party in the kitchen, and I could go sound asleep, but never could I sleep until they were home safe.

The pool was outside for summer, so Don made a game room in our basement for winter months. He placed a pool table in the center, for this is a favorite of his. I love the saying, "The little boy in a man never changes, only the price of their toys." Don built an air-hockey table, drilling hundreds of little holes for air to come up through to slide the puck. We also had a fuse ball table that was very popular with the young men. We wanted our children to know their friends were our friends and were welcome anytime.

Kim had a date with a nice-looking young man, and when Don and I shook hands with him, his mannerisms were impressive. The girls always had to bring their date into our home so we could meet them before allowed to leave the premises. This young fellow called Kim several times after this first date to ask her out again. When she refused, I asked her why. She said, "I didn't like his attitude!" *Bravo!*

Senior year in high school Kim, had the lead in the musical *Brigadoon.* She certainly was beautiful as she stood on stage singing about the "Heather on the Hill." I attended all three productions. After the last, we hosted a cast party in the basement. Kim had other honors in high school like being part of "royalty" around a basketball court, but *to me,* she stood head 'n' shoulders above others.

Kim will always be "royalty" to me!

Jacque was my busy little bumble bee. She buzzed around a lot with friends, but since the eighth grade, she really only wanted to be with one fellow. We asked her to date others so as to know a variety of personalities but always went back to her "true love." When in junior high, I remember taking her out in the country to the farm of Jerry and Alice to attend a birthday party for Rick. Country folks are sure all right with me!

The high school years for Jacque were busy and, like her personality, "bubbling"!

There were places to go and things to do for her, and she *had to be there*. It seemed everyone loved being around for her generous and wanting-to-please ways. This also won her several honors of being part of "royalty."

Jacque loved being a cheerleader. This took her to all games at home and in neighboring towns. I remember one evening she had gone to an "away game" and was riding home in a car with friends. When the curfew hour came and went and she finally did appear, Don and I met her at the door.

"Where have you been?" we asked.

Jacque said, "The car had a flat tire, and I was the only one that knew how to change it!"

She was just a beaming because of a job well done! Don had always insisted that when the girls learned how to drive a car, they also learned how to change a flat tire.

We always had a curfew hour for our children to be at home. This was so important not only because I could sleep better but all the dangers that lurk after dark!

Jacque will always be my "royal princess"!

You will not fear the terror of night. (Psalm 91:5)

Kris was my beautiful but shy girl. She loved being with friends at church functions and having overnighters with girlfriends. All the activities we did as a family, Kris joined in with it all. Swimming, waterskiing, snowmobiling, sled-riding, ice skating, roller rinks were all her favorite things to do, but what interested Kris the most were the animals. Dogs, cats, hamsters and especially horses were what she wanted to be with.

Our dear friends Bob and Donna have a niece who boarded horses across the road from us, and Kris would ride horses with her. Anna Marie, daughter of friends Richard and Joyce, allowed her to ride her horse many times. One of the times was when Kris was up for Rodeo Queen. She was required to ride a horse in front of a stadium full of people. As she galloped the horse around the arena, Kris's hat flew off. I was so proud of her when she nonchalantly got off the horse, picked up the hat, and remounted and headed the steed out the gate. The people clapped and shouted for her performance.

Kris will always be a queen in my book!

But ask the animals, and they will teach you. (Job 12:7a)

Beautiful Weddings

Daughters are never as beautiful as on their wedding day. Mine were no exception but to me the most beautiful of all. They were tired and exhausted from all the preparation, as were a lot of others, but their radiance was brilliant! I was so blessed at their weddings and so very pleased with the mates they were given.

Rick and Jacque, high-school sweethearts, married in December after graduation in May. Their wedding was the very first event in our new church building. Our church purchased a former retail store which before this was a car dealership building. Members had been working for months to be able to have services here, and before invitations were sent, we were assured the remodeled building for church would be ready. There can be so many delays in construction, and rehearsal night the sanctuary was a "swarm of busy bees." People were everywhere, putting trim around doors, fixing the lighting, sound, cleaning, polishing, and even laying carpet. Rick and Jacque drew a big heart on the boards of the altar with their names written there before carpeting was in place. I was thankful that these two kids had their all on the altar.

(You must worship before one altar. (2 Chronicles 32:12)

A coworker of Kim was also a very gifted seamstress. Nicki's desire was to create a masterpiece with her sewing, and a bridal gown was her ideal. Creating a masterpiece, I'm sure, is the thought of all artists, but she also readily agreed to make all the dresses for the wedding. Nicki, Kim, and Jacque put their heads together, and they designed a beautiful wedding gown for our princess. With no pattern, Nicki took an old sheet and draped this over Jacque to get the correct fit. Bridal material was so expensive. We bought disco satin from a local retailer and curtain material from a department store in the city. From the bolt of material for curtains, we spent many an evening cutting lace to put on ruffles that flowed all the way from the waist to the end of a long train. A veil was also made from the curtain material. She looked sort of like a Spanish senorita and so beautiful!

Don was equally as busy using his talents, for he made out of wood twelve stands to place candles and greenery on. These were placed on either side of the center aisle where the bridal couple would walk. The theme was Christmas. After discovering at rehearsal the kids didn't have anything to kneel on when prayed over, the day of the wedding, Don made a kneeling bench. Made out of wood, on each end was a cross with a heart shape in the center. The bench was padded and covered with new carpeting to match the altar. Rick and Jacque were first to use this bench. Kris, Kim, and many others followed.

There were over five-hundred people at this wedding. I know because we catered a tea room popular in our town, and the plates were counted by them for their fee. Jerry and Alice's family were four generations, and mine was three generations. Don's family and the girl's dad's family were well represented and a host of neighbors and friends. Rick and Jacque had recently graduated; I thought the whole local high school student body came. We were blessed!

I couldn't help thinking how beautiful and appropriate that a wedding took place in our church's sanctuary the first time the doors were open for service—December 6, 1980.

Jesus did His first miracle when attending a wedding!

The last years of Kris's high school was at a private school on the southeast edge of Tulsa, Oklahoma, two hundred miles away. I was proud of her making the decision to go there, for they had a Scripture teaching program, and she lived with a youth pastor's family. Kris met her true love when furthering her education and her intended was attending school at Oral Roberts University. RaMon lived in Western Oklahoma and was also two hundred miles from his family. A mutual friend introduced them. Kris brought him home to meet us, and RaMon won me over when he fixed the family a kettle of borsch soup. He loves to cook!

When they started talking of marriage, Kris was living with three other girls and working at a toy store. Her girlfriends were working at fast-food restaurants, and no one thought it necessary for their living quarters to have a refrigerator. The girls snacked and ate hamburgers out. The plan was after getting married, RaMon and Kris would keep the apartment. I asked Kris if she wanted a refrigerator or a bridal gown for her wedding.

She readily said, "Refrigerator!"

RaMon and Kris thought having the wedding in the chapel of the school would be fair to both families since each were of equal distance from there, plus neither one could take too much time off from their jobs.

The wedding was planned for November, and the previous April, Phil and Laura had their wedding at our church. I knew Kris and Laura were the same size, and I asked Laura about borrowing her gown. "Yes!" And it fit Kris to a tee! Daughter Kim had recently been in Mike and Kathy's wedding and had her bridesmaid dress in her closet, so I asked Kathy about two more lookalikes from the wedding. And "yes" again! We had the wedding party outfitted. I had bouquets and corsages made and bought ferns for the altar. I took mints and nuts and the ingredients for punch. I ordered the wedding cake on their end. I didn't want to chance hauling a cake for that distance.

I loaded everything, including the kneeling bench, in our RV camper. Don strapped the new refrigerator on the back of the camper, and we headed south to Oklahoma for a wedding! I loved it!

Kris was so beautiful on her wedding day—November 21, 1982!

Kim was working as a secretary in the city and shared an apartment with Debbie. Bob's home is in Shreveport, Louisiana, and he was in the city attending college. He roomed with a friend who is the brother of the pastor's wife where Kim attended church. Kim was actually dating the roommate of Bob's.

I think one of the first times Kim brought Bob home to meet us was in the wintertime. We had the snowmobiles out and were riding them in the snow and roasting hot dogs and marshmallows in the fireplace. Being from the South, this was very unique!

Kim's favorite hobby was sewing. Friend Nicki, who did so much at Jacque's wedding, was a big instigator in helping Kim to develop such skilled abilities. When Bob and Kim decided to get married, the wedding was planned "Southern style."

Kim designed and made her own wedding gown. No one else helped. She knew exactly how it should be. From beneath a huge bow at the back waist, a train flowed long and wide. The gown had capped sleeves, and she made lace mitts to wear on her hands and covering her arms; the fingers were free. A big picturesque hat crowned her head, and our daughter Kim was the most beautiful Southern bride ever—June 25, 1983!

Extended Families

The families our daughters married into have been an extended family for them. Each girl is fortunate, and I am honored to see them so accepted and loved. They seem to fit right in, and that is what family is all about. Not only our homes but our church family should be an extension of our own. Families that pray together stays together.

I have three sons-in-law whose first names begin with an R. I have called them *"Readin', Ritin', and 'Rithmetic."*

RaMon's parents live on the plains of W. Oklahoma. Dannie and Dorothy love *the Lord*, and this is obvious the first time you meet them. They have told me of a time when they sponsored children's church. They love to teach little ones about Jesus! Telling Scripture stories to children is an art. When you hold a child's interest, you have their heart. This is so needed in our world today.

Dorothy said after sharing the Scripture stories she and Dannie would pray for the children. Dorothy would be in front of the child, and Dannie placed his hand lightly on their backs. She said they prayed, and so much of the time this little person was filled with the Holy Spirit and spoke in tongues.

Rick's parents live on a farm west of our town. Jerry and Alice have four sons—Denny, Scott, Steve, and Rick—and one daughter, Debbie. I am told they would all fill up a pew in church on Sunday mornings, and they are country folks! Rick has gone to the sale barn with his dad the way I used to with mine. The atmosphere and aroma at those barns—now that's real country. Alice plays the accordion and blesses others so much with her talent. She volunteers her time quite often for community events. Practically the whole county knows this family and loves them for their outgoing ways.

Robert (Bob) lives in Shreveport, Louisiana. Bob's Dad went home to glory several years ago, and what a legacy treasure he left. Bob's brother Bill, an ordained minister, helped to give the eulogy. A Bible full of marked scriptures was the treasured legacy.

I have three grandsons that were in this service for their grand-dad, and what treasured legacy for them to have. *I believe the Bible, God's Word, is the greatest treasure ever!*

Pat, Howard's widow, has always been there for my daughter Kim. Pat has worked most of her adult years as a lab technician and really has a heart for people. I know by Pat's actions that my daughter Kim is loved, and that blesses this mother's heart.

CHAPTER 26

OUR SON

Delight yourself in THE LORD and He will give
you the desires of your heart.

—Psalm 37:4

On one of our ski trips to Colorado, Don and I met Pastor
Vernon and wife, Hazel. He was the administrator of our
church denomination's home for unwed mothers. We were
told the need to have foster parents, preferably a couple that would
take a newborn baby into their home and keep until adopted. I
thought this would be good training for my teenage daughters, so we
applied and were accepted.

I love babies especially newborns! There is something so special
about new life.

A tiny new little human being only *our Lord God* can create.
I am so amazed every time I hold a newborn; their uniqueness and
functioning of all their little body parts is so miraculous! I love babies!
If it were possible, I would have had at least a dozen.

My daughters were intrigued as I was when we brought our first
baby home—a little girl—and Kim named her Heather, a temporary
name for her because the adopting parents will give her the identity
name, perhaps a name off the family tree. I had a great time helping
my girls learn how to hold, feed, and diaper her, and baby's bath

is always a special time. Nothing smells as sweet as a newly bathed newborn!

We kept our baby Heather for about two months and then received the call to bring her to headquarters to give her over to the waiting parents. Knowing how attached my girls had become as well as myself, I made arrangements to take them out of school for the day. They too needed to meet the people that were taking our baby girl.

The new parents had driven to the city from the southwest part of the States and had with them their older child, a young boy approximately seven years of age. The new dad was a stocky-built truck driver, and mom was average built and her profession a registered nurse. When the little baby girl we had loved on so was placed into the arms of that big man, tears started rolling down his cheeks. The new mom leaned over her husband's arms and started to love on the baby, and the now-older brother hugged his daddy's leg. I don't think there was a dry eye in that room. My daughters and I went home sad without our baby but ever so happy because of her being so wanted by her real family. We were told that this baby was the first girl in that dad's family for four generations.

Oh! If we could ever get message out to the world that it's *adoption not abortion*!

Come on now! Listen up! *It is time to recognize life!*

When a seed is planted, the germination time begins—begins to grow or sprout. When walking with my daddy in the garden, he would tell me to be careful where I walked; there were 'young sprouts growing! *The womb is the garden where our Father plants the seed! The sperm is alive which connects with the egg, producing life!*

> And now THE Lord says—HE WHO formed me
> in the womb. (Isaiah 49:5)

> BEFORE I FORMED YOU IN THE WOMB I KNEW
> YOU. (Jeremiah 1:5)

The people of Israel. Theirs is the *adoption as sons*; theirs the divine glory, the covenants, the receiving of the law, the temple worship and the promises. (Romans 9:4–5)

Theirs are the patriarchs, and from them is traced the human ancestry *of Christ, who is God over all, forever praised! Amen.*

Come on now! Listen up! *Our Lord Jesus* when He walked this earth took special time to show affection and love to children. *Our Lord* knew the genuine need children have for affection *from both parents. Jesus understood the importance of a meaningful and loving touch.* Babies come out of the womb needing *to feel* the warmth and security of being loved. After all, they just were born into a cold ole world, and it's up to adults to supply a baby with all their needs! Even an older child has need of sitting on their Father's lap. I did! *I wanted to hear the ticking of his heart!*

> JESUS SAID, "…OF SUCH IS THE KINGDOM OF GOD." (Matthew 19:14)

Dear ones! Listen up! Now is the time to come to the aid of children everywhere!

A baby and small child already have the kingdom of God in them. These little ones are constantly looking for a like Spirit! Their instincts are *touch and sound.*

People were bringing little children to Jesus to have Him Touch them but the disciples rebuked them. When Jesus saw this, He was indignant. He said to them, "Let the little children come to Me, and do not hinder them, for the Kingdom of God belongs to such as these. I tell you the Truth, anyone who will not receive The Kingdom of God like a little child will never enter it." "And He took the little children *In His Arms, Put*

His Hands On Them And Blessed Them! (Mark
10:13–16)

Jesus Loves The Little Children
All The Children Of The World
Red And Yellow, Black And White
They Are Precious In His Sight
Jesus Loves The Little Children
Of The World!

And if anyone gives even a cup of cold water to
one of these Little Ones in the name of a disciple, I tell you the Truth, he will certainly not lose
his reward. (Matthew 10:42)

Our next baby, the scenario of when we picked her up might
have looked like we were smugglers!

Don and I were in the city for most of the day, picking up
supplies for the cabinet shop. We were driving the furniture van, the
truck used to haul cabinets. It was winter and ever so cold! We had
a designated time to meet Pastor Vernon at headquarters, and this
was after working hours. The staff had left the premises. We waited
on the parking lot in the truck behind the building. We were there
quite a while when a car pulled up beside us, and Hazel got out telling us that Pastor Vernon had just called her from the airport. The
weather was severe enough that the plane flying in from California
was delayed. Air traffic was backed up, and they had been circling
the city, waiting to land (this was before cell phones), and would it
be possible for us to wait at least forty-five minutes longer for Pastor
Vernon to drive from the airport to where we were waiting? And yes,
we did wait.

It was now dark, no street lights in that back behind the building parking lot, and the wind was blowing something fierce! It was
such a spooky place to be. We saw the headlights of a car coming
around the side of the building, and for more reasons than one, I was
sure hoping it was Pastor Vernon. In the vision of the car's lights, I

recognized his body form, and he was clutching a small bundle close to him. He had his head down because of the strong winds and was walking toward my side of the truck.

I opened the door, and he quickly placed the baby in my arms and said, "All I have is this one baby bottle, and I'm out of diapers!"

The air coming through the open door was so cold I quickly said, "I've got everything this baby needs," and I closed the door.

He walked back to his car, drove away, and there Don and I sat in the cab of that truck and I had a new baby in my arms.

This little baby girl was Polynesian, and was she gorgeous! She had lots of dark hair, brown button eyes, and lovely olive complexion. She was very petite and ever so active but such a good-natured baby. She became Kim's favorite and Jacque named her Andrea and we nicknamed her Andy. What a joy! I think we had her for about three months. When the call came to bring her to the city, arrangements were made to go to the assistant administrator's house because he lived on the way to the airport. He was flying with that baby to the northwest part of the States where this precious baby girl would be the daughter of a pastor and wife so wanting a child. Little Andy "flew in and flew out!"

Home from Hospital

I shall never forget the day this momentous phone call came from Pastor Vernon. He said, "A boy baby, six days old, still at the hospital, had a very traumatic birth. In the process of being born, he received a broken collarbone. He needed weekly trips to the doctor that delivered him. Would you be able to care for him?"

I said, "Sure! I am in the city at least once a week, picking up supplies for the shop. No problem!"

Don was involved at the shop, so I took my dear friend Judy with me. Harry and Judy had moved to our town, and we were getting acquainted; I felt Judy and I had a kindred spirit!

We arrived at the hospital, and I gave a nurse at her station my credentials.

She said, "Come on in. We've been expecting you."

The nurse led me into the nursery and over to a basket where my protégé lay sleeping. I leaned over slightly and looked to see a very-fair-skinned baby, long and lean.

My next thought was, *Blond hair...his features remind me of Don! A son we always wanted!*

The next moment can only be described as divine, for I heard the words from our Lord speaking to my heart strong, loud, and clear: "This is your son!" I immediately had such a surge of love for this little baby. I picked him up into my arms and held him close.

The nurse gave me instructions on how to care for him with the broken collarbone. His arm was taped to his chest, but the little hand was free to wiggle. The nurse said that babies' bones are so soft but they mend quickly, and the doctor would probably remove the bandage on his first visit which would be in a couple of days. She gave me the doctor's name and the appointment time. I had brought "take baby home from hospital" clothes for this little one; the nurse had me change him. I couldn't put his one arm in a sleeve, just drape the shirt over the arm and button the front. He looked so happy! His eyes were wide open, looking at me. Not a peep out of him! I think he knew he was going home!

I walked out of the hospital, clutching my boy to me like an ole mother hen. I drove, so I reluctantly gave the baby for Judy to hold. She also knew more about boys than I did; she had mothered four sons. This was also in a day when car seats for infants were not required and Judy and baby boy were in the front seat right beside me.

It was close to lunch time, so we drove to a favorite eating place. We were going into the restaurant, and I started to walk very slowly, straddle legged!

Judy started laughing at me and asked, "What are you doing?"

I told her that bringing a baby home from the hospital, I needed to walk as if I had given birth! Judy and I both started laughing so hard. We were so joyous and happy with this new baby boy.

On the way home, Judy needed to purchase a gallon of milk, so we stopped at a convenient store. She placed the baby again in my arms and went into the store. As I sat behind the steering wheel, holding this little one, my thoughts were on what I was feeling. Four different times I had given natural birth to a baby and felt the excelled excitement when a newborn was placed in my arms. At those moments, there was such a certainty of love and the fact the baby in your arms was yours. I felt so strongly in my bosom for this baby I thought to breastfeed him. I had nursed all three of my daughters, and I knew the feeling. With this impression in my breast, I thought to myself, *Could this baby boy really be mine? Would my Lord really bless me with such a gift?*

I began to think of all the reasons this could never be possible: We both had been married before; we had three girls at home and, in my past, three nervous breakdowns. I thought no adoption board would ever approve us!

As I sat in the car, looking down at the precious bundle that I held, I looked out the window on that beautiful September day and looked up into clear blue sky and thought once again *to pray a prayer of release!*

> But now, by dying to what once bound us, *we have been released* from the law so that we serve in the new way of the Spirit, and not in the old way of the written code. (Romans 7:6)

Dear Lord, thank you for this moment; and if You want this baby boy to be Don's and my son, work out all the details!

I also prayed that Don would have the fatherly instincts strong enough to raise a boy, for I always heard "a son follows in the footsteps of his father!"

Judy and I traveled on to our town, and I drove straight to the cabinet shop. I carried the baby boy inside and placed him in Don's arms and said, "Here's your son!"

Don is a very emotional man anyway, and as he held the newborn baby, he was heaving and almost sobbing. He looked at the baby and then looked at me. He looked at the baby and then looked at me. He couldn't say anything; he was speechless. I too started to cry at the sight of them, and as I stood there looking at the two, I thought, *They definitely go together*, and in my heart I couldn't help realize a baby boy had indeed come home.

After leaving the shop and taking Judy home, I took the new baby to our home. The girls all took turns holding him, and I readily told them about changing a baby boy's diaper.

"This could be a challenge for us all," I said. They understood.

In a little over a year, this was our third baby to keep in our home, and this was Kris's turn to decide the name. She named him Matthew Don.

Among Matt's first visitors was his Aunt Vernita. I have a picture of my sister holding him sitting on our porch swing. In her family, "Dan the Man" came along after she had three girls—Marilyn, Myrna, and Marla. I knew my sis was hoping this little fellow could be ours to keep. My dear friend Barb also came those first days we were home, and I took him to see Bob and Donna. Bob would always call him Tiger.

The next evening, after bringing Matt home from the hospital, Don and I went to the city to our scuba-diving lessons. Don had been on the rescue diving team in our town for years but had not been certified. I was just learning. To qualify for the class, a person had to swim a mile but could do any swim stoke they wanted. To complete the mile I did every swim technique possible, mostly doing the backstroke and floating awhile to rest. The girls were old pros at taking care of babies after the two previous foster ones, but I didn't want them to have the responsibility this night because of the baby's broken collarbone. Seven days old, and this baby boy sat in an infant seat on the patio of a swimming pool.

I had fun telling people, "Yeah! I just came home from the hospital with him yesterday!" And I quickly did another dive under the water and let Don do the explanation.

Legally Ours

Praise be to the God and Father of our Lord Jesus Christ,
Who has blessed us in the heavenly realms with every spiritual
blessing in Christ. For He chose us in Him before the

creation of the world to be holy and blameless in His sight. In love He predestined us to be adopted as His sons through Jesus Christ, in accordance with His pleasure and will.

—Ephesians 1:3–5

The first six weeks of Matt's life, I took him weekly to the doctor who delivered him. By the third and fourth visit, Doctor O could tell how attached I was, and he asked me if I had considered adoption.

I said, "Yes, but there have been complications in my past, and besides, we have three girls."

He quickly pulled a wallet from his back pocket and took out a picture to show me. The picture was of three boys and a little girl. Doctor O said the boys were his and the girl was his by adoption. He also told me at this hospital there in the city he doctored this premature baby in an incubator and really became attached to her. Doctor O and his wife contacted this home for unwed mothers to see about adoption. They were able to adopt this baby girl and had three boys at home. This is when he started helping to deliver babies for this same home. *Wow!* Way out wonder! This doctor sure gave my faith a boost that day!

I so enjoyed those first months of Matt's life. He was so agile and seemed to develop all skills on schedule in a baby's growing process on time, if not sooner than most. One thing I noticed different than my girls was the crawling stage before a little one pulls himself to heights. I used to place my daughters lying on their stomachs on the floor with a blanket underneath them and put toys around to entertain them. They would stay on this blanket the longest time, playing more of a docile, laid-back way about them. Matt, at the same stage, wouldn't stay on the blanket but go exploring. He would roll himself under the coffee table and clasp his little hand on the wood leg; he would pull on a cord to a lamp or play on the wood runners of a chair. I thought this must be the difference of feminine and masculine gender, and he just had the curiosity of a boy.

About this same age, Matt loved to chase our housecat and pull his tail. The cat was so tame Don could even pull him around by the tail. I guess what the son sees the father doing, it seems to be a "guy thing" to do likewise. Tiger didn't seem to be hurt by either tail pulling; "ole yeller" lived twelve years—a good lifetime for a cat.

When Matt was a toddler, he fell into the deep end of our pool. Don and I had our backs turned and were bent down working on the pump. We heard the splash of something hitting the water, and Don was out the door and went immediately to the edge of the pool. He saw Matt under the water but coming to the top reached down and grabbed him and pulled him up to safety. For two summers, Matt walked two feet away from edge of the swimming pool.

I really believed Don and Matt bonded from the start. Matt was still in diapers, and Don took him fishing with him. I can still see the two of them walking out the gate leading to the pond south of our home. Don would be carrying the fishing gear, and Matt carried his bottle or sippy cup and an extra diaper. He toddled along behind his dad!

Out of this same pond, when Matt was four years old, he caught a four-pound bass. This won Matt first place in a bass tournament sponsored by a local retail store.

The girls enjoyed Matt as well, but being girls, they liked to paint his finger nails and curl his hair. Matt didn't mind; he loved their attention. When we talked about adopting Matt with our daughters, they seemed all for having him for their little brother; only Kim told us of her reservations. Being nineteen years old now and always thinking with her head on her shoulders, she expressed concern about our age. Don was then forty-five, and I was thirty-eight years of age. Don would be over sixty-five when Matt was only twenty years old. Kim asked us if this would be fair to Matt. I assured her my mother was over forty years when I was born and my parents were very active my growing-up years. We had the example of our beloved Granny Alta, and besides, we didn't mind being called Abraham and Sarah.

I was trusting Don would make the initial call to Pastor Vernon about adopting Matt. I guess my thinking was that by him calling, he would be confident and assured from *our Lord* Matt was our son. We were at a wedding reception in the city where close friends George and Joanie married. At the table enjoying the jubilant celebration, Don told me of making a phone call, talking with Pastor Vernon. Don said he asked him about adoption, and Pastor Vernon said there were quite a few children at our denomination's home in neighboring states.

Don said, "No, we want the one that is already here in our home!"

Silence for a bit.

Pastor Vernon said, "We don't usually adopt to foster parents, and besides, we have fifteen hundred on a waiting list for babies."

More silence, and Don replied, "Isn't possession nine-tenths of the law?"

Pastor Vernon said, "I'll put this before our board of directors and let you know."

I am so thankful to this day that this board of directors were praying, Spirit-filled, godly group of men. They prayed over every baby until a decision was peaceably made on what family a little one belonged in. Don and I felt the leading of *our Lord*, but to have these directors give approval was so miraculous! We were at a Christmas party of the sponsoring home and again sitting at the table when Pastor Vernon walked over and told us we had been approved by the board! What a joyous first Christmas we had with our son. I made a huge Christmas stocking and put MATT in it and hung him on the fireplace mantle for a picture. The grin on his face says it all. Matt was a very content and happy baby—but then we still had all the legal work to do.

Don and I had to have medical physicals, write an autobiography of our lives, and send an initial fee to the headquarters of the home. The lawyer there would put everything together legally the law required. After months of waiting, the lawyer called and said he had completed the legal papers and Don and I had an appointment and he would go with us when we went before the judge. The courtroom would be at the big courthouse in downtown of the city, and before going before the judge, we would be allowed to see our baby at headquarters for the first time.

"But sir," I said. "We have had our baby here in our home since he was six days old!"

The lawyer said, "I'll have to call you back!"

It seems the lawyer was not aware that Matt had been in our home since leaving the hospital after birth, the problem being we lived in Kansas, and the baby needed to reside in Missouri—a legal technicality but one that needed resolved. When the lawyer called back, he said to bring Matt with us the day of court appointment. We would place him in a crib at headquarters located in the state of Missouri. The secretaries there knew plenty how to care for little ones. Pastor Vernon, the lawyer, Don, and I would go downtown before the judge. *If* the judge asked if this baby now resides in the state of Missouri, we were to answer yes—because Matt at that moment was asleep in a crib in Missouri. We were prepared.

Don and I walked down a long aisle leading to the judge's bench. The desk he was sitting behind was taller than we were. Don and I stood looking up to the judge who was intently looking down at some papers, obviously reading.

The judge said, "I am reading a letter of recommendation sent to me from Doctor O."

At this point, I got so excited on hearing about this letter because we knew nothing about it! I'm not sure what the judge's next statement was. He either said, "I went to school with Doctor O" or "My son went to school with Doctor O," but I sure didn't mistake what he said next. The judge said, "I know this doctor well. If he says you will be fit parents for this child, that's good enough for me! Case dismissed!"

What a miracle! Our Lord had indeed worked out all the details!

At our church, we have baby dedications. Matt was dedicated to *our Lord* on Father's Day in June 1979. He was nine months old. Pastor Derrell and Gayle looked up meanings of names for these occasions. It was on this day we learned the meaning of Matthew: "gifted" or "gift of God." Amen!

Young Years

When Matt was in kindergarten, the teacher asked the children to draw using stick people in a picture, showing others what they thought their mom did best. He loved going through a drive-through restaurant for those little boxes filled with a hamburger, French fries, and a drink. I think the surprise inside these boxes intrigued him the most! We would be traveling down the highway with Matt playing with his little cars and trucks in the backseat, and he invariably would pop his head up just in time to see the golden arches. He spotted them miles ahead and I think every billboard advertising them.

The picture he drew the teacher was a car going through a drive-through with the golden arches in the background. This is what he thought I did best!

Matt would play in the sawdust at the shop like most kids would play in a sand pile.

At church, a boy's group sponsored a pine derby race. These are little cars made of wood, and on an incline board, the boys raced them. The car was made at the shop and was fun for both Dad and son. Matt, at a very early age, was sweeping up the sawdust to earn money. We put three jars on his dresser and labeled them TITHE, SAVINGS, and SPEND. We wanted him to know the first 10 percent of what is earned belongs to *the Lord*.

Around the house, Matt had responsibility of taking out the trash, feeding the dogs and cat, and making his bed. I enjoyed taking him to the grocery store with me; he was always quick to spot the item needed on the shelf. He was very young when he learned to drive the lawnmower and consistently kept the yard neat; this was over an acre. Matt loved to play board games, checkers with his dad, and together we played Uno, Battleship, Sorry, but Monopoly was a favorite. He really liked being the banker and buying property. Baseball was the all-time high! He loved collecting baseball cards, and I think knew every player that ever played. Every statistic about the players he seemed to have memorized. I thought he would be a sports announcer, and his love for baseball brought about one of my most embarrassing moments.

Matt did a season of playing little league baseball. With so many activities and interest our family was involved in, Don later gave him a choice of baseball or going fishing—and of course, he chose fishing. At little league, they are required to wear helmets when at bat. This is definitely a good safety precaution.

I went to the beauty shop to get a haircut. When I sat down in the chair, the beautician was fastening the cape she sheepishly came around and stood by my side and said, "I can't cut your hair. The state board would revoke my license if I did. You have lice!"

I couldn't believe what I was hearing. I was mortified! Humbly I asked her what could be done. She told me of a product at the drugstore that would kill off the lice, but my hair had to be free of all nits before she could cut it. I felt so ashamed and hurried to the drugstore. At this time, I had not a clue where the lice came from; but when I got home, checked Matt's hair, obviously the lice came from the baseball helmets.

Matt loved all the sports that Don did, and hunting was no exception. Don gave him a BB gun when eight or nine years old. A bull's eye circle was placed on a bale of straw in the backyard for target practice. He also did this with a bow and arrow. They went on hunting trips to Western Kansas for pheasants and locally hunted doves in season. Deer are also plentiful in our area. When Matt was twelve, he passed the hunters safety course with great ease. I don't think a question on the test was answered incorrectly.

I returned from the grocery store one day and walked into my office, and there sat Matt, holding a gun and staring straight ahead. Immediately alarm rose up within me!

He said, "Mom, I didn't think the gun was loaded! It went off and the bullet hit the picture above the bookcase and cracked the glass."

The number one rule at our home with guns was that they are kept in their cabinet and no bullets left in the chamber. All I could do at that moment was go hug on my son! I thanked and praised *our Lord* for protecting Matt. Today, the bullet is still in the wall, and the picture with the cracked glass still hangs above the bookcase as a reminder of our Lord's grace and mercy that day. The picture is of Christ kneeling in the garden of Gethsemane.

Matt came down with chicken pox the day before a scheduled trip of going west for pheasants. Not being able to go on the hunting trip hurt him worse than the illness.

On one of the return trips to Western Kansas, I went into Matt's room, and the smell of a skunk was very strong. On his dresser he left the collar of a dog that had been sprayed.

The first deer Matt brought down was just north of our town. Matt was upon a hillside, and Don was down lower out of sight. All at once Don heard the gun shot and a loud, "Yippee!" The deer was an eight-point buck, and the head hangs at the cabinet shop. My two avid hunters going with friend Charlie made a trip to Texas near San Antonio for a hunting expedition. A boar's head also is hanging on the wall at the cabinet shop.

For Matt's sixteenth birthday, Don bought him a used Ford Ranger pickup. It was Matt's responsibility to buy the gas and keep the truck serviced. I guess a man will always remember his first vehicle. Don still talks about the old Maxwell car his grandparents gave him.

How can a young man keep his way pure? By living according to Your Word. (Psalm 119:9)

Matt asked Jesus into his heart and was water baptized. Don and I were elated! Matt attended the academy affiliated with our church; at school the teacher required an essay on who they admired the most. Matt wrote about his dad.

For a short time, I homeschooled Matt. He diligently did the work, and the music class was playing the piano. He memorized one short song, and that is the extent of his piano repertoire. The religion class we studied Proverbs; I thought this book was extremely important for a young person.

The proverbs of Solomon son of David, king of Israel: for attaining wisdom and discipline; for

understanding words of insight; for acquiring a
disciplined and prudent life, doing what is right
and just and fair; for giving prudence to the sim-
ple, knowledge and discretion to the young—let
the wise listen and add to their learning, and let
the discerning get guidance—for understanding
proverbs and parables, the sayings and riddles of
the wise. *The fear of THE LORD is the beginning of
knowledge, but fools despise wisdom and discipline.*
(Proverbs 1:1–7)

At this time, I tried to encourage Matt to attend college. Randy,
a young man who had worked at the cabinet shop, helped me put
the business books on computer. This machine amazed me on how
much easier bookkeeping became. I talked with Matt about taking
classes to learn computers. All he ever thought of doing was working
at the cabinet shop with his dad.

While attending the academy, Matt made a small two-door wall
cabinet. He routed a design of a basket of flowers on each door. He
entered this in a competition statewide and won a top honor for his
school. Matt graduated from the academy in 1997.

Matt worked several years at the cabinet shop as full-time
employee. Don could count on him to install a set of cabinets as if he
himself did the job. Matt bought a fairly new but not new Honda car
making monthly payments. He was about twenty years old when he
felt led to attend our church's discipleship program in Mission, Texas.
The school required a student not to arrive with a vehicle, meaning
Matt needed to sell his car and have no transportation. Matt's brother-in-law, Bob, agreed to take over the payments if we could bring
the car to Shreveport, Louisiana. That would mean a way back home
to Kansas would be needed. It's a miracle! It just so happened our
friends Jon and Linda had a Honda car in Shreveport they needed
back in Kansas. Matt drove his pride and joy of a car to Louisiana
and drove another Honda back to Kansas for Jon and Linda. He
attended a year's session of disciplined discipleship and did a mis-
sions trip to El Salvador.

When Matt came home for a visit before the next term started, he began again helping Don at the shop. He made a decision not to complete the disciple course and stay working at the shop. He told me he felt his dad needed him. Close to this time, a very close friend of Matt's was killed in a car accident. Freddie was a faithful witness for *his Lord*, quick to tell others of Jesus's love with his bubbling, outgoing personality. At the going-home service, many a young person raised their hand to accept Jesus. Freddie was home with Jesus. My heart went out to parents, Fred and Debbie, and Matt was devastated!

Matt had dated some in later years of high school and the two years after when working at the cabinet shop. He told of girls that were interested in him when at Mission, Texas. It seemed like older, mature girls were the ones interested in Matt, but then, he grew up in a household of older sisters.

There were times at the cabinet shop Don and Matt were at odds. On cabinet-making decisions they weren't seeing eye to eye. I think it was the age-old conflict of who's boss. Matt knew enough about cabinet building; he thought some changes would help. Don's way of thinking—why change now? It has worked for me thus far! Really, the way I saw it, they were both right! They are just two peas in a pod.

Frustrated at work and the loss of a dear friend, Matt became involved in worldly ways. He either came home in wee hours of the morning or spent nights with friends. The look in his eye and his actions undoubtedly told me that drugs were involved, and he was now a man and could not and would not communicate with his mother. Knowing I was loyal to his dad was probably a factor in our relationship. Matt was wanting to stand on his own two feet, but this ole world has such evil lurking everywhere to tempt our young people. Matt was twenty-two years old, and I was really concerned for my son.

The battle is ever so strong for the hearts of our young people. The fear I had for Matt was intense, but because of happenings in my past, the nervous breakdowns and defeats in my life, I could not allow fear to come inside of me.

There are over 365 "fear not" in Scripture, and I was claiming all of them!

I had to realize a child is given to us for those early years of training.

> Train up a child in the way he should go: and
> when he is old, he will not depart from it.
> (Proverbs 22:6)

Don and I had dedicated Matt to *our Lord* when he was nine months old. At this time, we pledged to *our Master and King* to do the best we could to be *godly* examples to our son. On dedication day, not only Don and I made this vow, *but the whole church body* said they would be *godly* examples to influence our son. In my mother's heart I had to accept the fact Matt belonged to *the Lord*.

The prodigal son, when he was out in the world, still belonged to *his father*. In fact, *the father* searched the horizons for *his* son to be walking toward *him*.

> *But while he was still a long way off, His Father saw*
> *him.* (Matthew 15:20)

Matt was now in the Father's hands and care for training.

> All your sons will be taught by THE LORD, and
> great will be your children's peace. (Isaiah 54:13)

CHAPTER 27

DESTRUCTION AT NOON

Noonday, December 18, 1983
"Cabinet Shop Destroyed, Lay Wasted Away"

Don and I were sitting in a Sunday school class in the church sanctuary in December 1983 when the pager my husband wears on his belt, being a volunteer fireman, announces another fire. What I heard the voice from the pager say created such a wave of unbelief, and I turned to look at Don to see his reaction. He was looking straight ahead as if in shock. Usually on the first beep of the pager, Don was up and moving toward a door on his way to put out a fire! But he sat there, stunned at the news, and I leaned over and told him, "Don, they said the cabinet shop is on fire!"

I knew better than to get in the way of a fireman on the way to a fire; I turned to my right and asked Frank and Lois, Don's sister and her husband, to take me to the shop. We quickly drove there to see firemen on the front steps getting ready to go into the burning building. Alarm gripped me when I realized the one putting on an air mask, coat, and grabbing a hose was Don! My husband was going into a burning building! I then realized he would know the inside of that building more than anyone—the neglect being he didn't put on gloves or helmet and headed toward smoke coming from the basement

As I stood across the street, watching, I knew I needed to pray, but how does one pray in these circumstances? I prayed in a language given me when *baptized in love*. The sight I was seeing was beyond my comprehension. I needed to talk with the *One who is above all!*

I waited, intently watching the front door of the cabinet shop while firemen in the front yard shot a heavy stream of water on the building. Another fireman was by the door, preparing to go in as a backup for Don. The day was bitter cold! There was ice and snow several inches deep on the ground and the temperature in the teens. I'm so thankful that the wind was not blowing. It seemed like hours but was probably only ten or fifteen minutes at the most. Don appeared at the door of the shop, threw off his mask, and staggered down the steps and fell down into the snow. I started running toward him, hearing a fireman and policeman closest to Don yelling, "Injured man! Injured man!"

I fell to my knees beside Don on the ground, bent close to his face, but couldn't speak words to Don because of still *speaking in tongues!* This I did for a few moments until becoming aware of those around us saying, "We need to get this man to the hospital!"

The policeman said, "I have a car all warmed up, and it's at the curb ready to go. I'll take him!"

They helped Don into the front seat of the patrol car. I sat in the back for the ride to the hospital.

Walking toward the emergency entrance, Don reached down and scooped mounds of snow on top of each hand. He was so in pain! Dr. B said he had third-degree burns and needed to be transferred to KU Burn Center. An ambulance was on the way to take us. The paramedics allowed me to ride in the ambulance with Don, and as we were traveling north out of our town, we could look over in the distance and see black smoke. It looked like the tail of a tornado, only coming up from the ground instead coming down from the clouds. Knowing this was the cabinet shop burning, our livelihood, we looked at each other and agreed maybe *our good Lord* wants us to be missionaries elsewhere.

Don said when he entered the burning building, his only intent as a fireman was to put out the fire. Inside the front door to the left, along the steps leading down into the basement, Don kept a pile of lumber. He knew the way around this obstacle, and that's why he entered. Also the steps down had a turn at the bottom; this he was also familiar with. To drag a hose this length around these corners was quite a challenge but would be more so for another fireman unfamiliar with the territory. In the basement, Don saw fire on the east wall about twenty feet away, sprayed it, and put it out. Thinking to spray down the rest of the basement, he hollered to Arlie, his backup, "More fire hose is needed!" The south side of the room was filled with smoke; the north where he was standing was clear; and not hearing any crackling sounds, he started to turn the nozzle on. Don said at this moment, a voice inside of him he can only describe as the Holy Spirit told him to "get out immediately!"

As Don fled the basement and on the stairs going up, his air pack on his back got hung up on a piece of trim molding that was protruding over the stairway opening. He struggled to free himself, and as he again mounted the next step, he felt the skin being peeled from his hands like pulling off a pair of rubber gloves. At the top of the stairs he saw a hole in the floor directly in front of him with flames all around the perimeter. He sprayed water on it and knew this was an illusion because the flames did not die down. Don then surmised it had to be a reflection from the glass of the air mask he was wearing coming from flames on the ceiling. Don walked through the area he thought before was a hole in the floor, turned, and came out the front door of the shop.

The people were gathered for worship that Sunday morning, and we were told later of church services that had prayers in our behalf. Don and I are so thankful we live in a town of praying people. When Don was diagnosed at the burn center in the city, he had second-degree burns, not third. We believe *our Lord* gave us a miracle. A building burned to the ground that day, but the real cabinet shop's life was spared.

Don had loaned the shop that day to a friend who was building a new house. Ron was familiar with the shop; he used to work there.

He needed to stain, sand, and lacquer trim, and the basement was the spray room to do this. With the temperature below freezing, a stove was burning for heat. Ron had a stained rag in his back pocket, and when close to the stove, the rag caught fire. He yanked the rag out of the pocket, and it fell to the floor. From years of lacquering and staining, the floor had quite a buildup of combustible materials. They were ignited by the burning rag, and fire spread quickly with all the flammable substances in a cabinet shop. Don and I are so thankful that Ron and no one else were seriously injured.

Visiting with Don at the hospital, he was concerned about the set of cabinets that burned up in the fire. They were nearly completed and ready to be installed in the customer's new home. He asked me to call Leonard and Helen and tell them to find another cabinet maker.

When I made the call, these precious people said, "No way do we want someone else to build our cabinets. We will wait for Don to be back in business!"

Don was very emotional about someone having this much confidence in him. We did not have insurance, and starting up another cabinet shop was a mighty big mountain to climb. The customer's decision to wait was the boost Don needed to start climbing!

When Don left the hospital, his hands were bandaged so big he looked like he was wearing boxing gloves—only they were white, not black gloves. My dear friend Sherry and I sterilized the bathroom in our home as best we could and put a sign on the door, saying, DON'S PRIVATE BATHROOM—STAY OUT! Don had to sit in a tub with a special solution added to the water, and I had to cut skin from off the burn wounds every day. I joked with my friends and said, "This did more for our marriage. Don had to sit naked in a tub with both hands in the air while I gave him a bath!" He sat there so brave and bold and didn't even flinch when I did the cutting; it had to be very painful. And this whole procedure of dressing those wounded hands, kneeling beside the bathtub was very humbling for me. What a sweet-natured husband was mine!

At this time in our town, there was a fairly new grocery store. Jim and Barbara let us have the use of their old grocery store building "rent-free" to help us get established again. Don and I attended an auction and purchased nearly new equipment for a very economical used price. With the banker, creditors, faithful hired man Frank, and all those people backing us with prayer, we delivered the promised set of cabinets to Leonard and Helen six weeks after the fire!

Little Red-Handle Saw

At the end of the year of 1983, our daughters were married and away from home, and son, Matt, was five years old. The day before the auction where the big equipment was purchased, Matt went with Don and I to check things out. The auction was being held in a long, tin-style building and was being heated by one portable heater at one end. It was so cold in that place; we all had to keep going back to this heater to warm up. Don found a table saw, shaper and planer that he thought would be worth coming back the next day to bid on. There was a long table to one side of the length of this building, and on this there were boxes full of odds and ends of small carpentry tools. Matt saw a small red handle sticking out from one of these boxes and expressed his "need of this tool" to be able to "help Daddy!" The little saw was only about twelve inches long, but it fit his hand perfectly, and he wanted to work. Don told him we could not take it home this day, but we would be coming back tomorrow for the auction, and "Daddy would buy the saw then."

The next day was again bitter cold, and knowing these auctions can be a long-drawn-out affair, I decided we would all have a better day if Matt stayed home with Granny Alta. Granny had been in our home since the Friday before the fire on Sunday when I picked her up at a hospital after having a heart attack. After much persuasion, she agreed to come to our home for rest and recuperation. Many a moment I thought of her and her age, having had this heart attack, when the cabinet shop fire happened; but what a blessing to have her in our home at such a time. Her jovial and spunky attitude gave us a boost many a time. Granny said the two of them would stay close to the stove on such a cold day and they would read books and Matt could play with his little cars and trucks. Ladies from church looked in on them too.

At the auction, the bids seemed to be in Don's favor; but then, the auctioneer had to be touched by a man waving his huge white boxing glove at him! Those hands had to be bandaged every morning, and a lot of gauze was required to keep germs out that might cause infection. Don would be emotional when another one of his bids was *accepted, knowing another tool had been purchased to do his artistic work. People gathered around* us, giving us their encouragement to keep going and "hang in there" words to motivate. We were *greatly blessed* and give *all glory and praise to our Lord God*!

The little stuff is auctioned off first, and I knew when Don bought his big table saw that we did not keep bidding on the box with the little saw. When a box is placed up for sale, a person has to buy the whole parcel and not just one item out of it. All the items in this box, Don knew what he could use and not. He said when the bid went so high that we could buy everything in this box brand new from wholesalers, Don quit bidding for this reason. At this time, we had to be frugal even with the small stuff. Off and on, the rest of the time at the auction, I would try to think of something to take home to Matt. The atmosphere in the home the past couple of weeks was "rebuild." Matt wanted some sort of tool, at five years old, to help his family build and make the product that provided our livelihood.

After Don purchased the equipment he went for that day, we had to wait until the building cleared of people so someone could operate the forklift. Watching the new shop machinery being loaded, I decided to go to concession stand for a hot drink; this was also by the heater. Walking around the corner from where the loading was being done, I walked by the long table that had the small boxes on, and I marveled that it was so clean. It amazes me that so much "junk" can be on a table before an auction, and it's cleaner than a whistle after.

I glanced down this long table in the direction of the concession stand and saw two men in their work clothes drinking their hot beverage. In front of these two fellows on the table was the little red-handled saw. This was all that was laying on this long stretch of table—at the very end of was this little saw.

Thinking it now belonged to one of these two men, I quickly went up to them to ask, "Did this little saw belong to either one of you?"

"No," they said.

And if I wanted it, since everybody was gone except the people out back loading their truck, I better take it. I grabbed that little saw and raced to tell Don about my find.

Don was still giving orders on how he wanted the equipment loaded in the truck, so after he acknowledged my find, I realized that no thank-you or words of appreciation did I say to those two men. I quickly walked back to the concession stand and found it to be all locked up. The long, bare table was there, but the two men that had stood at the end of the table had disappeared.

I don't have any words of explanation. *Only I know we have a loving Father who cares about all our needs and also the desires of our hearts.* Don and I went home that day and presented a little red-handle saw to our son. They had a father-and-son picture taken, both grinning from ear to ear. Don was standing by his new-powered table saw that fit his expertise, and Matt had the little twelve inch saw to help Daddy build cabinets. Both came from that auction on a cold January day in early 1984.

Early that spring, thinking we could not afford the building we had temporally set up shop in, Don was looking into other possibilities. Other buildings around town didn't seem large enough, and he was thinking of building out in industrial park east side of town. We were in debt to the bank for the equipment and wasn't sure which way to go on a future location for the cabinet shop.

We were negotiating with the city and library board on their purchasing the vacant lot where the old cabinet shop had stood in hopes this could be a down payment on a new building. Don had bought the old shop that was the former Baptist church, and this was located next door to the city library.

When Don bought the Baptist church building, he called his mom and said, "Mom, don't worry about me anymore. I'm going to be in church every day!"

One item that was heartrending to lose in the fire were the beautiful stained-glass windows in front of the building. After the fire, the library board thought expanding the library by way of the now vacant lot would be ideal for them. I say "vacant lot" because no building stood there. We still needed to clean up the debris left by the fire. The long cold winter past with spring budding—this too was in our plans.

The mail carrier delivered a registered letter to our home from the city. Thinking an agreement had been made on the purchase of the lot, I gleefully opened it. To my astonishment, the letter stated that Don and I owed the city sixty-five thousand dollars for damages to the library because of the fire. I immediately thought, *Where will we get this kind of money?* And the next thought, *We will have to sell our home.*

I knew how close the library building stood next to the old cabinet shop; there was approximately six feet between. After Don and I left the burning inferno because of his injuries, the fireman and a lot of the townsfolk really fought a battle. The Presbyterian church across the street from the library and old shop had dismissed their services that day and carried books from the library to safety in their church building. I have newspaper pictures of choir members in their robes carrying stacks of books down icy steps. Even with their efforts, a lot of books were charred and the inevitable water damage from the water sprayed by fireman hoses. Their need of money to replace the damages was justifiable.

After opening the registered letter, I turned to Don and said, "We need to pray! We really need to pray." As a woman, I derived a lot of comfort from my home sort of like an ole nesting bird. I appreciated my home and enjoyed the neighborhood it was in, but if it was *the Lord's will*, I wanted to be obedient. Don and I always told each other that everything we have and are belongs to *the Lord*. If we were to leave this house, we would make a home elsewhere.

On the other hand, is the enemy trying to destroy us? We needed to fight! The ole devil is a defeated foe, and Don and I needed to bombard heaven until we had victory in our situation!

That afternoon, sitting at our kitchen table, we bowed our heads, and Don prayed, "*Lord, keep all of this a spiritual matter. Amen.*"

I agreed wholeheartedly with Don's prayer. The prayer had settled in my heart, and *peace came.* I realized the few words my husband prayed covered the whole situation. I didn't have to bombard heaven with a lot of words or to speak in tongues in order to have prayers answered. *Our Lord God knows our hearts!*

> Again, I tell you that if two of you on earth agree about anything you ask for, it will be done for you by my Father in Heaven. For where two or three come together in My Name, There Am I With Them. (Matthew 18:19–20)

With the warm days of spring, the lot at 103 E. Peoria needed cleared off. Walking through the ashes that was once the cabinet shop was a sad endeavor. We really felt at home in that ole church building, and we were reminiscing as we raked and gathered those remains, throwing it on a truck to haul to the dump. The heavy metal and iron that once was table saws, joiners, shapers, or sanders were thrown on friend Les's truck to get rid of. We were busy in clearing the lot, for the city did buy it, and we had so many days to get this job done. Rainy weather had delayed us in cleaning the lot and getting a shop set up to do business at the old grocery store location. We had been busy. Don's wounds were healing very well, but this too seemed like a slow process. The burns on his forehead and sideburns on his face were healed, but on his hands, he still had to wear tight-fitting gloves. The gloves were necessary to have less of a scar.

The love of the people in our town that was shown Don and I is precious to us beyond words. There was even an account set up for us at a bank, and donations were deposited for us—all the prayers, visits, phone calls, letters, donations, and the time individuals gave of themselves to help us. It's great to live in a small town in these United States. We are a blessed nation to have such a brotherhood!

A small bucket of coins had been found in the ashes, all black, covered with soot, but Don thought they could be cleaned. Randy found a small tin box that had the titles to the vehicles, charred around the edges, but each vehicle number was legible. There was also an important paper Don needed for a job. Everything else in the tin box was bits 'n' pieces, but the little cedar box that Ron found can only be described as *a miracle*!

The old cabinet shop was an old wood-frame building; the ashes ended up in the hole in the ground that was the basement. Ron was raking around in about three feet of ashes where up above would have been Don's office. The fire happened one week before Christmas, and Don never does any shopping until Christmas Eve or a day or two before. He had fifteen hundred dollars tucked away in a three-by-ten-by-two-inch cedar box in one-hundred-dollar bills. Ron found this box in all those ashes. The box badly burned, but the fifteen one-hundred-dollar bills inside were just charred around the edges. All the serial numbers were legible, and the bank sent them off to the mint for us, and we were reimbursed. We still have this little cedar box. It is always a wonder to look at now and then. How a little wood box survived a fiery inferno when heavy iron and metal equipment melted? *It's a miracle!*

Our daughter Jacque gave us the poem "Footprints in the Sand." She told us that the poem reminded her of how *our Lord* had brought us through so much during the fire and rebuilding of the business. The story in the poem: there were two sets of footprints and then there was just the one set. The one set indicates the time *our Lord* carries us *Himself* through the sands and storms of life.

The Lord God himself did indeed carry Don and I through the fire!

Don and I did not have insurance on the cabinet shop, the building, or the contents thereof. At the time of the fire, we just thought everything was a total loss. Imagine our surprise when Ron, the man in the shop at the time of the fire, approached us and said he had two policies—the one policy being on his present home and the other on the new house he was building. Both policies had liability clauses, and both would pay off. He thought each policy would pay us twenty-five thousand dollars. We were rejoicing over such good news. With fifty thousand, this would make a big dent with the equipment we purchased. We were elated!

Then Ron's insurance agent called. He said the two policies weren't worth just twenty-five thousand a piece but fifty thousand a piece. *Wow!* Way out wonder! We could buy the new drum sander and pay off the equipment and have a little left for a down payment on a shop building. We were praising *our Lord!*

Then a few days later, Don again heard the voice of the insurance agent on the phone. He was very solemn in speaking and asked if Don and I would come to his office that afternoon.

"Yes, we would be there right after lunch!"

He wanted to talk with us in person because he himself was in a state of unbelief. When we were seated in front of his desk, the agent looked at Don and me and said, "You people must be living right!"

It seems on the 15th of December 1983, *three days before cabinet shop fire on the 18th*, this insurance company decided to increase the amount of coverage of all policy holders' liability, automatically throughout the company, to a larger amount. Ron didn't know of this change or the agent in our town until the claim on the cabinet shop fire was filed. The change did not increase the premium. The liability coverage of Ron's policies was in the amount of *one hundred thousand dollars each!* When the claim was submitted and arrived at the home office, *someone* reading our claim had to associate with the ruling just made on the 15th, with our fire on the 18th of December. *Our Lord* put it in *someone's* heart to recognize the three days grace period. *This has to be a miracle!*

The library to the west of the old cabinet shop received their money and now has a lovely new addition. The Smith home which was to the east of the old cabinet shop had damages repaired, and we were able to purchase the grocery store building we had already set up shop in—the building we didn't think we could afford.

> My Grace is sufficient for you, for my power is
> made perfect in weakness. (2 Corinthians 12:9)

But thanks be to God, which gives us the victory through OUR LORD JESUS CHRIST. (1 Corinthians 15:57)

Thou shall not be afraid for the terror by night: nor for the arrow that flies by day; nor for the pestilence that walks in darkness; nor for the *"destruction that lays waste at noonday."* (Psalm 91:5–6)

CHAPTER 28

DOA—DEPRESSION, OFFENCES, APATHY

For years depression was the culprit that kept me from experiencing the presence of *my Lord*. I was looking inside of me and concentrating on what bothered me. It wasn't exactly me but what I had allowed to enter my think tank with problems and situations that dominated my thinking. I couldn't think about me because to my way of thinking, *I wasn't worthy to think about*. Hence—I was depressed.

Then along came the offences, and on top of the depression, at times I was a basket case. My thoughts would not only turn to the offence but to the offender. I needed to *forgive my offender* no matter how big or small the offense, but I *would think* over and over again about the offense, *thinking it was somehow my entire fault*, and this turned my thoughts to me, me, and me—a big vicious circle.

It seemed like the depression with the offences led me to apathy. Apathy was when I lacked interest in things generally found exciting or interesting. I had lack of emotion or feeling to so much and was indifferent mostly to the people around me—the very ones I loved the most especially my *Lord God and Savior Jesus Christ*.

I was grieving the Holy Spirit and causing Him pain by ignoring *His presence*.

Depression plus offences plus apathy made me dead on arrival—DOA.

I had to quit my stinkin' thinkin, make myself get off the fence, and I had to learn what Scripture says to "keep yourselves" *so I could start looking forward.*

Dear ones! Listen up! Now is the time to get rid of all hindrances. Scripture tells us to "not let any unwholesome talk come out of your mouths." Before a word comes out of one's mouth, it has to be a thought in the mind. I was grieving the Holy Spirit of God, *my Lord and Savior, who* did so much for me, by *thinking thoughts that hindered and grieved the Holy Spirit of God.* I didn't speak out loud my thoughts, but *our Lord God knows every thought we think*!

> Do not let any unwholesome talk come out of your mouths, but only what is helpful for building others up according to their needs, that it may benefit those who listen. And do not grieve the Holy Spirit of God, with whom you were sealed for the day of redemption. Get rid of all bitterness, rage and anger, brawling and slander, along with every kind of malice. Be kind and compassionate to one another, forgiving each other just as in Christ God forgave you. Be imitators of God, therefore, as dearly loved children and live a life of love, just as Christ loved us and gave Himself up for us as a fragrant offering and sacrifice to God. (Ephesians 4:29–5:2)

Dear ones! Listen up! I didn't just grieve *my Lord* but those closest to me. The countenance I gave to them was not the love, joy, and peace of the Holy Spirit. The answer to my entire dilemma is found in Scripture.

> Instead, be filled with the Spirit. Speak to one another with psalms, hymns and spiritual songs. Sing and make music in your heart to the Lord,

always giving thanks to God the Father for every-
thing, in the name of our Lord Jesus Christ.
Submit to one another out of reverence for
Christ. (Ephesians 5:18–21)

Dear ones! There is a story in 2 Chronicles 20 about Jehoshaphat
who was told a "vast army was coming against the people of Judah"
(verse 2). Jehoshaphat resolved to inquire of the Lord (verses 3–12):
"We do not know what to do, but our eyes are upon You" (verse 12).
"Then the Spirit of the Lord came" (verse 14). "For the battle is not
yours, but God's" (verse 15). Jehoshaphat appointed men to sing to
the Lord and to praise Him for the splendor of His holiness as they
went *out at the head* of the army, saying, "Give thanks to the Lord,
for His Love endures forever" (verse 21). "As they began to sing and
praise, the *Lord set ambushes*" (verse 22).

Dear ones! Listen up! When I started to put praise out in front of
all my battles and all my thinking, actually *putting praise the top part
of my thoughts*, the enemy was defeated. I believe *the Lord Himself* set
ambushes that defeated depression, offences, and apathy so I could
enjoy more fully *His Holy Spirit's presence*.

Now faith is being sure of what we hope for and
certain of what we do not see. This is what the
ancients were commended for. (Hebrews 11:1)

The ancients in the eleventh chapter of Hebrews all had faith
because they sought *our Lord*. The more we are in *His presence* by
prayer and fellowshipping with *Him*, the more we read and study
Scriptures and meditate on them, the more *faith* will rise up within,
and the *victory comes! When victory comes, maintenance begins! We
keep and maintain the victory by praising and worshiping our Lord God!*
The ancients in this chapter also all had a forward look. When I
started looking forward, I didn't have to look back on depression,
offences, and apathy again.

Everyone who believes that JESUS IS THE CHRIST is born OF GOD, and everyone who loves THE FATHER loves HIS CHILD as well. This is how we know that we love the children OF GOD: by loving GOD and carrying out HIS COMMANDS. (1 John 5:1–5)

This is love for God: to obey his commands. And his commands are not burdensome, for everyone born of God overcomes the world. This is the victory that has overcome the world, even our faith. Who is it that overcomes the world? "Only he who believes that Jesus is the Son of God."

I will bless THE LORD at all times: HIS PRAISE shall continually be in my mouth. My soul shall make her boast IN THE LORD: the humble shall hear thereof, and be glad. O magnify THE LORD with me, and let us exalt HIS NAME together. I sought THE LORD, and HE heard me, and delivered me from *all my fears.*" (Psalm 34:1–4)

We know that we live in HIM and HE in us, because HE has given us of HIS SPIRIT And we have seen and testify that THE FATHER has sent HIS SON to be THE SAVIOR of the world. If anyone confesses JESUS is the SON OF GOD, GOD lives in him and HE IN GOD. And we know and rely on THE LOVE GOD HAS FOR US. (1 John 4:13–18)

God is love. Whoever lives in *love* lives *in God* and *God in* him. In this way, *love is made complete* among us so that we will have confidence on the day of judgment because in the world we are like *Him.* There is *no fear in love.*

But perfect love drives out fear because fear has to do with punishment. *The one who fears is not made perfect in love.*

Dear ones! Listen up! After the deliverance of my second break-down, I was free and my inner being empty of fear. The third break-down happened because *I did not keep myself in the love of my Lord God. Keeping yourselves by reading God's Word, studying, and applying God's word is a must! The only way to have victory—keep victory—is applying the Word, Jesus Christ, to our lives! And doing this, we find the comforter and helper, the Holy Spirit.*

> I will pray the Father, and He will give you another Helper, that He may *abide with you forever*—the Spirit of Truth, whom the world cannot receive, because it neither sees Him nor knows Him; but you know Him, for He dwells with you and *will be in you.* (John 14:16–17)

> *For we are the temple of the living God. As God has said: I will live with them; walk among them, and I will be their God, and they will be my people.* (2 Corinthians 6:16)

The prayer my husband Don said during the loss of the cabinet shop destroyed by fire is a precious reminder to us that *our Lord* does indeed know our heart's desire: "O, LORD, keep all this a spiritual matter!"

A beautiful prayer found in Scripture to pray frequently or even daily is found in Psalm 51:10:

> Create in me a clean heart, O God; and renew a right spirit within me. Cast me not away from Thy Presence; and take not Thy Holy Spirit from me. Restore unto me the joy of Thy Salvation; and uphold me with Thy Free Spirit. Amen!

CHAPTER 29

DOWN TO THE FARM, OUT TO THE FARM, ON THE FARM

Eldon and Vernita lived in the big cities of Kansas City and Topeka, Melbourne lived east of our town, and Lawrence was *on the farm.* Whenever a gathering was planned, Eldon and Vernita would say they were going "*down to the farm,*" and Mel and I would say, "*out to the farm.*" This was the gathering place.

The farm was where our dad and mom were. We gathered to see them and each other. On one of Dad's birthdays, we all purchased the *same card.* Out of millions of cards, we managed to all give Dad the very same greeting card, and we all signed it the same way: all our love. Miles apart and years spanning the gulf of time, we were thinking alike—that's how close we are. We will always think of Dad as "in the garden."

Vernita graduated from high school when sixteen, taking two years in one, and was awarded, her name registered in the National Honor Society.

I'm sure the closeness I have for my brothers and sister is because they had to help take care of me from the day I was born. In fact, I don't think I would be alive to write this if they hadn't been there.

I undoubtedly bonded with my sister Vernita when she was required to share her bed with me from the time I was one year old. After the warmth of my mother's body, my ten-year-old sister was next in line. When I was six years old and sis went to work in the city, only coming home on weekends, I felt deprived. The big ole feather bed was too big for just me. I counted the days for the weekend. Our neighbor to the north lived and worked in the city during the week and came home on the weekends. Pauline provided sis the transportation when Vernita obtained a job at a bank, and she found a room in a widow lady's home. In the city, Vernita's only way of getting around was a street car. She told me all about ridin' the street cars and promised to take little sis for a ride on one.

The day arrived, and I was going to the big city with my big sister. First, I had to put on the new clothes she bought me to be presentable "up thar in the city." My feed sack clothes just would not do. The front door to the building sis worked in had a huge revolving door. I was so fascinated. She let me go round 'n' around; it was like a merry-go-round. The street car ride with the clackedy-clack of the tracks and the ringing of the bells for the stops was a sure-enough thrill! We rode it all the way to Swope Park! This is where we went to the zoo; all the animals I had only seen in books—I was so amazed! We ate hamburgers and went to the big cement pond for a swim! What a day we had, and what a sister I have! I love ya, sis!

In February 1951, Vernita married her true love, Ken. We call him by his middle name, Reed. I was ten years old when Reed and Vernita would take me to a little country community south of us, where Reed grew up. He has a sister, Deanna, and we would have a good time fishin' at the creek and swingin' on a rope in the haymow of the barn. Reed was a wonderful new brother. What I didn't like was he took my sister from me! Reed was in the Air Force stationed in New York and had to finish his line of duty, and of course, Vernita went with him. My sis being so far away I couldn't see her now and then was quite an adjustment for me. I eventually forgave him. Love ya, Reed!

Brother Eldon joined the Air Force sometime after high school and when stationed in Great Falls met his true love. Eldon and Peggy were married on my birthday in August 1951. Peggy brought a lot of refined ways to us country bumpkins' way of life especially when they moved to the city and were down to the farm most every weekend. I looked forward to their visits so much! My brother was home, and Peggy with her humorous wit, quick laugh, and sparkling ways all had a good gathering. It was great to have a new older sister!

The summer I was twelve, Mom had a ruptured appendix. The recuperation time was lengthy for her, and a lot of household chores became my responsibility. Dad and brothers Lawrence and Mel helped too! They were the ones that could cook! I had made oatmeal cookies and forgot to put the oatmeal in—a real soggy mess—and biscuits were so hard brothers played catch with them. If they fell to the floor, there was a big thud! We worked together in the kitchen, peelin' taters and frying eggs. My favorite meal today is still cornbread and beans. Daddy taught me how to make gravy, and we all knew how to fry those chickens. There were plenty of fruits and veggies down in the cellar, so I didn't have to work too hard!

Sometime after Mom was back on her feet, Peggy flew to Great Falls to spend some time with her family. Eldon was driving there to pick her up and bring her back to their home in Kansas City. They asked me to make the trip, riding up in the car with Eldon, saying this was my reward for taking care of Mom after surgery. I was elated! The longest distance I had traveled was to Iowa to see Uncle Mart, Aunt Irma, and cousins, but this trip would be seeing the mountains!

Eldon was driving straight through. He especially liked to drive at night, make better time! Somewhere on the Wyoming prairie, early in the morning before daybreak, we hit a deer. Asleep on the back seat, I rolled to the floor and abruptly awoke! Eldon got out of the car to check the damage; he was concerned about the radiator. Eldon is a great mechanic, so when he kicked and beat on the front of that car, it had to be okay. We did make it on to Great Falls, but the expense of repairing the damage to that car was our trip to Yellowstone Park. But being assured Glacier National Park was more beautiful, when I saw the mountains there and Lake McDonald, this country gal hadn't seen a prettier sight!

Peggy has a younger sister, Barbara, nickname of Bibs. It was great getting acquainted with her. I was amazed how well she knew her way around in the jungle of that city. We were given permission to go by ourselves on a bus all the way downtown to see a movie. To have such a privilege, I thought this is big-time stuff!

Peggy's mom was quite a lady. They celebrated Christmas while we were there, and while having the dinner celebration time, a dish blazing with fire was brought to the table. I really liked Peggy's dad—he was a hoot! He had painted their bathroom ceiling (they had indoor plumbing) and in the corner over the toilet stool ran out of paint. He didn't want to pay the price of a whole new can of paint, so he put a sign over the spot on the ceiling, saying, WHAT YOU LOOKING UP HERE FOR? GET BACK TO BUSINESS!

I don't think anyone ever forgets their first glimpse of the mountains—especially being from the plains of Kansas. The mountains represent such majesty, beauty, splendor, and freedom. The vastness of them is a big part of our America, and I will never forget the generosity and consideration of my brother who took me to see them. I love ya, Eldon and Peggy!

Melbourne joined the Army and had a tour of duty in Korea. He was the most distance away from home and for the longest length of time; I was really homesick to see my brother. When the day finally arrived, there wasn't a more elated little sister than me. He was so handsome in his uniform I thought he was the Prince from the East arriving back out on the farm. Mel had a way about him that whatever I thought to be in need of, he would find a way to provide it for me. Sometimes I didn't even have to ask. In remembering him, his ways of thoughtfulness to me still blesses me very much!

I remember when quite young, I would run off to the neighbors without permission. Mom couldn't trust me, so she would put a harness on me and tie me to the clothesline. I could run up and down the clothesline as much as I wanted and jerk and twist my body, but the harness was strapped secure. Before my family tied me up, I remember running as hard as I could to see my friend across the road. At their house, I heard the call of my name loud and clear but ignored it. Mel found me playing in their yard and told me to get home pronto! As I was going out their gate, I glanced back to see Mel break a twig off a tree. I started to run, but this was when he could run faster! It seemed every step I took I felt a whack on my behind all the way home.

Mel dated quite a bit; most every Saturday night found him sprucing up to pick up his present friend. I don't think there was a girlfriend he had; at some time or other, he asked me to go on the date with them. I went to the movies, drive-in theaters, square dances, and lots of eating places at his invitation. Not too many big brothers want a little sister tagging along on a date, is there? Dad and Mom got up so early and went to bed so early, knowing I would be spending an evening entertaining myself. Mel was thoughtful enough to bless little sis with having a good time too!

If Mel's date was in the town to the north and a good double feature was playing at the theater in our town, he would drop me off to see these Saturday night shows. If he didn't show up to pick me up at the theater after the last show ended, I was to wait at the post office across the street. It was always open. I would fall asleep on the floor in a corner. There was no thought of danger—at least on my part. We were a country town, and everyone trusted each other.

One wintry night after our evening out, Mel and I headed back out to the farm. We left town going south on Highway 7 and turned on the country road east in the direction of the farm. The snowstorm had turned into a blizzard; it was so cold, and the wind was blowing something fierce! The snow drifts were getting so deep the car was barely making it through them. We made it to the top of the first hill on that road and became stuck in the snow. We sat there for a little bit. Mel was so serious; I could tell he was contemplating what to do.

He turned to me and said, "Sis, there is barely enough gas in the car to run the rest of the night to keep us from freezing with the heater running! I need to walk home to get the tractor to pull us out! It is too far for you to walk with me, and I'll be all right if I keep moving. I have my boots on. We'll roll the windows down a little bit on each side. You lock the doors after I get out. I'll be back at daybreak."

I was left alone that cold dark night, but Mel had four miles to walk in a storm.

I fell asleep, and the next sound I heard was my daddy's voice calling my name. There was scratching on the window on the side of the car I was lying on. The snow and ice had thickly covered the window, and it took a bit of scraping for a hole to be big enough to see in. About the time I was awake enough to answer Daddy's call, he was peering at me through the scraped-off opening.

I was then sitting up, and I heard Daddy start to shout! "She's all right! She's all right!"

Lawrence had driven the tractor to pave the way, and Daddy and Mel were in the ole farm truck. The sun was shining, and the freshly fallen snow was sparkling like diamonds. What a beautiful morning it was!

My brother Mel seemed to have such an interest in the activities I was involved in; he became the leader of the 4-H club I was in. Lots of evenings, he and I would head to a meeting or some function pertaining to my 4-H project. I had cooking and sewing classes to attend, but these were mostly in the daytime. Daddy took me to these sessions. My last year in 4-H, I made a white formal and won the county's reserve champion style show award. But every farm kid needs to raise a farm animal to take to the county fair. Mel said we would start out with hogs, have them for a project for a couple of years, and switch over to cattle. But he wanted me not to have just a common breed of a pig; a rare kind would win more top honors. Dad and Mom went with Mel and me on this adventure. We drove way over in the hills of Missouri where Mel purchased a purebred Hereford gilt. We had registration papers on her, and I put the name of Queen Elizabeth on my hog and called her Queenie for short. Hereford hogs have the same markings as Hereford cattle—red hair and a white face. I washed this hog, curried her hair, and polished her toenails with clear polish. When time for the fair, it was Mel who loaded Queenie and I into the truck and helped enter her for judging. And just like Mel said, she always won the grand champion ribbon because of being the only one in her class. No other Hereford hogs were known in our area.

It was at a 4-H square dance in the northern part of our county that Mel met his intended true love bride. I remember the night well.

On the way home, he talked of no one else at the party but Margie. He was impressed she was a farm gal and knew the work ethics of farm life. Margie's dad had a dairy farm, and twice a day, those cows have to be milked! And the glow of Margie's countenance and her sweet-natured personality was impressive to Mel. He had danced a few rounds of squares with Margie, and he definitely wanted to date her. I love ya, Margie!

When I was fifteen and sophomore in high school, I had my driver's license because of living on a farm. The year was 1955, and Mel had a brand-new blue-and-white Chevrolet. Mel was in the National Guard and for two weeks every year was required to be at a training camp. The night before he left for camp, we were sitting at the kitchen table. Mel reached into his pocket and pulled out his car keys and handing them to me said, "Sis, here are my car keys. I'll be gone for two weeks. When the car needs gas, I've made arrangements for you to charge at the service station south of town. Have a good time!" To this day, it's hard for me to imagine any older brother doing this for a fifteen-year-old sister—and his new car! And yes, I had a good time with my friends cruising up and down main street most every evening. What a generous brother not only with possessions but time spent with little sis. His memory I treasure.

Mel and Margie were married in June 1957. A son was born to them on Mel's birthday, August 23, 1958. He is named Melbourne Francis Kim II. I love ya, Mel!

I have always had a big brother in my oldest brother Lawrence. It seems like a tradition that one brother in a family stays on the farm to help Dad and Mom carry on. Uncle Walt was the bachelor of Mom's brothers, and Lawrence is our family's. He didn't complete the third grade therefore doesn't read or write. My brothers and sister attended a one-room school about a quarter of a mile south of the home where I was born in. If the tractor or machinery needed repairing, Lawrence was the one to put it back together. Not only did he keep things running on our farm but Lawrence worked for over forty years at a dairy farm that bottled and sold milk in town. He is just a good ole farm boy!

Early childhood memories of Lawrence: I picture him and I sitting by a radio, listening to Fiber Magee and Molly, The Lone Ranger, Amos and Andy, The Shadow Knows, and Let's Pretend. The latter program had a theme song: "Cream of wheat is so good to eat we eat it every day!" Lawrence would play games with me. A favorite of mine was Chinese checkers, a game played with marbles you skip across a board. Mom liked games too! Many a cold winter afternoon Mom, Lawrence, and I played a card game called Canasta. This was Mom's favorite when we could entice her away from sewing.

In the wintertime, Lawrence chopped holes in the ice on the pond with an ax so the cattle could drink water. In summertime, he had a hay hook in his hand to grab a bale of hay and swing it up on a stack. It was one of these times in the haymow of the barn he saved his little sister.

The center of our barn had a wide and tall alley with paneless windows at the top opening into the haymow. When in the haymow, this put a platform down the center with a lower level on each side. There was a board propped up against the platform from a lower level, and I was running up and down on this board. When looking out the huge front opening of the barn where they brought the hay in, the board was on the right lower level. All at once, I lost my balance and started to fall. I still have a vision of the ground coming up to meet me through that side opening. Lawrence just happened to be on this right lower level of the haymow and with quick reaction managed to grab my foot. I felt like my body swung like a pendulum coming down and my forehead met with the edge of that board. Lawrence said I bled like a stuck hog! Daddy carried me to the house where Mom cleaned me up as best she could, then they took me to the doctor for stitches. Today, I wear a hairstyle with bangs to cover up the scar. I've told people that the fall in the haymow would have killed me if I hadn't lit on my head!

Another time at the barn, Lawrence was doing chores. It was milking time, and he was coaxing ole Bossy with a bucket of grain to come to the stanchion. This cow had long horns, and to place her head through the boards of the stanchion, he had to turn her head a little sideways. Lawrence had grain in the trough to entice

Bossy to do this. I was just standing there watching and listening to Lawrence's voice coaxing Bossy: "Here, Bossy! Come on, Bossy!"

All at once, before Lawrence could drop the board to lock Bossy in, she flipped her head to one side, kept on turning, and was coming right toward me. I froze in place, and how I remember Bossy coming at me with her head down. I felt my body being lifted up and looked down to see a cow's horn on either side of me. Lawrence said the cow just lifted me out of her pathway with her horns, set me to the side, released me, and walked on out the door.

I remember Lawrence telling me, "Now you get to the house!" and I did run to my dad and mom as fast as I could! But Lawrence now had to start coaxing Bossy all over again as she had to be milked!

Eldon and Vernita are enjoying retirement elsewhere, and they don't come *down to the farm* anymore. Lawrence and I live in the same town and have taken drives *out to the farm*, or more correctly stated, where the farm buildings were. The ole house and barn are gone, and a brushy wooded area is in their place. A new modern house stands like a castle on the backside of those eighty acres. Lawrence and I drive by the ole home place and talk of memories *on the farm*.

Lawrence is nearly eighty-five years old—a mind as sharp as a tack and clear as a bell. Eldon and Vernita have fair complexions, blond wavy hair, and blue eyes, taking after Mom's side of the family. Lawrence, Melbourne, and I have darker skin, thick brown curly hair, and green eyes after Dad. But we all came out of the same mold.

Lawrence is my counterpart, and we have gone country. I love ya, Lawrence!

CHAPTER 30

TITUS

Titus was an extra-large yellowish cat that was a kitten when I was a baby. Brother Mel named him, so this was thought to be his pet, but I played with him every day. My brothers said Titus was so big and became so docile because he was castrated. Every farm kid knows what this is. When Dad and my brothers would perform this surgery, I held the pan that the testicles of the pigs were placed in. I would then carry them to the house for Mom to finish cleaning for the mountain oyster fry! My brothers castrated the male farm cats by placing them head down in one of Daddy's long rubber rain boots. Watching them, I knew those boots were their protection from being severely scratched. I'm sure this procedure was done to keep the population of cats in low number on the farm, but every now and then, I would discover a litter of kittens. They would perhaps be in the barn or under the smokehouse. After a few days, they would strangely disappear. I would ask my brothers, and they would tell me that a skunk or a coyote kidnapped them. But then, I had plenty of barn cats to play with that were kept to keep mice from eating the grain.

And I had Titus! He was so tame and potty-trained our house was his home too! If Titus wanted outside, he would go to the door and let out a loud meow, and someone quickly let him out. I dressed Titus in baby clothes complete with bonnet. He was so cute! We polished the living-room floor by sliding around in our socks and pulling one another on old blankets. Paste wax was all there was. Titus let me pull him around on a blanket to help polish the floor. Poor ole cat got very dizzy because I would pull him around and around!

One day, sitting on the back steps, I noticed Titus's long whiskers protruding out from either side of his face. I knew Daddy shaved! As long as those whiskers were needed, Titus needed shaved too! I got the scissors and clipped those hairs off his face as close as I could. Mom found me as I was sitting there, petting and talking to our extraordinary docile cat. She told me that Titus would probably not be able to catch mice anymore and that the whiskers were a cat's way to gage where the mouse was.

Oh! I felt so bad! I knew how much Titus was needed in the house as a mouse catcher. Mom would see one of those pesky little critters and holler, "Get the cat! Get the cat!" We would scramble to get Titus while Mom kept her eye on where the little varmint was hiding. And after getting a good sniff and smelling the mouse, Titus waited ever so patiently. When the mouse ventured out, Titus would catch him in one of his big paws and put him in his mouth. Mom didn't want the cat-and-mouse game to be played in the house because the mouse might get away again, so at this time, she would pick Titus up with the mouse in his mouth and put him outside to play the game. He would release the mouse and let the mouse run a short distance and then go pounce on him again. This Titus did until he got tired or hungry. Then the mouse went in his mouth head first, and the last of that varmint to be seen was his tail sliding through Titus's front teeth. Then he smacked his lips and licked his paws. Titus was such a happy cat.

I don't know what prompted me to do the most awful disgusting thing to an animal especially one as good and helpful as our Titus. I don't remember him scratching anyone; he was so calm. If he did put his paws on you, his claws never cut very deep; but perhaps I did get a scratch from him, I'm sure, as you know by now he would have done so to protect himself.

My folks didn't have indoor plumbing until I was in high school. There was a path out the backdoor of the house leading to the toilet. Taking care of business, I opened the door and saw Titus waiting for me. Why he followed us around the farm like a dog does was so unusual for a cat, but there he was. I must have been angry or didn't get my way about something and felt like I needed to take it out on something or someone. Whatever, Titus was there and received the brunt of my action.

I picked Titus up and went in the outhouse with him and slid the board off the middle hole. We had three holes in our outhouse—papa bear, mama bear, and baby bear. The baby bear hole was on the end lower to the floor and was made especially for me. The catalog had to be kept between papa bear and mama bear hole, a most important rule; but I didn't spend any time looking at the catalog that day; I was sabotaging Titus!

Yes, I did! I threw Titus down the hole of that ole outhouse and turned to leave. But then, I heard Titus's faint meow; and hearing that low, faint cry pricked my heart. Yes, it did! And I turned back to rescue Titus. I leaned over the hole, seeing two very large green eyes staring back at me and a very begging meow. I reached down as far as I could, but my arm wasn't long enough. I was really feeling sorry for this cat now and knew he had to be brought up out of that hole. I thought if I was down there with him, I could lift him out to freedom. Yes, I did! I went in, feet first, and discovered to be knee high in you know what!

I tried to lift Titus out, but the hole was too high. Just the top of my head and eyes were peering out. We were some distance from the house but sure hoped someone had the need to use that ole outhouse. But yell and scream I did! Brother Mel rescued us, and I'm not sure if he was more concerned about Titus or me. I told him his cat fell in and I was trying to get him out when I fell in. Mom was washing clothes in the ole wringer washing machine, and I was the last batch of the day. The water with homemade lye soap sure felt good, and I'm sure I was doused many times. I think I was put in the tub with clothes still on and maybe the agitator of the washing machine still on. Mel went and jumped in the pond for a long lengthy swim and took Titus with him.

Yes, Titus was quite the pet cat. I was over twenty years old and away from home when I received word that Titus had died. I think he lived this long because of the good dose of fertilizer he received when he and I were three years old.

CHAPTER 31

STENCH IN
THE WORLD

The story of the stinky ole outhouse has a filthy and grotesque connotation. There are people, places, and things in this ole world that is stinky, filthy, and grotesque, and Scripture tells me we are not to even think or talk about the evil or wickedness.

> Do not put out the Spirit's fire; do not treat prophecies with contempt. Test everything. Hold on to the good. *Avoid every kind of evil.* (1 Thessalonians 5:19–22)

> Finally, all of you, live in harmony with one another; be sympathetic, love as brothers, be compassionate and humble. Do not repay evil with evil or insult with insult, but with blessing, because to this you were called so that you may inherit a blessing. For, Whoever would love life and see good days *must keep his tongue from evil and his lips from deceitful speech.* He must turn from evil and do good; he must seek Peace and pursue it. For the eyes of the Lord are on the righ-

teous and His ears are attentive to their prayer, but the face of the Lord is against those who do evil. (1 Peter 3:8–12)

IF MY PEOPLE, who are called by MY NAME, will humble themselves AND PRAY AND SEEK MY FACE and *turn from their wicked ways*, then will I hear from Heaven and will forgive their sin and will heal their land. (2 Chronicles 7:14)

Dear ones! Listen up! Now is the time to be free!

Until the age of thirty-four, I was not experiencing the fullness of the Holy Spirit *my Lord* intended for me to have. At the age of twenty-four, I was institutionalized with my first nervous breakdown. I was coming out of my third breakdown at the age of thirty-four. A lot of good things happened in these ten years. At age twenty-nine, I had asked Jesus into my heart and life, was baptized in *His love*, my marriage to my Christian husband, and the wonderful new church family I have; but it was coming out of the third breakdown when I learned how *powerful our Lord's Word is, and on his Word, I needed to make my stand!*

The offences that had come my way were deeply rooted inside of me with a bitterness of hurt and rejection that hindered the free flow of the Holy Spirit. Because I had been so rejected, I was rejecting the *only One who could help me*. At this time, I didn't take to heart *the words of our Lord* in John 14:16:

I will pray the Father, and He will give you another Helper, that He may abide with you forever.

It wasn't until *I forgave my offender* and started praying for him and until *I asked my Lord to forgive me* for harboring resentment and bitterness for so long did I receive *freedom!*

If someone strikes you on one cheek, turn to him
the other also. (Luke 6:29)

This scripture about turning the other cheek, if practiced, has a
humbling effect; and when we humble ourselves, *the Holy Spirit will
flow freely!*

God opposes the proud but gives grace to the
humble. (James 4:6)

Being a farm gal, I'm reminded of the story about a mule: A
mule fell into an abandoned well and stood on all four feet, looking
up. No way could he climb out. The farmer finds his mule in the
well and thinks this mule is a goner, decides to bury him, and starts
to shovel dirt into the well. The mule feels the dirt on his back and
shakes it off. When the mule found he was standing in dirt ankle
deep, he stepped up out of the dirt on top of it. And this was the
mule's procedure: feel dirt, shake it off, and step a little higher; feel
dirt, shake it off, and step a little higher. This the mule did until he
stepped out of the well to *freedom!*

Dear ones! Listen up! *We need to forgive, forgive, forgive, and we'll
find freedom!* No matter how small the offense or how petty, like taking cookies from a cookie jar, if there is guilt or bitterness festering a
sore of any kind, *we need to ask forgiveness and forgive others!*

Learn to confess and repent quickly so that the
death process that is set in motion each time we
violate God's rules is not given time to do it's full
damage, "for the wages of sin is death. (Romans
6:23)

During the healing process after my third breakdown, I knew
that the Word of God is what I needed. After the miraculous deliverance of the second breakdown, my curiosity led me to reading books
about other people's deliverances and to study about demons. I again
opened my being, my mind, to evil. Hence, the third breakdown.

After this, I didn't want to subject myself to any sort of evil; I didn't want to read about or hear about evil. After my third breakdown, my healing did not come in a miraculous way but was gradually by every word of God I read. I knew a healing was taking place when I read my Bible, but also I felt the effects of *the stench of this ole world.*

Dear ones! Listen up! It is time we all realize the effects of the media and airways of broadcasting. Every newscast, so many of our television shows, radio, and songs that are aired, newspaper headlines and articles and billboards along our highways promote evil. We are in such a battle *in these end times,* and I am greatly concerned about *the minds of our young people.*

It was during the first breakdown at the state institution when I had such realistic visions. There were good visions and bad vision, and at the time, both appeared so real! Now I know these visions were fantasies—just a figment of my imagination—but because I can't forget how very real they were, today I have a hard time telling a little child a fantasy or make-believe story. *The stench of this ole world is after the minds of our children!* So much of what our precious little children hear, see, and feel comes from the fantasy in cartoons, books, and even toys they play with. My heart aches for our children, and we adults are giving this to them by allowing the stench, the evil of this ole world, *into our homes!* Pray, pray, pray for revival!

I remember as a child being told real-life animal stories and real-life Bible stories. The animal stories were very real to me because of growing up on a farm. The Bible stories *became real to me* the more I heard them.

I learned about how bees make sweet honey, how the butterfly gets their wings, and how beautiful birth is by stories about and watching the animals.

When I had a little chigger bite, Mom had a little ditty of a song:

> There was a little chigger and it wasn't any bigger
> than the point of a very small pin. But the bump
> that he raises, itches like blazes and that's where
> the rub comes in.

Mom was a little ornery when she told me the story of a mule:

A farmer was feeding his animals and was asking each, "How much oats do you want?"

The cow said, "Mooore"(more).

The horse said, "Nay" (none).

But the mule lifted up his tail and said, "A feewwww" (a few)!

Mom also told a story about a happening on Noah's ark. It seems the ark sprung a leak, and Noah thought, *What can I put in this hole to plug it up to stop the leak?* Noah sees his dog and calls him over to the hole and had the dog put his nose in the hole. This is why a dog's nose is always cold. The hole gets bigger. Noah calls his wife over and has her put her feet in the hole. This is why women's feet are always cold. But the hole in the ark gets bigger. Noah decides to sit in the hole. And this is why a man will always back up to a stove.

The Bible story got my attention and my curiosity. I loved to hear and read stories about David killing the giant, Daniel and the lion's den, the crossing of the Red Sea by the Israelites, and oh, the birth of *our Lord and Savior* in a manger and how He came into this world in a barn surrounded by animals. And the star that shone so bright would prompt the song:

> Twinkle, Twinkle little star, how I wonder what
> you are. Up above the world so high; like a dia-
> mond in the sky. Twinkle, Twinkle little star, how
> I wonder what you are.

Dear ones! Listen up! It is time our children are taught what is alive and real! They need to be taught the *Word of our Lord that is alive and real!* This will be how our *little ones, who already believe in Jesus, can remain alive and real and stand on the Word* against the evil and stench in this ole world. The teenage years come so quick when they want to follow what they see and hear around them. *The only solid foundation for us all is the Word!*

> Beloved, if our heart does not condemn us, we
> have confidence toward God. And whatever we

ask we receive from Him, because we keep His
commandments and do those things that are
pleasing in His Sight. (1 John 3:21–22)

The contents of a stinky ole outhouse is gross and ugly to think
about, but the grossness and ugliness of this ole world is *eternal dam-nation*. When a person follows the ways of this ole world, it will lead
to *an eternity in hell*. This is why we need to *abstain from all appear-ances of evil*! If there is anyone on the fence undecided about what
side to jump off on, they need to *jump to the side of green pastures
quickly*! One of these days, this fence will no longer be the dividing
line between good and evil but will become a *great impassible gulf*—
the kind *our Lord Jesus* told about in the story of the rich man and
Lazarus (Luke 16:19–31).

My brother rescued me from that stinky ole outhouse, and there
is a world of people needing rescue from the filth and sin of this ole
world. I waited that day to hear a voice when I yelled, and how long I
waited, I don't remember. But I yelled and waited, yelled and waited
for my rescue. My brother came.

Come on now! Listen up! *It's time to help rescue the perishing!*

*I cannot save another person! There is only one Savior given to the
world, but we can be the rescuing party that leads someone to our risen
Lord! Jesus saves, Jesus keeps, and Jesus satisfies!*

A man of many companions may come to ruin,
but *there is a friend who sticks closer than a brother*.
(Proverbs 18:24)

You are My Friends if you do what I command.
I no longer call you servants, because a servant
does not know his master's business. Instead,
I have called you friends, for everything that I
learned from My Father I have made known to
you. You did not choose Me, but I chose you and
appointed you to go and bear fruit—that will
last. Then the Father will give you whatever you

ask in My Name. This is My Command: Love
Each Other. (John 15:14–17)

Dear ones! Listen up! When I read the Scripture written above
when Jesus says, "Do what I command," this made me think of the
Ten Commandments. During my eighth grade year of schooling in
the parochial school, an assignment was to memorize these commands given by *our Lord God* to Moses. These commands, first written on stone by the finger of *our Creator, our Father God*, were given
to mankind *for freedom*! If human beings all over this world would
know and obey these Ten Commandments, what a free world we
could all live in.

The Father, Son and Holy Spirit are one! Jesus is our God!

He is known as Jehovah in the Old Testament and Jesus in the
New Testament.

Jesus didn't come to do away with the Old Testament *but to ful-
fill all Scripture*! The Ten Commandments need to be taught, memorized, and obeyed in lives today.

The Ten Commandments

1. Thou shalt have no other gods before me.
2. Thou shalt not make unto thee any graven image.
3. Thou shalt not take the name of the Lord thy God in vain.
4. Remember the Sabbath day to keep it holy.
5. Honor thy father and thy mother.
6. Thou shalt not kill.
7. Thou shalt not commit adultery.
8. Thou shalt not steal.
9. Thou shalt not bear false witness against thy neighbor.
10. Thou shalt not covet anything that is thy neighbors.

I received an email recently about the Washington Monument in Washington DC. This 555 feet, 5 inches high monument facing skyward to the Father of our nation has an aluminum cap atop displaying these two words: *Laus Deo*. These are Latin words meaning *"Praise be to God"*!

From the vantage point atop this granite-and-marble structure, *a perfect cross* imposed upon the landscape with the White House to the north. The Jefferson Memorial is to the south, the Capitol to the east, and the Lincoln Memorial to the west.

Yes, a cross—separation of church and state was not—is not—in the Constitution.

The first president of our nation, George Washington, gave the following prayer:

> Almighty God; We make our earnest prayer that Thou wilt keep the United States in Thy Holy protection; that Thou wilt incline the hearts of the citizens to cultivate a spirit of subordination and obedience to government; and entertain a brotherly affection and love for one another and for their fellow citizens of the United States at large. And finally that Thou wilt most graciously be pleased to dispose us all to do justice, to love mercy, and to demean ourselves with that charity, humility, and pacific temper of mind which were the characteristics of The Divine Author of our blessed religion, and without a humble imitation of whose example in these things we can never hope to be a happy nation. Grant our supplication, we beseech Thee, through Jesus Christ Our Lord. Amen.

The last verse of *"America,"* a song I sang in grade school, is very meaningful:

> *Our fathers God, to Thee, Author of liberty, To Thee*
> *we sing: Long may our land be bright, With free-*
> *dom's Holy Light, Protect us by Thy might, Great*
> *God, Our King.*

My favorite spectator sport is baseball. Don and I sponsored a girls' softball team with the cabinet shop name. We had more fun going to the games and cheering for our girls. I was surprised at how aggressive girls could be at this sport. The team won the state championship two years in a row.

Having had the three nervous breakdowns, I liken my life to a game of baseball. The three bases all covered are the breakdowns and I've rounded third and I'm on the homeward stretch. Home base is getting closer. I'm just so thankful to *my Lord and Savior Jesus Christ* I won't have to slide into home by the skin of my teeth; for a born again believer this won't be. My entry into home, I'll be standing— standing on the promises of *God my king.*

The bases, the breakdowns, were the hardest maybe because I had to make such a sharp turn at each one. These turns only came into my life to keep me on the right path. Oh, I stumbled and fell many a time between those bases, but *Jesus* sticking closer to me than a brother *was always there to pick me up.* In fact, *the love of my Savior* is the motivating power in this game of life.

Having rounded third base, I'm moving onward and upward and looking forward to my eternal home. I know Scripture tells us of "gates of pearl," but fancy pearly gates are not what I first want to see. *My Jesus*, just inside those garden gates, *who* is there waiting for me is the first sight my eyes want to behold.

My life has been quite a journey, and what amazes me—the older I have become in years, the more exciting life is. There is an adventure every day—new people to meet and places to see. Oh, there are those days when this ole body says, "Stay put where you are today," but I have a phone (cell phone too!), and I can write notes and letters to dear ones!

On those mornings when it's a little hard to get out of bed, I lie there, listening to the birds chirping. This is when I decide to ignore those aches and pains and get out of bed. If those birds are up so early singing and praising *their Creator*, then so can I! But I don't sing it out loud like the birds do; mine is in my heart. And this has become my favorite time of day, for I now take the next minutes or hours—however long I desire—*to commune with my Lord.*

I am so thankful our Lord is always available. I have found when I make myself available, my Lord is always waiting for me. Day or night I can commune with my Lord God. Having been in His presence is what will see me through my day!

I love to read and study *God's Word.* I have found within the pages of my Bible *all that is needed for this life and for the life to come.*

I am blessed!

All glory and praise to my Lord God and Savior Jesus Christ!

> For You have been my refuge, a strong tower against the foe. (Psalm 61:3)

> My soul finds rest in GOD ALONE; my salvation comes from HIM. (Psalm 62:1)

Come on now! Listen up!
It is time to think about going home and where you will spend eternity!

CHAPTER 32

ETERNITY

Winter is past. Spring has sprung! Flowers are popping up through the cold dark ground. Buds are showing up on lifeless-looking tree branches indicating life is still there; the sap inside the tree flows freely. From a dark dreary color, pastures are turning green. The winter wheat is inches high, waving green. Oh! Glorious! That which is dead is now showing life! One little seed has produced many a sprout.

Dear ones! Listen up! It is time to look on the *inside of you and see Jesus!*

For years I looked inside of me and saw me. I focused on me and didn't find life. I found only defeat by thinking only on myself and seeking after people, places, and things in this ole world. Nothing satisfies! *Only Jesus!* When I asked *Jesus to come into my life and I continued to seek Jesus, peace came*! The only way to retain was to remain *in the Lord God's holy Word.*

> He must turn from evil and do good; he must
> *seek peace and pursue it.* (1 Peter 3:11)

> You will seek Me and find Me when *seeking Me*
> *with all your heart.* (Jeremiah 29:13)

Dear ones! *Listen up!* Only when I got alone in my prayer closet and totally surrendered *all* did I find the relationship my whole being was looking for. So real does *Jesus completely satisfy.* Jesus is the first person I want to talk to every morning. The time is just Jesus and I alone communing with *the Father.* His presence becomes so real most mornings I do not want to leave. But I'm assured the mountaintop experience gives me the victory needed for the task of the day; the work is down in the valley.

> Land that drinks in the rain often falling on it and that produces a crop useful to those for whom it is farmed receives the blessing of God. (Hebrews 6:7)

> Now He Who supplies seed to the sower and bread for food will also supply and increase your store of seed and will enlarge the harvest of your righteousness. (2 Corinthians 9:10)

> Still other seed fell on good soil, where it produced a crop—a hundred, sixty or thirty times what was sown. He who has ears, let him hear. (Matthew 13:8–9)

Dear ones! Listen up! *It is time to seek the Lord your God with all your soul, strength, and might!* Your life depends on you yielding to *your Creator* and also the lives of those you love on this earth. By you, at this very moment surrendering *all to Jesus*, others through you will also receive their salvation. Whatever your decision now, *this very moment, you will carry with you into all eternity!*

CHAPTER 33

"FIRST LOVE"

For years the deep yearning within me was to have a deep companionship with my husband—soulmates with intense desires fully satisfied. In the first years of marriage, the lovemaking is so satisfying and gratifying to both partners. The wife longs to give herself fully and completely to her husband and believes his only desire is her—not just gratification of his desires. Spending the day with each other in hobbies and activities that both enjoy is so pleasurable with one's mate. I love to watch Don when he is fishing. I'm usually at one end of the boat, and he is at the other. I usually catch the most or the biggest fish, but I've heard it said: "A wife doesn't know what a patient man she married until she goes fishing with him." He has pulled my line out of many a snag many a time in more ways than one.

We have enjoyed the fellowship of each other for many years. Skiing and snowmobiling in Colorado is probably at the top of the list, for this is where I first knew I loved that man. The fresh mountain air, whiteness of snow, clear blue skies—everything so clean and pure—and so was our relationship. Conversation flowed freely between us about anything and everything. Just being alive took on a whole new meaning. Life became wholesome and with a purpose especially when I was with my husband. I definitely felt he was the better half of the two of us, someone I could always look up to and confide in. Love is a safe and secure place.

I have always been so thankful that Don has work to go to every day which he enjoys so much. It is so satisfying and rewarding to accomplish a job well done, but sometime after the children left home and we were empty nesters, the times I felt most secure in my relationship with my husband was when we were on a trip. Those were the times when all the cares and responsibility of the cabinet shop were left behind, and it was just Don and I on an adventure. Every mile we traveled together, thousands of miles, was pleasurable because of the not knowing what was around the next corner or over the next hill. And what sights our eyes did behold! God's creation is so beautiful! We both love to travel and sightsee, but the real reason I felt so loved and secure at these times was because I had my husband all to myself.

Back home and back to the routine of work schedules and Don was back at the cabinet shop, I would feel a tinge of desertion and rejection but would dismiss these thoughts from my mind with Bible reading, praising my Lord, and Christian fellowship. I also kept myself busy at home. I do appreciate my home and enjoy keeping house, especially those times of getting ready for company. The times I enjoy our home the most is when others are there to enjoy it with us. I love trying to make people feel at home in *our home*.

The attacks of the old enemy with thoughts of abandonment when my husband was working kept coming, and a new one added with Don loving his work more than me. The old devil knows our weakest points. After all, Satan came to "kill, steal, and destroy." But I know the rest of this verse when Jesus says,

> *I have come that they may have life, and that they may have it more abundantly!* (John 10:10)

In December 2004, we parked our RV at Potter's Point on Caddo Lake in Northeast Texas. The previous year Don had finished chemo, so we wanted a place to dock our small fishing boat and just go fishin'! With my husband's strength not being what it used to be, I knew he would rest best with a fishing pole in his hand. At this writing, Don has been cancer-free for over twenty years. I am so thankful to Our Lord for His grace and mercy providing for all our healings—physically, mentally, emotionally, and financially. We serve a great God!

> But my God shall supply all your need according
> to His riches in Glory by Christ Jesus. Now unto
> God and Our Father be Glory for ever and ever.
> Amen. (Philippians 4:19–20)

The last five years we have spent most of the winter months at our second home in Texas which Don and I have greatly enjoyed. I am so grateful that we are healthy enough to do this and my husband is still with me. No matter the weather, Don gets up every morning and goes fishing. If he needs anything, there is rain gear, umbrella, and a portable propane heater in the boat; and yes, lots of times he will take a lunch. Being a farm gal, I enjoy playing in the dirt, so I have flowers all around the RV to attend to. On days weather doesn't permit me to go outside, I read, write, cook, crochet, and there is always a cell phone to keep in contact with friends. The nearest town is fifteen miles away, and I go in several times a week to the library for emailing. There is a lot to this southern hospitality as everyone is so friendly and helpful, but one morning, watching Don go through routine of leaving for fishing, knowing he would be gone for hours, I thought to myself he acts like he is going to work. Getting ready for his day was like preparing to leave for the cabinet shop. I should have rejected my next thoughts and got busy with some task but was caught up in thinking, *Why, he even loves fishing more than me!*

> When the enemy shall come in like a flood, the
> Spirit of the Lord shall lift up a standard against
> him. (Isaiah 59:19b)

I knew this scripture and believe wholeheartedly that the *word of God is the only way to defeat the enemy.* But remember, dear ones, we choose the direction in our minds.

The mind can be a battleground, and we can think on the Word of God or think on the dart the enemy attacked our mind with. *It's the dwelling or action on the thought when it becomes attached.*

The fact that Don likes to go fishing isn't the object of frustration here, for I love to fish too. It's especially enjoyable on a clear, blue-sky day and not too windy when waves are rockin' the boat—and I never want to be out in a boat on a cold day. Those days I like staying indoors close to a fire. I'm a fair-weather fisherman. On a cloudless warm day (and not too hot!), the scenery and being so close to nature is beautiful! I love being outdoors in God's great creation. It is the thought that he loved fishing more than me.

Other thoughts tried to penetrate my brain like *He only needs you to be his cook!* Don comes in from either work or fishing and is just famished. A balanced diet is especially needful to one's health. A lot of my thinking involves planning meals nutritionally and, in the days we are all living in, economically, but I have always enjoyed doing this. A lot of satisfaction and accomplishment can be derived from putting a meal on the table and knowing you were successful in your efforts. I especially like to have friends share their recipes and know the outcome is tried and true. Now to really reject the thought the enemy threw at me, *the Word of God says,*

> Whatever your hand finds to do, do it with all your might. (Ecclesiastes 9:10)

> And that you study to be quiet, and to do your own business, *and to work with your own hands,* as we commanded you; that you may walk honestly toward them that are without, and that you may have lack of nothing. (1 Thessalonians 4:11–12)

> Whether therefore you eat or drink, or whatsoever you do, *do all to the glory of God.* (1 Corinthians 10:31)

I couldn't be happier with the area we are in. I can see the lake from the RV, and there are trees all around. The redbuds and dogwoods bloom beautifully in the spring, and the cypress trees are so unique, standing so majestically in the water. We feed birds all winter long and every morning wake up to them praising their Creator. How very peaceful and serene it is here.

The little country church we attended is down the road, approximately five miles, and the people really love Jesus and Pastor R preaches the Word. This is so refreshing every Sunday morning and Wednesday evenings. The messages are inspiring and sometimes bring conviction, which is needed, because it hits the nail right on the head. The music is so encouraging and uplifting because we sing so many songs about heaven. I am so *looking forward to my eternity with my Lord and Savior.* This time is definitely getting closer to reality where we are promised seventy years. Time is getting shorter for us all! I like to think about the rapture, where we all go together and not one at a time. Whatever way He chooses, eternity starts with our life on this earth.

Come on now! Listen up! *It is time to once again make sure you have made preparation for your eternity in heaven!*

I really enjoy our little fishin' camp nestled here in the woods, but RV living can also be extra straining on one's efforts. In keeping house, two people being in such small quarters sometimes will cause both to bite the lip. There isn't too much room to walk around if there isn't a place for everything and everything in its place. Besides, the aroma or smell the fisherman brings in from the great outdoors isn't too pleasant. I've heard the joke that "ole fishermen never die, they just smell that way"!

We were even having a problem with ants in the RV. I have to be so careful to not leave a crumb anywhere and everything packaged tightly in containers so the little critters can't partake. Just when I think the victory is won, something sweet is left out, and those little black specks are seen nibbling, filling their appetites. Instead of being disgusted with the ants, I would think Don needs to come on these fishing trips by himself.

It just seemed that our marriage of forty years was again being put to the test. I tried to find some humor in this by saying, "Forty years I've been going around the same mountain!" But the words of a song came loud and clear:

> Take another lap around Mount Sinai until you
> learn your lesson.
> Till you stop your whining and you quit your
> rebellion
> Till you learn to stand in your day of testing
> by trusting and obeying The Lord. (chorus)

Words and Music by Al Poirier

Mount Sinai is where Moses received the Ten Commandments.

> When the Lord finished speaking to Moses on
> Mount Sinai, he gave him the two tablets of the
> Testimony, the tablets of stone inscribed by the
> finger of God. (Exodus 31:18)

Moses was the leader that our Lord used to accomplish many miracles by his obedience. The people had seen these mighty miracles and were even blessed by the great Exodus, or deliverance from Egypt themselves.

What a miracle when they walked through the Red Sea on dry ground with Egyptians in pursuit. Waters came down and drowned the enemy. Then the miracles done for them in the wilderness, turning bitter waters into sweet to drink, providing manna for food, clothes not wearing out—but they murmured, complained, and were disobedient (Exodus, Leviticus, Numbers, and Deuteronomy).

I too have seen mighty miracles in my behalf, and I sure don't want to grieve my Lord with complaining and a bitter attitude. I definitely don't want to be a bitter ole woman that speaks only of negative circumstances, but I want the excitation that comes from a good attitude and plenty of gratitude. When I start thinking of all the good my Lord has blessed me with, there are so many ways I can't even count them! Besides, I knew the scriptures that says,

> And be content with what you have, because
> God has said, "Never will I leave you; never will
> I forsake you." (Hebrews 13:5b)

> Peace I leave with you; My Peace I give you. I
> do not give to you as the world gives. Do not
> let your hearts be troubled and do not be afraid.
> (John 14:27)

Dear ones, come on now! Listen up! It is time that we all realize when anything disturbs our peace that our Lord intends for us to have—it's time to seek the Lord!

Taking my "troubled thoughts" to my Lord, the scripture that came to me is found in Psalm 37:23 KJV:

> The steps of a good man are ordered by The
> Lord, and He delighted in his way.

In prayer, I felt like the Lord said He made my husband the way he was so He could make me the way He wanted me to be. Ouch! Sort of like back to the mill and the grinding stone, or "on the Potter's wheel." I so want to be yielded to what my Lord's purpose is for my life. In fact, I have prayed over and over again, "Not my will but Thine," with adding, "And don't let me get in the way!" What is so astonishing and amazing—when we completely place ourselves into our Father's hands, there is peace and serenity and absolutely no fear.

A CD that I recently had started listening to is "Songs 4 Worship SANCTUARY." The song "No Need to Fear" has really ministered to me. Music and lyrics by Habib Bardowell:

No Need to Fear

No need to fear *No need to hide inside*
Just need to come alive *And trust in God alone**
No need to fear *Our God is still alive*
He still moves stones *You're not alone no need
to fear**
Even when the darkness comes up on you*
Even when a storm has blown your way*
He will never leave you nor forsake you*
Remember you're the reason that He came**
Even when your friends have turned against you*
Even when you're lost and all alone*
He is not against you He is for you*
And He's coming back again to take you home*

This is the word that came to Jeremiah from the
Lord: Go down to the potter's house and there
I will give you my message. So I want down to
the potter's house and I saw him working at the
wheel. But the pot he was shaping from the clay
was marred in his hands; so the potter formed
it into another pot, shaping it as seemed best to
him. (Jeremiah 18:1–4)

Study Note from Full Life Study Bible (NIV) by Donald C. Stamps

Jeremiah 18:2 THE POTTER'S HOUSE. Jeremiah was
told to go to a potter's house where he watched a
potter fashioning a pot from clay. Because the vessel was not suitable for what the potter intended,
he had to remold it into something other than
what he had first designed. This parable contains
several important principles for God's work in our
lives. (1) Our submission to God as the One who

molds both our character and our service to Him determines to a large extent what He can do with us. (2) A lack of fervent commitment to God can frustrate His original purpose for us (cf.v.10). (3) God remains free to change His intentions for our lives. If He has planned goodness and blessing for us and if we rebel against Him, He may then shape us into pots destined for destruction (vv.7–11; cf. 19:10–11; Ro 9:22); on the other hand, if we are, through our own stubbornness, pots headed for destruction, but we repent, God will began to shape us into instruments of honor and blessing (cf. 2Ti 2-20–21).

But now, O Lord, Thou art Our Father; we are the clay, and Thou Our Potter; and we all are the work of Thine Hand. (Isaiah 64:8 KJV)

Does not the potter have the right to make out of the same lump of clay some pottery for noble purposes and some for common use? (Romans 9:21 NIV)

Dear ones! I want to clarify again that I love my husband Don very much! The battle inside me was not against him; I just needed assurance of love and, as always, when seeking my Creator, found an abundant supply. There is nothing to compare with the love of Jesus Christ, our Lord and Savior.

But the enemy is so subtle and sneaky. The devil is made up of lies and will throw these darting lies at us continually if we don't fully realize *Satan is a defeated foe.*

For our struggle is not against flesh and blood, but against the rulers, against the powers of this dark world and against the spiritual forces of evil in the heavenly realms. (Ephesians 6:12)

> I give you the authority…and to overcome all the
> power of the enemy and nothing will harm you.
> (Luke 10:19)

> We demolish arguments and every pretension
> that sets itself up against the knowledge of God,
> and we take captive every thought to make it
> obedient to Christ. (2 Corinthians 10:5 NIV)

Lies, lies—how many marriages have been broken up with the start of one little lie like "they love something else more than me," "I don't *feel* loved," "I'm not happy."

Oh, dear ones! Real happiness is not based on happenings or with what we can or cannot receive from another human being. Instead of always looking to receive something from our mate, if we would just give in to the other person's desires and wants, we will find more happiness and satisfaction with this frame of mind. The giving of oneself in time, efforts, and the work of our hands is the best gift of all to another. A coffee mug sitting by my kitchen sink that I keep a fingernail file and clippers in has this saying: *Love isn't love 'til you give it away!*

> It is more blessed to give than to receive. (Acts
> 20:35)

The following is a quote from *The Ultimate Gift* by Jim Stovall:

> When we truly love others, our
> love makes each of us a different
> person and it makes each one we
> love a different person too.

When I started cooking meals, washing dishes and dirty underwear, scrubbing toilets and sinks, vacuuming floors, etc., I did it all *to the best of my ability*. Even in some of these menial tasks, I seek the help of my Lord to do a better job. By dedicating the day, the hours, and sometimes minutes and seconds *to the Lord and for his glory,* I am blessed and gain a victory. My husband was happier, and so was I. The ole saying "when mama ain't happy, nobody is happy" can be so true. All I can say, "Mama, get happy *in the Lord!*"

> Happy is he that has the God of Jacob for his help, whose hope is in the Lord his God. (Psalm 146:5)

The first of every year, our pastor in Kansas calls for a corporate fast. This year in particular is crucial with a new president taking the helm on January 20th and the economy and moral decay of our nation. Horrible happenings are taking place all over this world, and we really need to pray for Israel and "the peace of Jerusalem." Depending on our health, our fast could be one meal or for a day or several days—whatever Our Lord would lay on our hearts to do. But all members were asked to spend more time in prayer and reading our Bibles. I choose a three-day fast because this reminds me of the time Jesus spent in the tomb and how I'm thankful for that third day when my Savior arose! Solid food wasn't eaten, but we drank plenty of liquids—juices for meals, sipped on our protein drink, milk at bedtime—and since it was winter and colder weather, maybe a hot lemon and honey drink to take away a chill. And I drank as much water as I wanted. We were to pray for the church, body of believers in Christ, and the direction our Lord wanted for the coming year.

The fast went really well, and this tired ole body was really rejuvenated. I felt energized in my physical being and soaring with the eagles in my spirit man. I knew in my heart our Lord was answering prayers. Our RV home is approximately five hundred miles from the body of believers that I had fasted and prayed with, but I felt a very close connection of unity with every brother and sister in the church; and what was so beautiful—a fresh, new current of love flowing within as only the Holy Spirit can supply—knowing our Creator God is love and because of His great love. *He loves us so much He gives us love! Our God is awesome!* I just want others to know Him and experience for themselves His love! Our Lord is alive and so real.

What a breakthrough! Just makes you want more and more and more of Jesus!

> But they that wait upon the Lord shall renew their strength; they shall mount up with wings as eagles; they shall run, and not be weary; and they shall walk and not faint. (Isaiah 40:31)

Study note from Life in the Spirit Study Bible (KJV) by Donald C. Stamps

> To wait upon in the Lord is to trust Him fully with our lives; it involves looking to Him as our source of help and grace in time of need (cf. Ps 25:3–5; 27:14; Luke 2:25, 36–38). Those who wait upon the Lord are promised: 1. The strength of God to revive them in the midst of exhaustion and weakness, of suffering and trial; 2. The ability to rise above their difficulties like an eagle that soars into the sky; and 3. The ability to run spiritually without tiring and to walk steadily forward without fainting at God's delays. God promises that if His people will patiently trust Him, He will provide whatever is needed to sustain them constantly. (1 Pet 1;5).

> See, I have engraved you on the palms of My Hands. (Isaiah 49:16)

After the fast, I was able to concentrate more so on *who* my Lord is and not so much on my feelings. Now and then, my heart kept being pricked in regard to negative thoughts about my husband's devotion, but I knew in my spirit that complete victory was forthcoming. I knew that my Lord was dealing with me and wanted to show me a different perspective or outlook with Don's and my relationship. Being on the potter's wheel, or enduring chastening of the Lord, if we will yield and look for His instruction, our lives will be for the better good. There is peace knowing we are in the Master's hands.

> My son, despise not thou the chastening of The Lord, nor faint when thou art rebuked of Him: For whom The Lord loveth He chasteneth, and scourgeth every son whom He receiveth. (Hebrews 12:5–6 KJV)

Study notes from Life in the Spirit Study Bible by Donald C. Stamps

> Note several facts about God's discipline of believers and the hardships and troubles He allows us to suffer. (1) They are a sign that we are God's children (vv.7–8) (2) They are an assurance of God's love and concern for us (v.6). (3) The Lord's discipline has two purposes: (a) that we might not be finally condemned with the world (1Cor 11:31–32), and (b) that we might share God's Holiness and continue to live sanctified lives without which we will never see The Lord (vv.10–11,14). (4) There are two possible consequences of the Lord's discipline. (a) We may endure the hardships God leads us through, submit to God's will and continue to remain faithful (vv.5–6). By doing this we will continue to live as God's spiritual children (vv.7–9) and share His Holiness (v.10); it will yield the fruit of righteousness (v.11. (b) We may "despise" the discipline of Our Father (v.5), rebel against God because of suffering and hardship, and thereby fall away from God (v.25; 3:12–14). (5) Under God's will, trouble may come (a) as a result of our spiritual warfare with satan (Eph 6:11–18, (b) as a test to strengthen our faith (1 Pet 1:6–7) and

our works (Mat 7:24–27; 1Cor 3:13–15), or (c) as a preparation for us to comfort others (2Cor 1:3–5) and to manifest the life of Christ (2Cor 4:8–10, 12,16). (6) In all kinds of adversity we must seek God, examine our lives (2Chr 26:5; Ps 3:4; 9:12; 34:17) and forsake all that is contrary to His Holiness (vv.10, 14; see Ps 60:1–12; 66:18 notes; see article on The Suffering of the Righteous, p.766).

Dear ones! Come on now! Listen up! Now is the time to realize our trials only come to make us strong! Strong, firm, and steadfast Scripture says,

And the God of All Grace, Who called you to His Eternal Glory In Christ, after you have suffered a little while, will Himself restore you and make you strong, firm and steadfast. To Him be the power for ever and ever. Amen. (1 Peter 5:10–11 NIV)

But The God of All Grace, Who hath called us into His Eternal Glory by Christ Jesus, after that ye have suffered a while, *make you perfect, stablish, strengthen, settle you. To Him be Glory and dominion for ever and ever. Amen.* (1 Peter 5:10–11 KJV)

Sometimes thoughts and emotions can run rampant, so I included the King James version for the fact that trials and chastisements will *settle me.*

We use the kitchen booth with table in our RV at mealtime, and it also serves as a desk where I do bookkeeping. So here I keep a little flip-over calendar with inspirational verses, and this particular one is by bestselling author Stormie Omartian. There was a definite message for me on January 24, 2007:

Your deepest needs and longing will only be met
in an intimate relationship with God. No person
will ever reach as deeply into you as God will.
No one can ever know you as well or love you as
much. That insatiable longing for more that you
feel, the emptiness you want those closest to you
to fill, is put there by God so that He can fill it.

I read it once then twice to make sure of my understanding
and then heard a still, small voice, not demanding, condemning, or
critical, just calm, gentle, and loving, ask me this question: *"Who is
your first love?"*

I quickly went back to the bedroom, knelt beside my bed, and
asked my Lord to forgive me.

I repented that I was trying to receive something from my husband
that *only my Lord and Savior could provide.* My deepest, most
intense desires can *only be met by my Creator.* Yes, this all made so
much sense to me now. My God is the Potter and designed and made
me from the inside out! He definitely would know my deepest longings.
No human being could possibly understand. I also needed to
ask my husband to forgive me—and what a relief for Don! I had
been acting like Don should be doing something else to satisfy me,
and how frustrating when no one on this earth could possibly know
what that something else is!

Only God can fill my longings!

From the calendar message, I had to look up the meaning of the
word *insatiable*, and the dictionary I have says "incapable of being
satiated or never satisfied." Then I looked up the meaning of *satiate*,
and the dictionary says "to satisfy fully, to gratify to excess; safe. Filled
to satisfaction."

Come on now! Listen up! *It is time to be filled to satisfaction!*

But the desires of the *diligent* are fully satisfied.
(Proverbs 13:4b)

Dear ones! Search no more from your spouse to fill the emptiness or longings that you have.

Companionship is meaningful; comradeship and marital relations are physically gratifying, as our Lord intended, and love of children are precious special times, but *only Jesus* can satisfy our deepest needs and longings.

For only Jesus saves, Jesus keeps, and Jesus fully satisfies!

> You open Your Hand and satisfy the desire of every living thing. (Psalm 145:16)

> All that I need, He will always be
> All that I need till His face I see
> All that I need through eternity
> Jesus is all I need.
> (Author unknown)

> The Lord God took the man and put him in the Garden of Eden to work it and take care of it. (Genesis 2:15)

I really enjoy what I call "playing in the dirt" and planting and tending to flowers in the garden. It really thrills me to see a little seed planted in the ground pop through the brown dirt with such vivid green color and grow into a beautiful flower. What a miracle! But it also reminds me that I should bloom where I'm planted. The length and time of my blooming, like the flowers planted, is in the jurisdiction of my Lord. How wonderful to be outdoors on a cloudless, blue-sky day with birds making music and flowers, nodding their thankfulness to me for pulling out the weeds around them. This reminds me of pulling the weeds and tares out of my life. Sometimes I really have to tug and pull on that ole weed. for the roots are really deep; but with my Lord's help, the root of that weed has to give way and surface. What a feeling of excitement and accomplishment when this happens. I also like to dig up a weed and plant a blooming flower in its place. When doing this, I think of the scripture:

> Do not be overcome by evil, but overcome evil
> with good. (Romans 12:21)

By thinking these thoughts, gardening is good therapy for me, and my hubby, Don, equally likes the outdoors. The challenge is a little different, but the outcome is much the same. I think most men like to have their minds challenged, like fishing and hunting. The pursuit is the challenge, and when the game is caught—the victory. Sports like baseball, football, golfing, soccer, etc.—all create challenges. When Don comes in from a fishing time so excited about the game caught, the cares and responsibilities in this ole world are momentarily forgotten. The outing outdoors, like the gardening I do, is very refreshing and uplifting. I believe as wives, we should be thankful for these pursuits and even encourage them.

There is such a fulfillment in just being outdoors in what I call God's great cathedral.

My Cathedral

> My cathedral has a ceiling of blue... My cathedral beneath the sky...
> Where I may lift up my eyes unto the hills and hear music from a stream rippling by.
> My cathedral has an altar of flowers—their fragrant incense fills the air.
> In my cathedral I am closer to Him than I could be anywhere...
> For here I pray in a place so grand...the carpet I kneel on was made by His own hand.
> My cathedral has candles lighted by the stars and mighty pillars of trees.
> No other cathedral is so beautiful for God made my cathedral for me.

This past Valentine's Day, I received a very special card from my hubby, Don. The card itself reads,

My Promise of Love—

What better time than Valentine's Day to promise you all my love...
today, tomorrow, always.

Happy Valentine's Day!

But what he wrote in his own handwriting touched my heart
deeply. He penned these words:

> P.S. I do love you more than my shop and fishing
> and or anything else in this world but God. So
> will you be my valentine forever. I love you and
> love you and love you.

Hubby Don

Now how about this for being married for over fifty years!
Eighty years on this ole earth and on the baseball diamond of
life I'm so close to home plate, and the excitement of reaching this
base is greatly anticipated. What a thrill to score and have a victory
won, to have the Umpire of Life call me at home *safe!* And I'll be with
Him, *Jesus, my first love!* The question "Who is your first love?" not
only convicted me but served as a warning. This reminded me to get
priorities in proper perspective and tell myself, "Woman, shape up!
I'm so close to home I don't want to fall down now.

Come on now! Listen up! *It is time to heed the warning given the
Ephesians in Revelation 2:2–5:*

> I know your deeds, your hard work and your per-
> severance. I know that you cannot tolerate wicked
> men, that you have tested those who claim to be
> apostles but are not, and have found them false.
> You have persevered and have endured hardships
> for my name, and have not grown weary. Yet I

hold this against you: *You have forsaken your first love.* Remember the height from which you have fallen! Repent and do the things you did at first. If you do not repent, I will come to you and remove your lamp stand from its place.

Full Life Study Bible (NIV) study note by Donald C. Stamps

Revelation 2:4 FORSAKEN YOUR FIRST LOVE. This refers to the Ephesians' first deep love for and devotion to Christ and His Word (John 14:15, vv.21; 15:10). (1) This warning teaches us that knowing correct doctrine, obeying some of the commands, and worshiping in the church are not enough. The church must have above all a heart-felt love for Jesus Christ and all His Word (2Co 11:3; cf. Deut.10:12). Sincere love for Christ results in single-hearted devotion to Him, purity of life and a love of The Truth (2Co 11:3; see 2Ch 30:6 note; Mt 22:37, 39 notes; John 21:15 note).

Dear ones! Come on now! Listen up! It is time to think about these legacy writings and compare with the warning to the Ephesians.
You might say that I've persevered under some pretty heavy trials, the proof being I'm still here! I detest the wicked things that come over the television and Internet and to the best of my ability keep from hearing and watching it and refuse to have it in my home. A preacher that says one thing from the pulpit and has a life style other than what he preaches makes me sick to my stomach! And for years, I was guilty of sitting on a church pew, knowing correct doctrine, obeying some of the commands, and worshiping the Lord with lips and not from the heart!
Dear ones! When I heard the words "Who is your first love," I knew. I knew because *the holy Word of God tells me in 1 John 4:19 KJV: "We love Him because He first loved us."*

But before this revelation came, I was being deceived. The dictionary says *deceive* means "to cause a person to believe what is not true; mislead. To catch by guile; ensnare." Deceive involves falsehood, or the deliberate concealment or misrepresentation of truth and with intent to lead another into error or to disadvantage.

Oh, dear ones! Listen up! I was being deceived by thinking the shallow empty longing I had needed to come from someone else namely my husband. I was fast becoming a contentious wife (look those scriptures up sometime), but for the grace and mercy of my Lord calling and warning me that *Jesus and Jesus only should be our first love!* The Word of God only promises me these eighty years, and I so want my children, grandchildren, great-grandchildren, and descendants from now on or whoever is reading this to realize that deception is out there! It is in the world—and is our focus on things in this ole world, our cares and problems or another person and even ourselves?

Dear ones! Listen up! It is what we do with that deception that will give us the victory!

Repent! Turn from everything else, and make Jesus your first love.

Dear ones! Listen up! It is time to realize I am trying with all that is in me to keep you from going through life with a mindset like out of my past. It is the thinking on other things, people, and always seeking for material gain—what benefited *me*—that kept my mind occupied. It cuts me to the core that out of my past there was a time "I knew God but didn't worship Him as God." How very heartrending is the following Word of God:

> *For although they knew God, they neither glorified Him as God nor gave thanks to Him, but their thinking became futile and their foolish hearts were darkened. (Romans 1:21 NIV)*

Our Father in heaven created us in His image to have fellowship with Him. God put Adam and Eve in a beautiful garden to have heartfelt companionship. They sinned by disobedience to a command of their Creator and ours. Listen to what Scripture tells us in Genesis 3:8–9:

> Then the man and his wife heard the sound of the Lord God as He was walking in the garden in the cool of the day, and they hid from the Lord God among the trees of the garden. But the Lord God called to the man, *"Where are you?"*

Dear ones! The above verse is also true today. People are not doing right by their Creator, and they are hiding. Now everyone should know that nothing and no one can hide from God, but human nature, when doing wrong, makes us want to hide under the covers or within ourselves and try to be obscure from the truth who is God! *But God, in his great love, mercy, and grace, is still calling out to mankind, "Where are you?" Our Creator is still calling us to an intimate relationship with Him.* Listen to this explanation:

The Full Life Study Bible (NIV) by Donald C. Stamps

> Genesis 3:8—THEY HID. The guilt and consciousness of sin caused Adam and Eve to shun God. They felt afraid and uncomfortable in His Presence, knowing that they were sinful and under His displeasure. In this condition they found it impossible to draw near to Him with confidence (see Acts 23:1, note; 24:16, note). In our sinful condition, we too are like Adam and Eve. However, God has provided us a way to cleanse our guilty conscience, *free us from sin, and restore us to His Fellowship—the way called Jesus Christ (John 14:6).* Through the redemption God provided in His Son, we can draw near to Him in order to receive His Love, Mercy, Grace and help in time of need (see Heb 4:16).

Oh, dear ones! Come on now! Listen up! It is time to make it a priority sometime in a twenty-four-hour day to meet personally with our Creator—no one else around, just you and your God, seeking fellowship, *one with the other*. Start making it a habit to start every day with a good attitude and plenty of gratitude with personal worship and praise to our Creator. Listen to this teaching I heard years ago and found it to be so beneficial in my life: *Inner praise will crucify my carnal nature.*

Dear ones! This very moment, determine in yourselves to start the flow of inner worship and praise that flows in and through and out of one's heart. Keep the music flowing as you go about your day. When upsets happen—continue to *speak to yourself* with psalms, hymns, and spiritual songs. This is what Paul and Silas did at midnight in prison.

> Speak to one another with psalms, hymns and spiritual songs. Sing and make music *in your heart to The Lord*, always giving thanks to God the Father for everything, in the name of our Lord Jesus Christ. (Ephesians 5:19–20)

> The crowd joined in the attack against Paul and Silas, and the magistrates ordered them to be stripped and beaten. After they had been severely flogged, they were thrown into prison, and the jailer was commanded to guard them carefully. Upon receiving such orders, he put them in the inner cell and fastened their feet in the stocks. *About midnight Paul and Silas were praying and singing hymns to God,* and the other prisoner were listening to them. Suddenly there was such a violent earthquake that the foundations of the prison were shaken. At once all the prison doors flew open, and everybody's chains came loose. (Acts 16:22–26)

Oh, dear ones! Come on now! Listen up! It is time to accept the fact that whatever problems and circumstances of life have beaten you—the problems you are facing—compare to what Paul and Silas did. Start singing those praises to the Creator of all and set yourself free and others will find freedom too.

A chorus we sing at church has great meaning with seeking a relationship with our heavenly Father and Creator:

> I want to sit at your feet, drink from the cup in
> your hands
> Lay back against you and breathe, feel your heart
> beat.
> This Love is so deep, it is more than I can stand
> Your Peace is so Real, it is overwhelming.
> The more I seek You,
> The more I find You,
> The more I find You,
> The more I Love You.

Come on now! Listen up! *It's time to seek Jesus and keep the love flowing!*

Dear ones! I know at this writing we are definitely in the last days. Listen to what the Word of God tells us in 2 Timothy 3:1 (KJV):

> This know also, that in the last days perilous times shall come. For men shall be lovers of their own selves, covetous, boasters, proud blasphemers, disobedient to parents, unthankful, unholy, Without natural affection, trucebreakers, false accusers, incontinent, fierce, despisers of those that are good, Traitors, heady, high-minded, lovers of pleasures more than lovers of God; Having a form of godliness, but denying the power thereof; from such turn away?

Life in the Spirit Study Bible (KJV) notes by Donald C. Stamps says:

> *3:1 In the last days perilous times.* The last days of salvation history began at Pentecost (Acts 2) and will be concluded with the second coming of Christ (see Acts 2:17 first note). Paul prophesies through the Holy Spirit (cf. 1Tim 4:1) that evil in the world will accelerate and intensify as the end approaches (cf. 2Pet 3:3; 1 John 2:18; Jude 17–18). (1) As the conclusion of the last days approaches, there will be a widespread collapse of the moral structure of the family and of society in general as people are arrogant "lovers of pleasures more than lovers of God" (v.4). These times will be especially grievous and trying for God's true servants.
>
> (2) Paul issues the warning that within organized Christianity many will have "a form of godliness," i.e., hypocritical religion, but will deny the power of the gospel that produces genuine godliness. Paul adds, "from such turn away" (v.5). The full blessing of salvation in Christ Jesus and the mighty end-time outpouring of the Holy Spirit will occur in and through the church that has passion for Jesus, longs for His coming as the Bridegroom and carries the fire of God in true NT faith and ministry. There will be even greater grace and power for those believers and churches who hold fast to the original faith entrusted to the saints (Acts 4:33; Rom 5:20; Jude 2).
>
> *3:2 lovers of their own selves.* Paul gives a list of sins that all have their root in self-centered love (vv.2–4). Today some teach that a lack of self-love is the root of destructive behavior and personality disorders. *Apostolic revelation teaches that the problem of sin lies in our self-centeredness—period.*

3:3 Without natural affection. Believers must be prepared to face an overwhelming deluge of ungodliness as history approaches the end of the age. (1) The apostle prophesies that satan will bring great destruction on the family. Children will be "disobedient to parents" (v.2), and men and women will be "without natural affection" This can be translated "without family affection" and refers to a lack of the feelings of natural tenderness and love, as demonstrated by a mother who rejects her children or kills her baby, a father who abandons his family, or children who neglect to care for their aging parents (see Luke 1:17, second note).

(2) Men and women will become lovers of money and pleasure and will pursue their own selfish desires (v.2). Many will consider parenthood, with its demands for sacrificial love and nurture, as an unworthy or undignified task (vv.2–4). Loving parents will be replaced more and more by those who are selfish and brutal and who abandon their children (cf. Ps 113:9; 127:3–5; Prov 17:6; Tit 2:4–5; see 2Tim 4:3–4 note).

(3) *If Christian parents are to save their families in the difficult times of the last days, they must shield them against the corrupt values of the society in which they live (John 21:15–17; Acts 20:28–30), separate them from the world's ways and refuse to let ungodly influences mold their children* (Acts 2:40; Rom 12:1–2; see article on *Spiritual Separation for Believers, p.1827*).

They must accept the plan of God for the family (see Eph 5:21–23, notes; see article on *Parents and Children, p. 1892) and live differently than the ungodly (Lev 18:3–5; Eph 4:17). They and their families must indeed become strangers and aliens on earth (Heb 11:13–16), even while they pray for and have compassion for the lost.*

3:5 *Having a form of godliness.* Paul refers to those who profess to be Christians and appear to be religious, but who do not manifest God's power that can save them from sin, selfishness and immorality. Such people tolerate immorality within their churches and teach that a person may practice the sins listed in vv. 2–4 and yet inherit salvation and the Kingdom of God (cf. vv.5–9; p.4:3–4; 2Pet 2:12–19; see 1Cor 6:9 note).

Dear ones! Listen up! Doesn't the above Word of God and study notes read like today's newspapers or words out of the mouth of a present day news commentator on television?

I urge you with all my heart to make sure Jesus is your first love, and teach your children from little on how to be overcomers in Jesus's love.

And they overcame him by the blood of the Lamb, and by The Word of their testimony, and did not love their lives so much as to shrink from death. (Revelation 12:11 NIV)

Revelation 12:11 (NIV) study note by Donald C. Stamps

12:11 THEY OVERCAME HIM. Faithful believers on earth overcome satan by being freed from his power by the blood of the Lamb, by determining to speak for Christ and by showing a willingness to serve Christ at any cost.

I See a Crimson Stream

1. On Calvary's hill of sorrow where sin's demands were paid

And rays of hope for tomorrow across our path were laid.
I see a crimson stream of blood. It flows from Calvary.
Its waves which reach the throne of God,
Are sweeping over me.

2. Today no condemnation Abides to turn away
My soul from His salvation, He's in my heart to stay.
I see a crimson stream of blood. It flows from Calvary.
Its waves which reach the throne of God,
Are sweeping over me.

3. When gloom and sadness whisper You've sinned, no use to pray,
I look away to Jesus, And He tells me to say:
I see a crimson stream of blood. It flows from Calvary.
Its waves which reach the throne of God,
Are sweeping over me.

4. And when we reach the portal where life forever reigns,
The ransomed hosts grand final, will be this glad refrain.
I see a crimson stream of blood. It flows from Calvary.
Its waves which reach the throne of God,
Are sweeping over me.

(Music and lyrics by G. T. Haywood)
Hymnal "Sing unto the Lord"
Word Aflame Press
8855 Dunn Road
Hazelwood, MO 63042

Who Am I

1. When I think of how He came so far from
Glory
Came and dwelt among the lowly such as I
To suffer shame and such disgrace,
On Mt. Calvary take my place;
Then I ask myself a question Who am I?

2. When I'm reminded of His Words, "I'll leave
thee never"
Just be true I'll give to you a life forever
I wonder what I could have done
To deserve God's only Son;
Fight my battles 'til they're won Who am I?

(Chorus)
Who am I that a King would bleed and die for?
Who am I that He would pray 'not my will thine
for?'
The answer I may never know; Why He ever
loved me so;
That to an old rugged cross he'd go for who am I?

Written by:
Charles (Rusty) Goodman
Cannanland Music
A division of
Word Music, Inc.
4800 W. Waco Dr.
Waco, TX 76710

I Am

While praying one day, a woman asked, "Who
are you, Lord?"

He answered, "I Am."
"But who is I Am?" she asked.
And He replied, "I Am Love,
I Am Peace,
I Am Grace,
I Am Joy,
I Am the Way, the Truth, and the Light,
I Am the Comforter,
I Am the Strength,
I Am Safety,
I Am Shelter,
I Am Power,
I Am the Creator,
I Am the Beginning and the End,
I Am the Most High."
The lady with tears in her eyes looked toward Heaven and
Said, "Now I understand, But Lord, who am I?"
Then God tenderly wiped the tears from her eyes
And whispered, "You are Mine."
(Author Unknown)

Thank You, Jesus!

2-12-08

My name is Marsena Charlene Kim Light Hadlock. I was born and reared in Eastern Kansas. My life has been given to me by my Creator, my Lord God, my Father, and He has blessed me with the love of Jesus, my Savior. I have given my life to Jesus. These writings are about my life; therefore, these writings belong to Jesus to do with as He desires.

All glory, praise, and honor be to my Lord God Jesus Christ!

EPILOGUE

There is nothing more important in life then for an individual to know Jesus—not just to know about Jesus but actually allowing Jesus to live in one's life with main objective to tell others they too can have a life in Jesus.

Remember: If not experiencing peace—do a checkup from the neck up. Start praising Jesus.

ABOUT AUTHOR

Marsena Hadlock was born and reared on a farm in Eastern Kansas. She is now over eighty years old. She has written her autobiography that others may be inspired to overcome depression and experience freedom too. Marsena has been married to husband, Don Hadlock, for over fifty-two years; and together they've enjoyed four children and their spouses, eleven grandchildren, and seventeen great-grandchildren.

CPSIA information can be obtained
at www.ICGtesting.com
Printed in the USA
JSHW021200060623
42778JS00001B/19